The Computer User's Legal Guide

CHILTON'S BUSINESS COMPUTING SERIES

The Computer User's Legal Guide

R. LEE HAGELSHAW

CHILTON BOOK COMPANY

Radnor, Pennsylvania

TO MY PARENTS.

**Special thanks to Staton Rabin for her
valuable suggestions, critique, and support.**

Library of Congress Cataloging in Publication Data

Hagelshaw, R. Lee.
  The computer user's legal guide.
  Includes index.
  1. Computers—Law and legislation—United States.
2. Computer contracts—United States. I. Title.
KF390.5.C6H33 1985   343.73'07800164   84-45690
ISBN 0-8019-7550-6 (pbk.) 347.3037800164

This publication is designed to provide accurate and authoritative information in regard to the subject matter covered. It is sold with the understanding that the author and publisher are not engaged in a professional relationship with the reader and are not rendering legal or other professional services. If legal advice or other expert assistance is required, the services of a competent professional should be sought.

The names appearing in this book have been contrived by the author. Any similarity to the names of actual companies or products is entirely coincidental, and no reference to any actual company or product is intended.

1 2 3 4 5 6 7 8 9 0   0 9 8 7 6 5 4 3 2 1

======================

Contents

Part Two
Acquiring Computer Software

Part Three
Legal Protection and Marketing of Computer Software

POSTSCRIPT: HIRING A LAWYER — 198

Part Five
Appendix

INDEX — 228

===================================

Introduction:
Law and the
Computer

Toulouse, France
The Committee to Liquidate or Stop Computers claimed responsibility for three bombs that badly damaged the Toulouse government's computer center yesterday. It was the first bombing of the year by the committee, which began attacking computer centers in the Toulouse area in 1980.

—Associated Press, January 29, 1983

"The first thing we do, let's kill all the lawyers."
—Shakespeare, *Henry VI, Part 2*

Many people see lawyers as an expensive obstacle to progress, at best a necessary evil. A few people, frustrated by inaccurate utility bills and stubborn automatic banking machines, have begun to regard computers in the same light. But the skepticism of the dissenters usually is based on a lack of knowledge of the importance of these two performers in our economic and social activities. For both the ancient practice of the law and the recent science of computers are essential to the prosperity of a modern society.

Every major technological advance of this century has been aided in its creation by our system of law. Although the law hasn't adapted itself to the changing technology as quickly as some would like, it has served as an important tool in the development of the computer and its many applications. A basic knowledge of law as it relates to the computer will help programmers and software developers, hardware and software vendors, consultants, and end users profit more from the technological changes now taking place.

HOW KNOWING THE LAW CAN HELP YOU

Let's say that you have decided you want to buy a personal computer. You've read all of the reviews and listened to advice on which computer is right for you. A nearby computer store is offering the machine you want at a good price, and you buy it. But what are all these papers that come with the computer, the ones that mention "disclaimers" and "limited warranties"? If the computer breaks down after the manufacturer's warranty period has expired, do you have any legal rights beyond those mentioned in the agreements you signed? If a service contract is available, what advantages does it offer beyond the rights you already have to a computer that works? If the salesperson told you that the computer would perform specific functions, are those promises enforceable even if they aren't in writing? If you're fortunate, your computer will operate smoothly from the start, and you'll have no need to be concerned with your legal rights. But a knowledge of those rights, as explained in Part I of this book, can save you money and trouble in the event of a dispute with your computer store.

Or let's say that your company needs to acquire software for data base management and financial analysis. None of the available off-the-shelf packages seems appropriate, so you hire a programmer to develop a custom program. This transaction raises a number of questions. Who owns the software when it's finished? Who's responsible for maintaining the software? Can your company modify the program for your particular needs, and if so, who owns the modified software? Can you use the software outside the office in which it was installed? Can you relicense the software to another company? The chapters in Part II dealing with the acquisition of software discuss these and other factors that you should consider when purchasing software or contracting for customized programming.

Or suppose that you're a computer programmer employed full-time by a company in its data processing department. During your lunch hour and at home, you're writing a program that you plan to sell on your own later. Does your employer have any rights in the software that you develop in your spare time? If you're free to market your program, should you do anything to legally protect your rights in the software while you're developing it? What should you know about the law concerning contracts, copyrights, and trade secrets before approaching a software publisher to market your program? What are the possible marketing arrangements? Knowing the basics of legal protection and marketing of computer software, as discussed in Part III, can mean the difference between wasted effort or success for your program.

THE MANY FACES OF COMPUTER LAW

The Computer User's Legal Guide provides the answers to the questions just posed and covers many other legal issues of importance to the computer user. However, the book does not attempt to address all areas of the new field of computer law. Computers are having a profound impact on many aspects of our business and personal lives, and computer law is becoming equally diverse. Traditional areas of the law such as contract, tax, and intellectual property are evolving to accommodate the new technology. Computers have also raised entirely new questions of law in the fields of communications, criminal law, and personal privacy. Many of these issues are beyond the scope of this book.

The Computer User's Legal Guide raises the most common legal questions of interest to the computer user and provides the answers in a manner that can be understood easily by nonlawyers. The book won't eliminate the need for the assistance of a qualified attorney when problems arise, but the information and advice offered here can help you avoid many legal problems *before* they arise and assist you in solving the inevitable complications that do occur. In short, it's a valuable reference source for every computer user.

PART ONE
Buying, Renting, and Leasing Computers

==

An Overview of
Contract Law
1

The subject of buying, renting, and leasing computers can't be explored without first gaining some basic knowledge about contract law. Of course, an understanding of contract law will be equally helpful when, in later chapters, we discuss the acquisition of software and the legal protection and marketing of software. Contracts are important because they can establish and qualify almost all legal rights and arrangements affecting two parties (whether individuals or companies).

Most commercial business and much of our personal business involve the use of contracts. A contract is essentially a promise that can be enforced through the law. A promise by a mail-order company to send you a box of floppy disks upon receipt of payment is an offer to enter into a contract, as is your promise to pay your neighbor's son $5 for mowing your lawn. However, a promise to take your bothersome nephew to the movies if he behaves himself during dinner will not lead to an enforceable contract (thank goodness).

Much of computer law is simply contract law adapted to the particular needs of computer users. However, computer-related contracts may be different from other contracts that you are used to working with. Computer law is a new field of the law that deals with a new technology. There are few established guidelines or generally accepted forms of contracts for many computer applications. If you are in a position to negotiate the terms of a contract, don't be afraid to be innovative and to use your imagination to find the best arrangement to suit your purposes. The more you learn about and work with contracts, the more you will appreciate the great flexibility of this legal instrument.

USING CONTRACTS TO AVOID DISPUTES

Many people believe that legal formalities unnecessarily complicate what would otherwise be simple and friendly transactions among friends or business associates. Why bring in a lawyer to draw up a contract, or even write a contract yourself, when it's more sociable and sporting just to trust the word and the handshake of a business associate? The need to state the terms of an agreement in a contract—a written contract, whenever possible—is simple. People have short memories, especially for detail, and inevitably two parties to an agreement will recall some of those details differently if a question arises. Although reasonable people can often work out their differences concerning their original agreement, they wouldn't be in the position of having to work something out had they taken a few minutes at the start to put it all down in writing.

For example, Mary, a data processing manager at Bigco, needed help in setting up a new procedure for handling customer accounts. She wanted to stagger the dates on which the monthly statements were sent out instead of mailing them all on the first of the month (the overtime work at the end of each month was wearing Mary out). Mary called her friend Jeff, who was an independent computer programming consultant. Mary told Jeff that Bigco would pay him $5,000 for "changing over Bigco's entire billing system." Mary explained exactly how she wanted the new billing procedure to work. Jeff didn't know how many customer accounts were involved, but he had a general idea of the scope of Bigco's operations. Neither Mary nor Jeff saw the need to put anything down in writing, since Jeff had done programming and consulting for Mary before, and there had never been any problems.

When Jeff was half finished with the project, Mary informed him that Bigco had just acquired a small local company, Smallco, and that the president of Bigco had told her that Mary's department would be taking over all of Smallco's customer billing. Smallco's accounts would add only 20 percent to the total of Bigco's accounts, but Smallco's billing system was somewhat different from Bigco's original system, and it would take some considerable rethinking by Jeff to fit Smallco in. Mary thought that the Smallco work should be included in the original $5,000 deal, since otherwise the Bigco billing system would be incomplete, and Jeff had agreed to change over Bigco's "entire" billing process. Jeff thought that he should receive more money for the extra work but finally agreed to do it for nothing as a favor to Mary, even though he felt it was unfair.

The situation of Mary and Jeff illustrates the need for establishing a written contract at the start. The Bigco contract could have specified the extent of the work involved, making clear that any additional accounts would be considered a separate project. This would have protected Jeff against performing more work than he had expected to do when he agreed to the $5,000 payment. A contract would have allowed Jeff to keep his consulting work separate from his friendship with Mary without the need for any favors that might strain the relationship. Contracts are intended not to involve lawyers and courts but rather to serve as a substitute for them. A good contract *anticipates* problems that might arise and provides the solutions, thereby avoiding arguments and phone calls to attorneys.

The idea of using a contract to avoid disputes applies to the printed "form" contracts that are included with the purchase of computers, peripherals, and software. Although the purchaser normally can't negotiate changes in the terms of such a contract, he or she can avoid problems by reading important clauses of the agreement at the time of purchase. If you have questions about the meaning of terms describing a warranty or explaining the conditions for re-turing a defective product, the time to ask those questions is when you buy the product, not later, after a problem has arisen. Always remember that the law is not carried down from the mountain anymore. It's created, to a large extent, by the private agreements that we make every day. Don't be afraid to ask questions and negotiate before you undertake any commercial or business transaction.

HOW A CONTRACT IS FORMED

As we have seen, a contract is essentially a promise or agreement that can be enforced by law. But some promises, like the promise to take your bothersome nephew to the movies, are not enforceable. What does it take to make a legally binding contract?

MEETING OF THE MINDS

As we are all too well aware, people often promise to do something without having any real intention of ever doing it. A casual acquaintance says, "We must get together," and you reply, "Yes, let's do it," but even as you say it, you doubt that the meeting will ever take place. In this kind of conversation, neither person expects that the other will be bound by his or her words. In contrast, if a concert promoter tells a musician that he will pay $500 for a Saturday night performance and the musician replies, "Fine, I'll be there," then there is a

Hagelshaw: The Computer User's Legal Guide (Chilton)

AN OVERVIEW OF CONTRACT LAW   7 *meeting of the minds* sufficient to form a contract. In other words, the circumstances and the statements are such that both the promoter and the musician expect that the other intends to perform as promised.

This meeting of the minds, or mutual intent to be bound by a promise, is often analyzed in terms of an offer and its acceptance. An enforceable contract is formed when person A makes a valid contract offer that person B validly accepts. An offer is made when person A communicates his or her desire to enter into a contract. That desire must be understood by person B, who in turn may decide to communicate his or her desire to accept the offer. Sometimes the two people aren't thinking along the same track, in which case there is no valid offer and acceptance, and therefore no contract. For example, Jane tells Belinda that she will sell her three "apples" for $1 each. Belinda, thinking that Jane is talking about computers instead of fruit, readily accepts the offer. There's no contract here, because there was no valid offer and acceptance (no true meeting of the minds) concerning either fruit or computers.

Even when person A's offer is understood by person B, there is no valid offer and acceptance, and no contract, unless both had the legal capacity to enter into a contract. Generally speaking, minors and mentally impaired people can't make legally binding contracts. For example, Junior, who is ten years old, offered to sell his computer to José, an adult, for $1,500. José, thinking that he could take advantage of Junior's youth, suggested that Junior throw two disk drives and a printer into the deal, to which Junior replied, "No way, José." José then accepted the original offer, but the next day Junior changed his mind and wanted his computer back. Can such a shrewd dealer as Junior back out of his agreement? The answer is yes, because the contract of a minor is voidable by the minor, normally up to a reasonable period after he reaches the age of majority (eighteen, in most states). Likewise, a contract made by a mentally impaired person is usually void or voidable.

Fraud and misrepresentation by a party also prevent the true meeting of minds necessary for a valid contract. Misrepresentation is the making of a false statement involving a material fact by one party to a contract if that statement is reasonably relied upon by the other party. Fraud is the same as misrepresentation, except that the person must make the statement knowing it to be false and intending to deceive the other party. Although outright fraud in the sale of computer goods and services is not common, there's a good deal of misrepresentation. Often this is the result of salespeople not knowing enough about some of the products they are handling. For example, if a salesperson tells a customer that a software package can be used with a particular computer and it turns out that the computer and the software aren't compatible, the salesperson has made a misrepresentation of a material fact. This may be grounds for voiding the sales agreement (but see later chapters concerning the effect of disclaimers).

Finally, there are prohibitions in the law that limit what two consenting parties can agree to. An agreement that violates a specific law or an important public policy can't be enforced. For example, if Hal agrees to pay Mike $10,000 in return for delivering information about the latest microprocessor pirated from Hal's competitor, Mike should not expect much help from the courts if Hal reneges on paying the $10,000. Contracts also can't be enforced if particular provisions are considered *unconscionable*, or grossly unfair, especially if one party had vastly superior bargaining power to the other. This becomes important in the case of standard "form" contracts, such as those that accompany computers and software, that purport to disclaim any responsibility for product defects or malfunctions. As we shall see later, under certain circumstances such terms may not be enforceable against the purchaser.

CONSIDERATION

Even when there is a valid offer and acceptance, there is no enforceable contract unless there has been *consideration* for the promises of the parties. Consideration means that each party will receive a benefit in return for the promise given. If Joe tells Harry that he will pay Harry $10 if he mows Joe's lawn and Harry accepts the offer, there has been valid consideration, and a binding contract is formed. The consideration to Harry is Joe's promise to pay $10, and the consideration to Joe is Harry's promise to mow the lawn. In contrast, if Joe promises to give Harry an old dot matrix printer that he doesn't need anymore and Harry agrees to accept the printer, there is no consideration, and no contract. Even if the parties fully intended that Joe's promise to deliver the printer be binding, Joe can later change his mind and keep the printer, because he received no benefit from Harry in return for the promise (however, if Joe physically delivers the printer to Harry, he may have made a gift that he cannot get back).

There are exceptions to the requirement of consideration. Terms of an existing contract for the sale of goods often can be modified without additional consideration. For example, if a seller originally promised to deliver a product at the end of the month and later stated that delivery could be made two weeks earlier, the seller could be held to the earlier delivery date, even if the buyer had given the seller nothing in return for the earlier delivery. Another exception lies in the case of promises that were relied on. If Joe promised to give Harry the printer for nothing, and Joe knew that because of that promise Harry was going to buy a computer that could only use Joe's out-of-production printer, Joe might be *estopped* (legally prevented) from backing out of his promise to deliver the printer after Harry bought the computer.

Sometimes consideration is not present when it appears to be. A promise to perform a preexisting obligation is not valid consideration. So, if a company president says, "I will continue to perform all duties required of me as president" if all employees will agree to donate $10 to the company picnic fund, the president cannot enforce the employees' promise to pay. The president has given no valid consideration, because he or she was already obligated to perform the duties of the position of president. By the same token, it is not valid consideration to mention past benefits as payment for the other party's promise. For example, if Martha and Tom agree that Tom will give Martha his television set in payment for the programming work that Martha performed a month earlier, there is no consideration and no contract. Tom will receive no future benefit in return for his promise to deliver the television, since Martha has already done the work. For the most part, the requirement of consideration is not an issue in a contract dispute, since both parties were motivated to enter into the contract because of an expectation of a benefit to each. The tougher questions involve performance and breach of contract, which we will examine shortly.

SPECIFIC TERMS

A contract that was formed through a valid meeting of the minds and that contains adequate consideration might still be unenforceable because of a failure to clearly specify certain key terms. For example, if Mary agrees to pay Jeff to perform programming services, but they don't specify when the work is to be done, Mary may not be able to enforce the agreement if Jeff never shows up. Generally a contract will not fail to be enforceable merely because the parties forgot to spell out every detail of an arrangement but because important terms of the arrangement—such as performance schedules and prices—were not mentioned. However, it's a good idea to clarify all aspects of the agreement, and as we shall see, it pays to put it all down in writing.

THE IMPORTANCE OF A WRITTEN CONTRACT

All the sample contracts we've discussed so far could have been made either orally or in writing, and everything we've said would apply in either case. The fact that a contract is written or oral makes no difference to the question of whether or not the contract is valid and enforceable (with a few exceptions that we will see in a moment). But an important transaction or arrangement should

Hagelshaw: The Computer User's Legal Guide (Chilton)

never rest on an oral contract. And once again, the reason is not to increase the involvement of lawyers and the legal system, but to avoid it.

First we should note the important instances in which a contract must be in writing to be enforceable. All states have a law known as the Statute of Frauds. This law requires that contracts that cannot be fulfilled within the period of one year must be in writing. This includes virtually all employment contracts. Although it's a good idea in any case to commit to writing all promises of fringe benefits made by your employer, you must put it in writing if you are being hired for longer than a year. A written contract is also required for the sale of goods if the price is $500 or more. If you don't have a written contract, the deal can be voided by either party. So if a salesman at a computer store promises to sell you the last computer he has on sale for $1,500 and tells you that he will hold the computer for you while you run home to get your checkbook, you're at the mercy of the salesman's sense of honor. He could sell the computer to the next customer who comes through the door, and you'd have no legal recourse.

Other than the two situations just mentioned (and a few more such as real estate contracts), an oral contract is just as enforceable as a written contract. But the value of having a contract in writing becomes painfully clear when you have to prove the terms of an oral contract, either to your formerly cordial business associate, who now claims you are trying to rob him blind, or to a judge. We learned earlier that one of the main functions of a contract is to avoid disputes and entanglements with attorneys. You defeat this purpose when you don't put your agreement in writing. Most disputes arise not because people are crooked or nasty but simply because they have short memories. We just can't remember all the details of our agreements. Not only does a written contract lengthen the memories of its authors, but it also discourages any legal challenges to the agreement, because a court will usually not accept testimony that the parties orally agreed to something that is not part of the written contract.

A written contract doesn't need to be a formal document, witnessed and notarized. Photocopies of typed letters signed by the parties, or even a simple handwritten note signed by both, can serve to document the important terms of an agreement. The main point is to get it all down on paper at the time when the contract is created.

BREACH OF CONTRACT AND REMEDIES

Once a valid contract has been formed, all parties to the agreement are legally obligated to fulfill their promises. A failure to substantially perform contractual obligations is a *breach* of the contract, and it entitles the other party to seek legal remedies, such as a court order requiring performance or payment of damages. Certain minor deviations from the terms of a contract might not constitute a breach, although an adjustment in payment or another modification to the contract might have to be made. Suppose, for example, that Mary contracts with System Corp for the installation of a computer system in her office. In exchange for the payment of $25,000, System Corp is to install the computer system by January 1 and provide Mary with six boxes of printer paper. If System Corp fails to have the system installed by January 1, Mary may withhold payment or seek other remedies for breach of the contract. However, if the system is installed and operating by January 1 but System Corp delivers only five boxes of printer paper instead of six, the contract has been substantially performed. Mary can't refuse payment, although she would be entitled to deduct the price of the sixth box of paper.

Under certain circumstances, a party to a contract may be excused from performing his or her obligations. The most obvious example is when the other party has already breached the contract. If you promised to pay $6,000 when a computer is delivered to you, you don't have to pay anything if the computer never arrives. And it isn't always necessary to wait for the other party to breach the contract. Let's say that you agreed to pay $6,000 on January 1 for a computer that was to be delivered on January 15. If the supplier calls you on December 31 and says he will not be able to deliver the computer on January 15, you may withhold your January 1 payment. Although the supplier has not yet breached the contract since delivery was not to be until January 15, you can reasonably anticipate a future breach, which excuses you from performing your side of the bargain. Other legitimate excuses for nonperformance include impossibility of performance (e.g., because of illness that prevents performance) and agreement of the parties to cancel the contract or replace it with an entirely new agreement.

When one party breaches a contract, the other party is entitled to seek all available legal remedies. When the contract involves an item that is unique (such as a Rembrandt painting), the remedy can be an order for specific performance of the contract. This means that the party that breached the contract will be ordered to provide the precise item that he or she promised to deliver. Specific performance is never ordered for a contract involving personal services, and it normally is not used in contracts for the delivery of products that can be replaced easily, such as commercially available computer hardware or software.

In most cases the remedy for breach of contract is cancellation of the contract or recovery of money damages. The party that breached the contract can be required to pay damages to compensate for direct losses and sometimes must pay indirect, or *consequential,* damages, but only if the breaching party knew or could reasonably foresee that the indirect losses would result. For example, suppose that a computer store agreed in writing to sell Jim a personal computer for $3,000. Later the store refused to deliver the computer. Jim bought the same machine at another store, but the price had risen in the meantime, and he had to pay $3,500. Jim could recover the difference in price ($500) from the first store, but he could not recover $50,000 in lost profits that his business suffered when it shut down because of the delay in obtaining the computer. The store could not have foreseen the lost profits unless Jim had told the salesperson about the particular application for which he wanted the computer. And if Jim had informed the salesperson of the potential for lost profits, the store probably would have disclaimed any responsibility for the losses before agreeing to sell the computer. We will learn about such disclaimers in later chapters.

Remedies, like all other terms of a contract, may be established through agreement. The parties may include a clause in the contract that limits the remedies available for a breach of the agreement. It is even possible to state that the parties will not go to court in the event of disagreement but instead will submit any dispute to arbitration. Always remember the purpose of contracts: to avoid courts and lawyers!

The discussion of contract law in this chapter was necessarily short and sweet. Many of the finer points of contracts were omitted in order to concentrate on issues of interest to the computer user. In the remaining chapters, you'll use your basic understanding of contracts to help you master some of the more complicated aspects of computer law. Return to Chapter 1 when you need a review of the basic principles.

======================================

Buying a Computer
2

Do you remember when you bought your first computer? Or are you thinking of buying one in the near future? If so, you know that your biggest problem is deciding which of the many systems to buy. A large amount of useful software is available for the IBM PC as well as for some of the less expensive computers. If you buy a computer from one of the smaller manufacturers, will you have problems with support or replacement should that company go out of business in a few years? Do you need a portable computer, a desktop model, or both? Is multiuser capability one of your requirements? What about the cost and availability of software packages to do the job you have in mind?

Identifying the right computer system (hardware and software) for your needs is clearly the most important step in the process of buying a computer. But other considerations ought to be taken into account. Most buyers pay little attention to the legal aspects of buying a computer. They ask few if any questions about their legal rights in the event there is a defect in the hardware or the system turns out to be inappropriate for the job. Many buyers make their down payments and sign agreements or accept documents without reading them. Often this lack of attention to the fine print has no serious consequences. Most personal computers are reliable and perform as expected. But when a problem does arise, the buyer's lack of knowledge can lead to misunderstandings and wasted time and money.

It's not surprising that computer buyers have paid little attention to the

Hagelshaw: The Computer User's Legal Guide (Chilton)

legal aspects of their computer purchases. The technology is new and unfamiliar at first, and many businesspeople and home computer users have enough trouble just trying to figure out which system they should buy and how to get started using it. Buyers have tended to rely on the salespeople at computer stores for advice and warnings concerning potential problems. Trusting in the computer sellers as the experts, buyers haven't taken the same measures to inform and legally protect themselves as they would when buying, for example, a house or a car. This lack of concern with legal rights has caused problems for some computer purchasers. After all, computer manufacturers and retailers are in business to make money and are primarily concerned with protecting their own interests, not yours, in the event of a dispute. With their greater experience and economic power, the sellers have been very effective in doing just that.

Unfortunately, the courts haven't fully recognized the unequal positions of the seller and the buyer in a computer purchase transaction. Much of the current law dealing with the purchase of computers was developed during the era of mainframe computers, when the purchaser was often a large company with experience in major equipment purchases and with access to legal advice. If an established computer manufacturer sold a large system to a major bank, the courts would enforce the fine print of the contract signed by the two companies. It would be assumed that the bank, as the purchaser, had been able to bargain for the terms that it wanted before it signed the contract. Today the vast majority of computers sold in the United States are small personal computers, and many buyers of these computers are small businesses that and individuals who lack the expertise and opportunity to bargain with the seller for terms that will protect their interests. Despite the unequal positions of seller and buyers, the courts have continued to enforce the terms of computer purchase contracts as if the buyer were fully aware of those terms and in agreement with them. Manufacturers have taken advantage of this situation by imposing on the buyer warranty contracts that are slanted in favor of the seller. Still, there are ways in which small computer buyers can protect themselves.

In this chapter we'll discuss the rights that computer buyers have in relation to manufacturers and retailers under a typical purchase arrangement, as well as other rights that buyers may have as consumers of computer products. We'll also learn what steps buyers can take to improve their legal position in anticipation of problems with the computer, and what they can do if the computer doesn't work as expected or promised. We should note that although the discussion in this chapter focuses on the purchase of computers, the points made apply equally to the purchase of disk drives, printers, and other peripherals. The legal aspects of leasing and renting computer hardware are dealt with in Chapter 3.

A TYPICAL COMPUTER PURCHASE

Let's look at a typical example of a personal computer purchase. We aren't interested here in the usual hardware concerns of the computer buyer—the amount of random-access memory, the number of disk drives, the suitability of bundled software, the availability of parallel and serial interfaces, and so forth. Instead, we will examine the transaction with an eye to the legal rights of the buyer, the terms imposed by the manufacturer to limit those rights if a problem occurs, and the ways in which the buyer can avoid misunderstandings and costly legal disputes.

Our computer buyer is Walter, a veterinarian who operates a small-pet clinic. Walter decided that he wanted a computer to handle his customer billing and to keep track of his appointments. Walter went to ComputerStore, a local retailer handling several models of personal computers. Walter explained that he needed a computer system that could handle billing for two thousand customer accounts, with the capability of generating daily lists of pet appointments and letters to clients advising them of new medicines and treatments. The salesman recommended that Walter buy the Pumpkin Deluxe personal computer. The Pumpkin came with a program to manage mailing lists, and the salesman said that customer-billing software was available at software stores or through mail-order retailers. Walter told the salesman that he didn't want to have to use a lot of disks, because anything left lying around would eventually get chewed up by one of his patients. The salesman assured him that he could use the billing program in one disk drive while leaving a floppy disk with the customer account data in the other drive, thereby handling all the billing without changing disks. Walter asked about printers, and the salesman told him that the Pumpkin was compatible with a good-quality dot matrix printer available at PrinterStore at a price of $800.

Walter bought the Pumpkin from ComputerStore and went to SoftwareStore to buy a program for his customer billing. There he learned that no billing programs for the Pumpkin were yet available. The Pumpkin had just been introduced, and billing software for other computers couldn't be used with it. At PrinterStore, Walter found out that the Pumpkin couldn't use the $800 printer that the salesman at ComputerStore had suggested. A comparable printer that worked with the Pumpkin would cost $1,200. Walter was told that he should have bought the Watermelon, a computer that cost the same as the Pumpkin. The Watermelon was just as powerful and was compatible with the $800 printer and several billing software packages.

Undaunted, Walter returned to the pet clinic and plugged in his Pumpkin. He followed all the instructions for installation, but when he booted the demonstration disk, the monitor screen filled with wavy lines. No matter what he did, the lines wouldn't go away. When Walter pushed any key on the keyboard, the computer just beeped at him. "This machine not only isn't 'user friendly,'" said Walter, "it's downright hostile." Later a friend told him that he should have bought a computer with a hard disk drive to provide more storage space for data, since, contrary to what the salesman had told him, there was no way he could handle all his client accounts on the Pumpkin without continually changing floppy disks.

By now Walter was very upset and wondered aloud what he could do. Would ComputerStore or the manufacturer of the Pumpkin fix his computer for him? He had assumed that the saleman at ComputerStore was an expert on computers, but the salesman had talked him into buying a computer that was clearly inappropriate for his needs. Was there anything he could do about that? Was anyone going to reimburse him for the extra money he had had to spend on the printer?

Walter was despondent now, and he began staring aimlessly into the bottom of the Pumpkin shipping box. His eyes rested on a small packet of written materials. Walter pulled out the first piece of paper and began reading: "Pumpkin, Inc.—Deluxe Limited Warranty." "What does all this mean?", he wondered.

What Walter was looking at is the principal legal form that accompanies a personal computer. This form explains any express warranty covering the computer and gives notice of any limitations placed on the buyer's legal rights. In this chapter we will refer to these documents as "warranty disclosure forms." We say "disclosure" because the document informs you of the rights that the manufacturer is willing to give you. As we'll see later in this chapter, the purchaser has other rights under the law beyond those in the warranty disclosure form. Let's now take a look at the provisions contained in these forms to see how they affect someone with problems like Walter's.

PROVISIONS OF THE WARRANTY DISCLOSURE FORM

Sometimes a buyer is asked at the time of purchasing a computer to sign a contract or agreement that defines his or her legal rights. But usually the buyer just plunks the money down on the sales counter and receives only a receipt or bill of sale from the salesperson. The buyer then finds a warranty form printed in the owner's manual or on a separate piece of paper tucked away somewhere in the box along with the instructions for unpacking and hooking up the computer, and the other documentation. Most often the buyer will read the warranty form, if at all, only as part of the process of registering the computer (i.e., after purchase). The buyer sends in a card or form to register the computer and other related hardware in case warranty service is needed.

The warranty form that you find in the computer packing box contains several clauses, some of which are intended to inform you of your rights, but most of which are designed to limit your right to make claims against the manufacturer. We're about to examine the clauses most likely to appear in the form. The papers for your computer may or may not contain all of these provisions.

EXPRESS WARRANTY

Most manufacturers offer an express warranty that the computer will be free of defects. An *express* warranty is an oral or written guarantee, as distinguished from an *implied* warranty, which is a guarantee imposed by law regardless of whether it is expressly stated. The manufacturer and the computer store often advertise their express warranties with pride: "Full warranty on all products," or "Extended six-month warranty on Pumpkin computer." What they neglect to tell you is that the limitations that they impose on your implied warranties take away more than their express warranty gives you. If the implied warranties were allowed to operate without limitation, the buyer would be entitled to receive a computer that is free of defects and works the way it would ordinarily be expected to work. That means, for example, that the buyer could get the computer repaired or replaced free if it blew out a circuit board after eight months of ordinary use.

Most express warranties don't give you that kind of protection. The express warranty is usually limited in duration, often to as little as ninety days. So the buyer has to discover the problem within ninety days of purchase, or he or she has no warranty coverage. It isn't always easy to find a defect within three months. Some users take months just to figure out how to get the computer working (although they'd be reluctant to admit it). It also takes a lot of time to learn and begin using the full capabilities of a computer, and bugs that weren't apparent during early, simple applications can show up later. Unfortunately, the limited express warranty period begins running from the date of purchase, no matter what you're doing with the computer.

In addition to a limit on the duration of the express warranty, the warranty is usually limited in the amount of protection it offers. The manufacturer usually warrants the computer only against defects in materials or workmanship. This means that if the computer contains a defective microprocessor chip or was assembled in such a way that damge occurs when you plug it in, the warranty would cover the problem. You could require the manufacturer to repair these kinds of problems or replace the computer. However, manufacturers have been careful to avoid warranting against defects in design. For example, a computer might be designed with insufficient internal memory to operate certain software packages or might have a problem-ridden operating system. The manufacturer, however, would not warant that the computer meets any such state-of-the-art standards of design.

LIMITATIONS ON IMPLIED WARRANTIES

Almost every product that we buy carries with it implied warranties. The *implied warranty of merchantability* guarantees that the product will operate as it would ordinarily be expected to operate. For example, we might expect a personal computer to be built so that a user could operate the machine for several years without the failure of a major component such as a disk drive or circuit board. If there were a failure after only one year, the manufacturer could be held responsible for the resulting damages in the absence of any limitations on the implied warranty of merchantability. The *warranty of fitness for a particular purpose* guarantees that the product will perform the particular function that the user had in mind when he or she bought the product. If a buyer told the salesperson at the computer store of the purpose he or she had in mind for the computer, the store, and possibly the manufacturer, could be held responsible for damages resulting from a sale to the buyer of a sytem that could not meet that purpose. Again, this assumes that no limitation had been placed on the implied warranties.

The warranty form accompanying your computer undoubtedly limits the effect or duration of the implied warranties or disclaims them altogether. For example, the form might state that any implied warranties are limited to a period of ninety days from the date of purchase. This would mean that beyond the ninety-day period you could no longer enforce the gaurantee implied by law that the computer will operate as it would ordinarily be expected to operate. The form might even say that all implied warranties are expressly disclaimed. This would mean that there are no legal guarantees that the computer will function as it should other than those guarantees stated elsewhere on the form, if any (normally there is a limited express warranty).

LIMITATION ON REMEDIES FOR BREACH OF CONTRACT

Ordinarily, when the seller of a product fails to live up to an agreement to deliver a product that works, the buyer is entitled to recover all damages that befall him or her as a result of the seller's actions. These damages could include the cost of the product, expenses for shipping a damaged product, the value of lost work time, and other related costs. In theory, at least, the buyer could recover damages for the loss of an entire business that collapsed because of a computer malfunction.

The typical computer warranty disclosure form limits what the buyer can recover if the computer hardware turns out to be defective. The buyer normally is limited to obtaining repair or replacement of the defective item, with the manufacturer having the right to choose between repair and replacement. In addition, your form will probably state that the manufacturer will not pay any consequential or incidental damages that might result from the manufacturer's breach of the agreement. These would include such indirect damages as lost work time, lost profits resulting from a nonfunctioning computer, the cost of shipping the computer back to the factory for repair, and the cost of obtaining replacement computer equipment or services. Through this clause in the warranty form, the manufacturer makes sure that the most the company will ever have to do is give you a new computer.

A SHORTER STATUTE OF LIMITATIONS

Under the law of most states, a buyer has as long as four years within which to sue a seller for failing to deliver what was promised. This period can be reduced to as little as one year by agreement of the buyer and seller. Your computer warranty form may specify a shorter period for the filing of a lawsuit than the usual four years. As we'll see later in this chapter, the form may have so effectively limited your rights that you have no basis for suing anyway, once the limited express warranty has expired. For this reason, some warranty forms make no mention of a time period for filing a suit. But if the form specifies a shorter period—for example, one year—it allows the seller to ask the court to throw out any lawsuit filed more than one year after purchase of the computer. Thus, the manufacturer doesn't have to pay an expensive lawyer to defend the suit.

INTEGRATION CLAUSE

As we learned in Chapter 1, a promise made by one person to another need not be in writing to be legally enforceable. Let's suppose that a computer dealer tells the buyer that the manufacturer will replace any defective computer with a more expensive model. Or perhaps the buyer bought the computer because he or she had read an advertisement claiming that the computer had more memory capacity than any other computer in its price range, or "your money back." The buyer might be able to enforce these promises against the manufacturer even though they were never put into the warranty form or other written document given to the buyer. To protect themselves against this possibility, some manufacturers include in their warranty disclosure forms a clause stating that any promises or representations that aren't expressly included in the written document are not binding. So if the warranty form doesn't promise to replace the defective computer with a more expensive model, then the buyer doesn't get the better model, at least not through enforcement of the warranties (the buyer might be able to sue for fraud). These clauses excluding statements and promises that aren't contained in the warranty form are called *integration clauses*, which are another way of saying that "what you see (in the printed form) is what you get."

OTHER PROVISIONS

Your warranty disclosure form may contain other clauses besides those already mentioned. It will probably say that no warranties are effective if the computer has been damaged by accident or misused or modified in any way. This protects the manufacturer from having to replace a computer that was dropped on the basement floor by cousin Ralph or that blew up when you tried to use it as the brain for your experimental robot. The form will also tell you that you may have other rights under the laws of your state that aren't mentioned in the form. We'll discuss these other rights later in the chapter. The warranty form may discuss additional points, depending on the type of computer or peripheral equipment that you're buying.

Now that we've seen how the manufacturer tries to limit the rights of the purchaser, we'll examine the rights that the purchaser still has and see how they can be enforced against the manufacturer and the computer store. The discussion will refer to the warranty disclosure form that came with Walter's Pumpkin computer (Figure 2–1). Let's see how Walter handles the troubles with his Pumpkin.

WHAT TO DO WHEN YOUR NEW COMPUTER BREAKS DOWN

You'll remember that Walter's Pumpkin monitor is full of wavy lines and that the computer only beeps at him when he uses the keyboard. What should Walter do?

Hagelshaw: The Computer User's Legal Guide (Chilton)

FIG. 2–1
A Typical Computer Warranty

PUMPKIN, INC.—DELUXE LIMITED WARRANTY

For ninety (90) days from the date of original purchase of this computer, Pumpkin, Inc., warrants that it will repair or replace the computer free of charge upon return of the computer to Pumpkin, Inc., or to any authorized dealer (shipping costs to be paid by purchaser), if the computer is defective in materials or workmanship. The decision whether to repair or replace shall be at the sole discretion of Pumpkin, Inc.

This warranty does not apply if the Pumpkin label has been removed or if the computer has been damaged by accident or misuse or has been modified in any way.

If the computer is found to be defective in materials or workmanship within the ninety-day period, the purchaser's only remedy shall be the repair or replacement of the computer, as specified above. Pumpkin, Inc., shall not be liable for any incidental or consequential damages arising out of the use of, or loss of use of, this computer. Any legal action against Pumpkin, Inc., related to this computer must be commenced within one (1) year from the date of purchase.

This Deluxe Limited Warranty is in lieu of all other warranties, express or implied. Any warranties, promises, statements, or representations made by any person concerning this computer that are not written in this document are void and without effect.

Some states do not allow the exclusion of consequential or incidental damages or limitations on implied warranties, so not all of the above restrictions may apply to you.

Note: This "Pumpkin" warranty is a condensed version of the type of warranty that will come with your computer. For an example of a full-length computer warranty, see the appendix.

First let's assume that Walter has just taken his computer to his clinic and he's still within the ninety-day express warranty period stated in his warranty disclosure form. Now he has to get the Pumpkin back to the manufacturer or to an authorized dealer such as ComputerStore within the ninety-day period. Walter will have to pay any transportation costs himself. These expenses would be the responsibility of the computer company or dealer under a normal implied warranty or merchantability, but as we've seen, most manufacturers

Hagelshaw: The Computer User's Legal Guide (Chilton)

replace that warranty with their limited express warranty. Under Walter's warranty form the shipping costs must be paid by the purchaser. Also, Pumpkin, Inc., can't be sued for damages to Walter's business caused by the absence of the computer from the pet clinic because consequential and incidental damages are excluded. But if Walter gets his computer back to the manufacturer or dealer within ninety days of purchase, they will repair it or replace it with a new Pumpkin.

Now let's change the facts a little bit and assume that Walter set his computer up at the pet clinic and it worked fine for ten months. Then, near the end of a day in which he had already been bitten by two of his patients and had seen his favorite tie eaten by a third, the Pumpkin decided to blow up. "There was a loud bang, and then smoke started pouring out the back," Walter told the salesman at ComputerStore. The salesman was sympathetic, but he politely reminded Walter that the ninety-day warranty had expired.

Does the purchaser have any recourse in this instance? Most of us would probably agree that a personal computer shouldn't give out so completely after only ten months, assuming that it has been used in a normal manner. Under the law of virtually every state, the implied warranty of merchantability would permit the buyer to get back the money paid for the computer as well as indirect damages such as shipping expenses. But these implied warranties were excluded under the Pumpkin warranty form and would be excluded with your limited warranty too.

Have the courts upheld these restrictions on the purchaser's warranty rights? For the most part the answer is yes. Computer manufacturers and suppliers learned long ago that the courts would impose full implied warranty obligations on them if nothing was done to disclaim or limit those warranties. In the mid-1960s a company that had bought a Univac 60 computer brought suit against Sperry Rand Corporation, the manufacturer, claiming that the computer did not perform as promised. A federal appellate court found that Sperry Rand had breached an implied warranty of fitness for a particular purpose because (1) Sperry Rand knew what the buyer intended to use the computer for, (2) the buyer was justified in relying on Sperry Rand's expertise in recommending the Univac 60 for this purpose, and (3) the computer turned out not to be able to perform as promised (Sperry Rand Corp. v. Industrial Supply Corp., 337 F.2d 363 [5th Cir. 1964]).

Computer companies soon began to insert disclaimers of implied warranties into their contracts with purchasers. The courts usually upheld the validity of these disclaimers, even as lawsuits against suppliers by disgruntled computer users increased in the 1970s. Some purchasers attacked the warranty disclaimers as unconscionable, or unfair, to the purchaser, and therefore unenforceable. But these arguments usually did not prevail. In the 1970s, before the age of personal computers, the typical computer purchaser was still a medium-to large-sized company. Courts believed that disclaimers of warranties should be enforced against such purchasers. As one judge wrote, "Although the plaintiff was less knowledgeable concerning computers than the defendant, [because he was] a businessman he must be deemed to possess some commercial sophistication and familiarity with disclaimers" (Badger Bearing Co. v. Burroughs Corp., 444 F. Supp. 919 [E.D. Wis. 1977]).

With the coming of the inexpensive but powerful microcomputer of the 1980s, the typical computer user is no longer a sophisticated buyer of computer equipment but rather just one of millions of small businesses or individuals without much knowledge of either computers or the law. The purchase of a personal computer is not so much a transaction between two equally positioned businesspeople as a consumer sale in which the manufacturer and retailer have a great advantage in resources and experience over the purchaser. Most purchasers lack the knowledge and experience needed to negotiate the legal terms of the sale. They may bargain over the price but feel they are really in a take-it-or-leave-it situation. Unfortunately, the courts have not recognized this unequal relationship by invalidating some of the disclaimers of warranties contained in personal computer warranty disclosure forms. However, the personal computer revolution is still young, and it can take years for cases to be decided in the courts, so it's possible that the courts will begin to invalidate disclaimers of implied warranties and extend more complete warranty protection to the buyers of personal computers.

A few states have laws that do not permit limitations on the duration of implied warranties. Kansas, Michigan, Nebraska, New Mexico, Ohio, Texas, and Utah have all enacted at least some aspects of the Uniform Consumer Sales Protection Act. Among other things, this act defines unconscionability in a way favorable to purchasers and permits lawsuits, including class action suits, against sellers that impose unconscionable or unfair limitations on their own liability. If you have a major problem with your computer after the express warranty period has expired, you should check with an attorney or consumer advocate in your state to determine the extent of your legal rights.

In addition to upholding the exclusion of implied warranties, the courts have also upheld the other restrictions on purchasers' rights contained in the warranty disclosure form. These include the shortening of the statute of limitations (the deadline for filing a lawsuit), integration clauses voiding any promises made orally or through advertising, and limitations on what the buyer can recover if he or she sues. We learned earlier that the buyer normally can obtain no more than the repair or replacement of the computer if a problem occurs.

The warranty form states that there will be no recovery of consequential or incidental damages. As with restrictions on limited warranties, some computer buyers have challenged limitations on types of damage on the grounds that they are unconscionable and therefore void. So far these arguments have not been very successful either (a court rejected such arguments in the case of Office Supply Co. v. Basic/Four Corp, 538 F. Supp. 776 (E.D. Wis. 1982]).

In fact, limitations on remedies may outlast the restrictions on the implied warranties. Limiting the computer user to the remedy of repair or replacement of the computer is not as unfair as allowing no remedy at all after ninety days. In other words, the evolving law may require sellers of computers to provide a more extended warranty protection, but the buyer probably could only receive the value of repairs or replacement of the computer and no other incidental damages. Even here, however, the laws of a few states don't permit any restrictions on what the purchaser can recover when he or she sues. Check with an attorney in your state if you have questions about the enforceability of warranty limitations.

So we have to conclude that the computer companies have been effective in reducing the chances that anyone can hold them responsible whan a computer breaks down after the express warranty period has expired—at least on the grounds that they failed to meet implied warranty obligations. There may be other grounds for legal action against the computer manufacturer or the retailer, and we will consider those in just a moment when we return to Walter's problems.

If you find a mechanical problem with your computer that has also been discovered by other users of the same model, you should consider notifying the appropriate government and consumer action agencies. There have been instances of widespread defects in personal computers, resulting in product recalls. When first released in late 1981, some IBM PCs contained a flaw caused by a defective ROM (Read-Only Memory) chip, which caused the decimal point to be positioned incorrectly. Apple III, when first introduced, had a defective clock-calendar chip. Texas Instruments warned its customers in early 1983 that the transformer of one of its home computers could fail, creating the danger of electric shock. If your computer fails or you discover a chronic problem and the manufacturer and the computer store won't help you, it's a good idea to write or call your local or state consumer protection agencies or private consumer organizations. If other people are having the same problem, it may be possible to pressure the manufacturer to correct the defect.

Whenever you're considering legal action of any sort against a manufacturer or computer store, stop and ask yourself how much the enforcement of your rights is going to cost you. We all know that lawyers can be very expensive. Their services are especially expensive for a field of law most of them know little about, like computer law. Learning takes time, and you may be paying for your lawyer's education. Of course, if you have a $15,000 system that has a major defect and needs to be completely replaced, then legal action may be cost justified. If the computer can be restored by modest repairs, then it may make more sense from a financial standpoint to pay out of your own pocket to get it fixed, instead of bothering with complaints or legal action against the manufacturer or dealer. Consider taking the computer to an independent computer repair shop. Often such a shop charges less than the dealer for repairs.

We have now learned enough about the law concerning defects in personal computers to know that Walter will have an easy time getting his Pumpkin fixed if he discovers the wavy lines on the monitor within his ninety-day express warranty period, and a very difficult time after ninety days. But you'll remember that he has troubles other than the mechanical problems: (1) The salesman at ComputerStore told him that customer-billing software was available for the Pumpkin (which wasn't true), (2) the printer cost him $400 more than the salesman had said, and (3) he was sold a computer that only had floppy disk capability when he really needed a hard disk drive system for his veterinary practice. In other words, ComputerStore sold him a computer that was inappropriate for his needs. Can he do anything about it?

HOLDING THE SALESPERSON TO HIS OR HER PROMISES

The first thing Walter should do is go back to ComputerStore and ask to speak to the salesman and his manager. He should remind them that he told the salesman about his particular computing requirements and point out that the Pumpkin model he was sold isn't right for him. If ComputerStore wants to have a satisfied customer who will keep coming back, the management may be willing to give Walter his money back or give him a different computer that will be more useful to him. Although this may sound like a good business practice, the store will probably be very reluctant to take such action. The main reason is that it would get stuck with a used Pumpkin. Pumpkin, Inc., would probably agree to fix the mechanical defects, but the company would probably not give ComputerStore financial credit for a computer that was returned because the salesman made mistaken promises. ComputerStore doesn't want a used computer that would have to be severely discounted on the used computer market, so the manager will probably try to talk Walter into keeping the Pumpkin. If Walter persists, ComputerStore will likely tell him that the sale is final and that he can get the mechanical problems repaired, but nothing more.

If Walter wants to challenge ComputerStore or Pumpkin, Inc., over the salesman's promises, does he have a legal leg to stand on? Reviewing the Pumpkin warranty disclosure form in Figure 2–1, we're reminded that the ninety-day express warranty covers only defects in materials or workmanship. There is no express warranty covering promises about the appropriateness of the computer for the user's needs. Such promises could create an implied warranty of fitness for a particular purpose, but the Pumpkin warranty form has replaced all implied warranties with the limited express warranty. If the law in Walter's state permits such limitations on implied warranties, he will have no grounds for claiming that ComputerStore violated any warranty obligations.

But Walter may have other legal rights against ComputerStore or Pumpkin, Inc. If Walter gets no satisfaction from ComputerStore and elects to have his lawyer write a nasty letter or even sue, he can base his claim for a refund or damages on two theories: intentional misrepresentation (fraud), and negligent misrepresentation (malpractice). Neither of these grounds for action relies on rights contained in the warranty disclosure form or on any contract between the buyer and seller of the computer. The integration clause, the restrictions on the statute of limitations, and the limitations on remedies would not apply because the claims Walter is making are not based on contract law.

INTENTIONAL MISREPRESENTATION (FRAUD)

A misrepresentation is a false statement that the purchaser has relied on, with a resulting loss of money or other damage. A misrepresentation can be either intentional or negligent (that is, careless). You can imagine an example of an intentional false statement. If the salesperson knows that a computer has only 64K of internal memory but tells you it has 128K in order to get you to buy it, he or she has made an intentional misrepresentation. That's another way of saying that the salesperson has defrauded you. The courts are quite willing to back buyers in such situations, permitting them to void purchases and get their money back. If Walter can prove that the ComputerStore salesman knew that billing software wasn't available or that the less expensive printer wouldn't work with the computer and told him the false information because he was trying to dump a slow-selling Pumpkin on him, Walter could sue Computer-Store to get his money back. He could also recover expenses related to the purchase, such as lost work time or profits and out-of-pocket expenses.

Of course, proving what the salesman knew or didn't know at the time of the purchase is difficult; these cases aren't easy to win. But the courts are recognizing that purchasers of computer systems, especially small businesses and others with little knowledge of computers, need protection against sellers who make false promises to close a sale. For example, a computer user was able to sue and recover damages and attorney's fees when the sales agents of a computer supplier made false statements about the capabilities of a computerized accounting system (Dunn Appraisal Co. v. Honeywell Information Systems, Inc., 687 F.2d 877 [6th Cir. 1982]).

Walter also might be able to sue Pumpkin, Inc., the manufacturer, for the fraudulent statements (if any) of ComputerStore's salesman. A manufacturer is generally not responsible for the noncontractual liability of the retailer, such as liability for fraud or negligence. But the manufacturer could be liable if the company was aware of the retailer's practices and encouraged or ignored them. For example, if ComputerStore had been telling customers that the Pumpkin had 256K of internal memory when it only had 64K and Pumpkin, Inc., knew about this practice but didn't try to stop it because it was helping sales, Pumpkin, Inc., might be sued as a participant in the fraud.

If you feel you've intentionally been given false information or have been misled by advertising when buying or inquiring about a computer, there is action you can take other than a private lawsuit. Your local district, state, or commonwealth attorney's office is interested in merchants that misrepresent their products. Private consumer organizations also may be able to offer assistance.

In practice, most sellers of personal computer equipment are reputable, so there is relatively little outright fraud in sales of personal computers, either in advertising or verbal statements and promises made by salespeople. The more common and more difficult case for the purchaser is when the misrepresentation is not intentional but negligent or careless.

NEGLIGENT MISREPRESENTATION (MALPRACTICE)

Although the sellers of personal computers are seldom fraudulent, they are often uninformed. In a few major cities, computer manufacturers sell their products directly to purchasers at computer marts staffed by manufacturer-trained personnel. But most personal computers are sold through retail computer stores. Many of the salespeople who staff these stores are young and relatively inexperienced in both computers and sales. They have difficulty keeping informed about all the details of their rapidly changing inventory. As a purchaser, you may ask a salesperson a question about a particular computer or peripheral unit that he or she simply doesn't know much about. You might ask the salesperson whether the computer you're interested in is compatible with a particular printer that is sold at a different store. The salesperson says it is, because he or she remembers reading that in one of the manuals. What the salesperson doesn't know is that the computer is compatible with the printer only if you buy and install a special interface card and cable. You don't find out about the card and cable and the extra $200 you'll have to spend to get them until after you've bought the computer.

Of course, if a salesperson says that a certain computer is "the greatest" or that "it will solve all the problems in your business and double your profits overnight," we tend to dismiss that as idle boasting. It wouldn't be reasonable to rely on such promises. But when the salesperson makes statements that give the purchaser specific product information, concerning such matters as compatibility with other hardware, availability of software, or ability to perform specified tasks and solve particular problems, we do tend to rely on that information to a large extent. Because the computer store personnel are supposed to be experts on what they sell, a certain amount of trust and reliance seems reasonable. When salespeople turn out to be wrong—and they often are—is there anything that purchasers can do about the money that they have wasted or the other problems that have developed? This is the question our friend Walter is now asking.

You'll remember that the salesman at ComputerStore gave Walter false information (not intentionally, we'll assume) about printer compatibility, the availability of billing software, and the appropriateness of using a floppy disk rather than a hard disk drive. As a result, Walter later spent more money than he had expected to when he bought the Pumpkin and lost time away from his business trying to straighten out the problems. Unfortunately for Walter, unless ComputerStore volunteers to pay the expenses he incurred and compensate him for his lost time (an unlikely event), he can't do much to force the store to pay.

In one case a computer user sued a computer company that had sold the user the wrong system. The user argued that people who sell computer products have special expertise in a highly technical field and therefore should be held to a higher standard of care in their dealings, much like doctors and other professionals. The court didn't buy the argument (Chatlos Systems, Inc., v. NCR Corp., 479 F.Supp. 738, 741 [D.N.J. 1979]). The courts may begin to impose professional malpractice liability on sellers of computer equipment in the future. But for now, computer buyers should expect to have to look out for themselves when making a purchase. Here are a few tips on what to do when you deal with a computer salesperson in order to avoid later problems.

PROTECTING YOUR LEGAL RIGHTS AT THE TIME OF PURCHASE

We have learned about the difficulties that computer purchasers like Walter can have in asserting their rights against manufacturers or retailers after they discover problems with their machines. The companies that are selling you your computer get good legal advice and have shielded themselves from much liability. But there are some steps you can take to protect your rights and avoid unanticipated expenses and headaches.

First of all, if you have the nerve and don't mind arguing with salespeople, tell them that you don't want the manufacturer's warranty. Earlier in this chapter, we learned that the implied warranty of merchantability gives you much broader protection than the warranty that the manufacturer wants to give you—a limited express warranty coupled with a disclaimer or limitation on the duration of all implied warranties. Tell the salesperson that you prefer to take the computer without any express guarantees from the manufacturer. The store may not agree to sell you the computer under these circumstances, but it might do it rather than lose a sale. If that ploy doesn't work and the warranty disclosure form turns up in your computer shipping box, mail it back to the computer company with a letter explaining that you're rejecting it. You take a chance this way, since without the express warranty you may have a tough time getting the manufacturer or dealer to fix a problem within the first ninety days after purchase (the duration of a typical express warranty). But if there is a major failure after ninety days (assuming the failure is not the result of ordinary wear and tear and that your use of the computer was "normal"), the manufacturer is exposed to liability for breach of implied warranty. You also stand a better chance of enforcing promises concerning the fitness of the computer for a particular purpose if you have rejected the manufacturer's warranty form.

If you were enticed to buy the computer by advertisements or brochures that you read, attach copies of them to the sales receipt. Have the salesperson initial them if he or she is willing. If the salesperson makes statements about characteristics of the computer that are particularly important to you, write the statements down and ask the salesperson to initial the paper and attach it to the sales receipt. This documentation of the transaction could help you tremendously if a dispute develops later. Of course, you'd like to have a good relationship with the computer store and don't want to anger anybody with unreasonable requests. But if the management runs a professional business, it should respect you for being careful with your money.

The best way to avoid trouble is to learn as much as possible about the computer you're buying before closing the deal. Consult books and magazines

Hagelshaw: The Computer User's Legal Guide (Chilton)

as well as friends and associates for critiques of various computers. When you go to the computer store, take your time and ask a lot of questions. Explain the particular uses you have in mind for the computer to make sure that the salesperson understands your needs. Ask to see software and peripherals demonstrated on the computer that you're interested in. Go to more than one store and compare the different versions of the capabilities and limitations of the computer, as well as its past problems. If you still aren't certain that the computer can do the job you have in mind, consider renting one for a while to try it out (see Chapter 3). *Remember:* Careful, informed planning can help get your computer operating smoothly and can save you the time and expense of legal quarrels.

MAINTENANCE CONTRACTS

Either when you buy your computer or later, you may have the opportunity to purchase a maintenance contract. Some manufacturers offer extensions of their warranty, which means that for the payment of additional money you will be entitled, during a specified period, to have your computer repaired or replaced if defects in materials or workmanship are discovered. Some computer stores offer similar maintenance agreements under which they will service what they sell for a specified period of time after the sale. You can also sign maintenance contracts with independent service companies such as TRW and Sorbus. These contracts are offered on a monthly, biannual, or annual basis, with widely varying fees.

When deciding whether these maintenance contracts are worth the price, you have to balance the cost of the contract against the product's reputation for reliability. If your computer model is known to be very dependable, you may not be willing to purchase the contract or to pay as much for it as you would if the model has a history of problems. The manufacturer's ninety-day express warranty period may be long enough to discover whether you have a lemon. Another factor to consider is the potential for business losses resulting from a nonfunctioning computer. If downtime will cost you a lot of money, a maintenance contract that ensures fast repairs is more valuable to you than to a business that isn't so computer dependent. Also ask whether the contract maintenance will be done at the computer store or at a local shop of the service company. If the computer has to be sent back to the factory for repairs, the inconvenience of such an arrangement may be reason enough to decline purchase of the maintenance contract.

You can certainly get your computer repaired without a warranty or a maintenance contract. Computer repair shops, both nationwide chains and local companies, are opening in great numbers around the country. These shops operate on the same basis as automobile or television repair shops. You pay an hourly rate for labor, and you also pay for parts. The independent repair shops should be able to do the same job at a lower cost than the manufacturer or the computer store, and this may be the cheapest repair alternative available. As with car repairs, the trick will be to find a computer repair shop that is competent and honest.

BUYING THROUGH THE MAIL

Throughout this chapter we've assumed that the computer user was buying the machine at a computer store and that the computer was new. If you elect to buy computer hardware through the mail, all of the issues concerning warranties, other contract rights, and suing the seller are the same. The big difference is that the computer store is close by and the mail-order company is likely very far away. If the computer has a problem, you can't walk into the mail-order company with your broken computer and demand action. You may have to send the computer to the company for repairs, which means delay and added cost (although some computers have warranties that are honored at authorized dealers nationwide). If the seller won't give you satisfaction, you may be faced with the difficult problem of carrying on a legal dispute with a company in another state. If you buy through the mail, make sure you know that what you're buying is exactly what you want and that the price is good enough to justify the added risk of a long-distance transaction.

BUYING USED COMPUTERS

You may also be interested in buying a used computer. People sell their old computers when they want to upgrade to a more powerful model or when they simply decide they can't use the old one anymore. You can buy used computers at computer "swaps" or at one of the growing number of stores that handle used computer hardware. Buying a used computer can be a good way to obtain one at a lower price than the same model would cost new. But make sure you test the computer first and clarify with the seller whether there is any express warranty with the purchase or whether you're buying it as is. If it's an informal sale, get the seller's address and phone number so that you can find him or her later in case you were sold a lemon. When buying a used computer, you have many of the same rights to sue for misrepresentation and fraud that you have in purchasing a new computer. Just the same, avoid spending more money for a used computer than you can afford to lose.

Renting and Leasing Computers
3

As with other kinds of office equipment, there are different ways to acquire computers. Besides purchasing a computer, you can lease one for an extended period or rent one for a few days, weeks, or months.

If you've heard that some computer leasing companies had financial difficulties, you may be thinking that computer leasing was a thing of the past. There were some spectacular failures, but they were largely related to the leasing of large mainframe computers. In late 1979, Itel Corporation, which leased computers and other equipment, collapsed into bankruptcy. Firms like Itel were hurt by the introduction of small but powerful computers that were easier for businesses of all sizes to purchase. This left the leasing companies with large unleased inventories of mainframe computers (the modern-day "dinosaurs"). But undeterred by these failures, companies in the mid-1980s are rushing back into the leasing and renting business, this time with smaller computers.

Computer leasing has long been used as an alternative means of financing the acquisition of a computer. Under the typical lease arrangement, the computer user makes a down payment and a series of monthly payments for a specified period, usually three to five years. At the end of the lease period, the lease may permit the user to own the computer. With the possible exception of maintenance obligations, there's little difference between this type of lease arrangement and an outright purchase with financing.

Even when lease payments are not applied toward the purchase price, the lease still functions primarily as a substitute for a purchase. The rapid technological changes in the computer industry may render the computer obsolete at the end of the lease period. If the leasing company takes the computer back after the lease expires, the machine may have little resale value. The computer's useful life was the life of the lease. So, as a practical matter, a lease is just another way of buying a computer. By leasing, the user can acquire a computer, usually with a smaller initial outlay of cash, to meet his or her long-term computing needs.

Renting computers is distinct from leasing. The reasons for renting a computer are usually different from the reasons for leasing or buying, as is the arrangement. A computer rental typically covers a shorter and more open-ended period of time than a lease. The computer may be rented on a monthly basis, with no limit to the total number of months. The user can return the computer after one month or renew the rental for as many months as he or she likes (there may be a minimum required period). The rental arrangement is designed to meet the temporary computing needs of the user. It permits the user to have a computer for only as long as it is needed. However, this flexibility has its price, since a month's rental costs considerably more than a month's lease. The price is higher to compensate the rental company for the added trouble and risk of frequent changes in users of the computer.

It's clearly cheaper to buy a computer for business or home use if you plan to keep the computer for any length of time. The potential attractiveness of renting computers is related to factors other than cost. For example, you can obtain a computer for a limited time or purpose without the expense of outright purchase; you can try out one or more models for a short period before deciding which to buy; and you can have a computer to work with while waiting for technological changes to result in availability of a more advanced model, which you might want to buy. These considerations will continue to be important to some computer users as the microcomputer industry matures, which means that the companies that rent computers are here to stay.

The companies renting computers range from established equipment rental and servicing companies, such as General Electric Company, to a host of small independent rental firms. A few companies rent inexpensive computers such as the Commodore 64 for home use, but most rent only the more popular and powerful models such as the IBM PC, the Apple IIe and Macintosh, and Hewlett-Packard personal computers. Typically, the user can rent a computer and related equipment (printer, extra disk drives, modems) on a weekly or monthly basis, although some companies also rent by the day. Under some arrangements the rental fee can be applied toward purchase if you decide you would like to keep the computer, or you may be given a discount on the purchase price. Prices vary widely among rental firms, but they are rarely low. Renting a computer is not a straight substitute for buying. You should identify a particular reason why your computing needs can be met better by renting than by purchasing. If there is no good reason for renting, then you should consider buying a computer.

ADVANTAGES OF RENTING A COMPUTER

As we have said, renting a computer can be expensive. A month's payment toward purchasing a computer is far lower than a month's rental fee. But under certain circumstances, renting may be worth the expense.

If you intend to use the rented computer for business, you can deduct the rental payments from your taxable income. The after-tax cost of the computer will of course be less than the cost to someone who cannot deduct the payments. But if you rent the computer for an extended period, the cost will still be much higher than the after-tax cost of buying the same computer. Tax considerations alone don't justify the decision to rent a computer.

Remember: Whether you're renting, leasing, or buying a computer, there may be problems in taking an income tax deduction when you are using the computer at home. Don't assume that you are always entitled to a tax deduction for your computer. (The issue of tax deductions for computers used at home is discussed in Chapter 9.)

You should rent a computer only when rental provides the solution to specific and temporary needs. There are several situations in which renting a computer makes sense. For example, a lot of people are confused by the great variety of computers available for business and home use. Renting a computer for a month or two is a good way to try it out before making a decision to buy. You might even discover that a particular office procedure that you had intended to computerize can be performed better manually. In that case you can return the rented computer and avoid the expense of buying a computer that would have ended up in the closet. The opportunity to compare different computers may be limited, since most rental companies stock only the more popular models such as the IBM PC. But even a limited selection can show you how different computers perform the functions you need.

Renting a computer is a good way to fulfill short-term or unanticipated computing needs. For example, a business might need extra computing power for a special, one-time planning project or a month-end billing backlog. Sometimes there are unexpected delays in delivery of computer equipment after purchase; rented computers can be used to begin the work until the purchased computer arrives. A business might also rent a computer to train an employee to use the computer or software without tying up the main office computer. A rented computer can replace a computer that has been sent out for repairs. Any important temporary or unexpected need can justify the cost of short-term rental. Some computer rental companies feel that the largest portion of their business will come from users in this category.

One of the biggest advantages of renting is that the rental company is responsible for maintaining the computer. If there's a problem with the machine, they will repair or replace it at no charge to you. This eliminates the expense of a maintenance contract and the risk of work delays and lost profits caused by a computer breakdown. In the long run it costs less to buy the computer and maintain it yourself, but in the short run it's nice to have someone else be responsible for maintenance.

Another advantage to renting is that you can have a computer installed and running immediately, without having to spend a lot of money at the start. You just pay month-to-month until you don't need the computer or until you are in a position to buy one. This might be an important factor for a company with a limited budget for capital expenditures. Of course, you end up paying less over the long run by purchasing, but there may be situations in which a temporary cash shortage or credit problem makes renting a necessity.

Renting is also a way to avoid the risk of technological obsolescence. Innovations in computer technology over the years have brought a steady increase in computer capabilities at lower cost to the user. For example, suppose you're having doubts about buying the latest computer to do your taxes because you have just read that next year's model will also make your morning coffee. In this case you might consider renting now, and when the more attractive model is available you can buy it and return your rented computer. Because of the high cost of renting, however, this is a strategy that should be employed cautiously. A computer that meets your basic word processing, planning, and other computing needs when you first buy it may still be adequate later, even after more advanced models have become available. You could spend a lot of money on expensive rental payments waiting for technological changes that you don't really need. Before you rent for reasons related to technological change, make sure you know what you are waiting for. If a current model is appropriate for your needs, you should probably buy it.

SOFTWARE RENTAL

Some computer rental companies also rent software as part of a complete business system. They feel they can rent more computers if the computer comes complete with word processing, spreadsheet, or other information management programs. Other companies decline to rent software with their computers. They don't believe they can make money from renting something that can be copied and returned immediately.

There may also be legal problems associated with renting software for use by businesses and other consumers. The typical software license agreement that accompanies the purchase of packaged software contains restrictions on transfer of the program to other users. The issue has not been decided finally in the courts, but it may be held that rental of software violates these license agreements or the copyright protection laws. For this reason, some computer rental companies are playing it safe by refusing to rent software with their computers. So keep in mind that you may have to buy software to use with your rented computer. (See Chapter 4 for a detailed discussion of software license agreements and other issues involved in the purchase and rental of software).

PROVISIONS OF THE COMPUTER RENTAL AGREEMENT

When you rent a computer, you'll be asked to sign a rental agreement that specifies the rights and obligations of the user and the rental company. Computer rental firms tend to be small, local companies that are developing the guidelines for a relatively new industry. For this reason there is less uniformity in computer rental agreements than, for example, in software license agreements or warranty forms accompanying the purchase of computers. But there are certain important terms that most rental companies put into their rental agreement forms to protect their interests. In the next sections we'll look at the key provisions contained in these agreements. A familiarity with them will help you assess potential costs and benefits of a computer rental arrangement and ask useful questions when you talk with a representative of a rental company. (An example of a complete rental agreement can be found in the appendix.)

RENTAL PERIOD

Computers are normally rented by the month, although it is possible to obtain one for shorter periods (a week, or even a day). The rental company normally requires a minimum rental period such as one or two months and of course will be happy to sign you up for a longer period. There may be a reduction in the price when you initially sign up for a period longer than the minimum required. If you rent the computer for only one month, you can renew the rental agreement by giving notice and continuing to make monthly payments.

PAYMENTS

The basic payment is the monthly rental fee. The rental company may offer discounts to users who rent a large number of computers. There may also be a reduction in the monthly fee when the computer is rented for an extended period, such as six months or a year. Because it is easier for the rental company to manage its inventory when it rents for specified periods of time, it is willing to give a price break to users who rent for such periods.

There will probably be other fees in addition to the monthly rental payment. Most companies require a deposit that they use to cover late rental payments or damage to their computers. They may also charge a delivery fee for bringing the computer to the user's location. Often the rental company will install the computer, both as a convenience to the user and as insurance that their computers are not damaged. For the same reasons they will pick up the computer at the end of the rental period. There may be a separate fee for pickup, or that may be included as part of the delivery fee.

There may be optional charges for services related to the rental. For example, the rental company may offer training in operation of the computer for an additional fee. It may provide other services such as advice in selecting software and instruction in its use.

SPECIFIED LOCATION AND USER

The rental agreement usually specifies the location where the user will keep the computer and requires that the computer remain at that location. The user must obtain permission from the rental company before changing the location of the computer. Change of location in this context means moving to a different address, not simply moving the computer to a different office within the same building. There may also be a restriction on who is to use the computer. If you want to rerent or loan the computer to another company, you may have to get permission from the rental company first. Moving your computer to different addresses could be grounds for the rental company to terminate the lease and take back the computer. These restrictions are meant to help the rental company keep track of its computers and make sure that they are used in reasonably secure environments. However, rental companies want to meet the needs of the user, who in the ordinary course of business may have to move the computer or allow another person temporary use of it. If the user knows of these special requirements at the time when the rental agreement is signed, the agreement can be modified to allow for them. If the changes in location or user have to be made later, permission in writing should be requested first.

REPAIRS AND MAINTENANCE

One of the biggest advantages of renting a computer, as we've said, is that the user does not have to worry about the cost, inconvenience, and potential business losses resulting from breakdowns. The rental company knows that the user will not renew the rental for another month if the computer has a problem that does not get fixed. The rental company promises to repair problems or replace the equipment immediately when there is trouble.

The responsibility for breakdowns or other damage that is not the result of ordinary wear and tear rests with the user. If the equipment is damaged through misuse or neglect, the user must pay the cost of repair up to the value of the damaged hardware. In other words, the rental company will fix internal defects and worn parts (things that go wrong during ordinary use), but you must pay for damage caused by accidents. The rental company may require a deposit to cover the cost of any damage for which the user is responsible. The user is also prohibited from modifying the rented hardware and if modifications are made, must pay the cost of restoring it to its original condition. The user must make sure that the computer is secure and take responsibility for thefts or unexplained losses of equipment. To ensure that the rental company's equipment is safe and being maintained properly, the rental agreement may give the company the right of reasonable access to the user's premises for inspection of the rented equipment. The agreement usually permits the rental company to terminate the rental and take back its hardware if it discovers that the equipment is being used improperly or has been damaged.

TERMINATION AND RENEWAL

The agreement gives the rental company the right to terminate the rental and take back the computer if the user fails to meet any of his or her obligations under the agreement. As we have already discussed, the main obligations of the user are to pay the rent, maintain the computer in its specified location, and avoid damage to the computer. The user also can terminate the rental if the rental company fails to meet its obligations. The rental company's most important obligations are to repair defects and to correct ordinary operating problems of the computer.

If rental is monthly, the user may terminate it at the end of any month. Of course, if the user has agreed to rent for a specified period such as six or twelve months, he or she is obligated to pay rent for that entire period. At the end of the specified period the rental will continue on a month-to-month basis until it is terminated. Typically the agreement provides for automatic renewal of the rental for another month unless the user notifies the company or returns the computer. The rental company would prefer that the user keep the computer and continue paying rent, so it is up to the user to decide when he or she no longer needs the computer.

DISCLAIMER OF WARRANTIES AND CONSEQUENTIAL DAMAGES

In Chapter 2 we discussed the implied warranties that accompany the purchase of computers, including the warranty of merchantability and the warranty of fitness for a particular purpose. We also discussed the efforts made by computer manufacturers to disclaim those warranties. Under a rental arrangement, the rental payments aren't applied toward the purchase price but are simply payments for temporary use of the computer. The implied warranties wouldn't go into effect because there is no sale of goods. Despite this fact, some rental agreements contain language disclaiming all warranties, because the rental company wants to make it clear that no warranties have been made concerning the rented equipment.

The agreement also contains a disclaimer of any liability for consequential or incidental damages that arise out of the use of the computer or out of inability to use the computer or other rented hardware or software. The most serious consequential damages are business losses resulting from breakdown of the computer. The rental company is responsible for repairing the computer if it breaks down, but while the repairs are being made, a business could lose money from delays in completing projects, billing customers, and the like. Equipment failure may also result in the loss of important data stored in the computer's memory or on disk. To protect itself from any possible liability, the rental company will insert a clause in the agreement disclaiming any responsibility for consequential damages.

INSURANCE

The user may be required to cover the rented equipment with insurance to protect against damage or loss. Some office insurance policies cover rented computer equipment; if your policy does not provide coverage; you would have to obtain additional insurance to cover the computer or seek a waiver of insurance. Rental companies often waive insurance requirements upon payment of an additional fee. Even if there's no insurance requirement, you are still responsible for loss or damage to the equipment while it is in your possession. The insurance just provides the rental company with a source of funds in case you are unable to pay for the damage or loss of the equipment.

OTHER PROVISIONS

The provisions that we have already discussed are the most important terms that you will find in your rental agreement. The agreement will contain other clauses, most of which are not unique to computer rentals but can be found in rental agreements for other types of equipment. For example, there will be penalties for paying the rent late, usually 5 or 10 percent of the monthly rental fee.

The agreement will probably contain an integration clause stating that the printed rental contract is the entire agreement between the parties. Integration clauses are intended to prevent the computer user from holding the rental company to oral promises about the capabilities and performance of the computer. If a representative of the rental company makes statements about what a particular computer can do for you, ask him or her to add the statements to the rental agreement. If it turns out that the computer can't perform as promised, you'll have stronger legal grounds for cancelling the agreement.

The appendix contains an example of a complete computer rental agreement. It's a good idea to read this form and familiarize yourself with the terms before talking with a rental company representative. This chapter should answer most of the questions you may have about how a computer rental works. If you have other questions, be sure to ask the representative before you pay. Read the entire rental agreement before signing it. Remember what we said in Chapter 1: Almost anything can be written into a contract. The rental company will present you with a preprinted form agreement, but you can still discuss adding clauses that you want or deleting something that you don't like.

ADVANTAGES OF LEASING A COMPUTER

Computer leases are made for computers of all sizes, from mainframes to micros. We noted earlier in the chapter that leasing is used primarily as an alternative means of financing the acquisition of a computer. But a leasing arrangement is not exactly the same as a purchase, and some computer users may find extra advantages in leasing.

One advantage of leasing is the ability to get a computer into the office with a smaller initial outlay of cash. Under a typical lease arrangement, the user makes a down payment, followed by monthly lease payments and a residual payment at the end of the lease. At that time the user owns the computer. The total after-tax amount paid may roughly equal the amount paid to make a financed purchase of a computer (this will depend on the user's tax bracket; the potential tax advantages will be discussed shortly). But leasing generally requires a lower down payment and lower monthly payments than purchasing. This may be important to some users who wish to preserve their budget for capital equipment.

There may be maintenance and repair advantages to leasing. If lease payments are not applied toward purchase (in order to avoid the tax consequences), the leasing company takes back the computer at the end of the lease period, and the user owns no interest in the computer. If the leasing company believes that the computer will still be valuable (i.e., technologically current) at the end of the lease period, it may assume responsibility for maintaining and repairing the computer during the lease term. This can save you the cost of a maintenance contract. But check your lease agreement carefully. Many leases require that the user pay for repairs.

The primary advantage of leasing comes from tax benefits. Of course, if you don't intend to use the computer for business, you can't deduct any portion of the cost from your taxable income. A computer leased for personal use would probably cost more in the long run than a purchase of the same computer. But a user who has a business use for the computer may pay less in the long run by leasing rather than purchasing, after taking into account finance charges and all tax deductions. Whether there's a financial advantage to leasing depends on the tax bracket of the computer user and the availability of certain tax savings. The following analysis, which is summarized in Tables 3–1 and 3–2, shows the approximate after-tax cost of leasing and purchasing a computer for users with incomes of $30,000 and $85,000.

Assume that two businesspeople want to acquire the same $5,000 computer. Johnson decides to buy the computer, but Smith leases her computer with a $500 down payment and equal monthly payments for thirty-six months. Both Johnson and Smith have a taxable income of $30,000, and neither has an incorporated business. Johnson can elect to deduct the entire $5,000 purchase price in the first year under the special allowances for business equipment given by Section 179 of the Internal Revenue Code. Assuming that Johnson paid cash for his computer, the total after-tax cost of the machine will be about $3,500. If Johnson were unable to take the Section 179 allowance, he could take an investment tax credit of $500 (Section 38 of the Internal Revenue Code) and

TABLE 3–1
After-Tax Cost of Purchasing and Leasing (income: $30,000)

	Purchase	Lease
Computer user	Johnson	Smith
Price of computer	$5,000	$5,000
After-tax cost		
Cash payments	$3,500–3,700	$4,300
Financed (at 15 percent)	$4,300	—

a normal depreciation deduction. In that situation the total cost would be about $3,700. In any case, Johnson has spent less money at the end than has Smith. Smith can deduct the lease payments from her taxable income and take the investment tax credit, if that credit was not taken by the leasing company. But Smith's total after-tax cost will be about $4,300 (see Table 3–1).

On the other hand, if Johnson buys the computer on credit, paying 15 percent interest on the loan, the total costs for Johnson and Smith will be much closer. Johnson can deduct the interest payments, in addition to taking the deductions and credits already mentioned. His total after-tax cost will be about $4,300 with the Section 179 depreciation allowance, and $4,600 without it. Smith's total after-tax cost on her lease of $4,300 now compares favorably with Johnson's total cost (see Table 3–1).

For users whose incomes are in the higher tax brackets, there can be a substantial financial advantage in leasing. Assume that the two businesspeople each have a taxable income of $85,000. Smith will pay a total of about $3,200 on her lease after all tax savings are accounted for. Buying with financing, Johnson will have a total after-tax cost of about $3,500 with the Section 179 allowance, and about $4,200 without it. But Johnson would still be better off purchasing with cash than leasing, as long as he can take the Section 179 depreciation allowance; he would pay $2,800 with the allowance, and $3,300 without it (see Table 3–2).

The figures in Tables 3–1 and 3–2 are intended only as a rough estimate of the relative cost of leasing and purchasing a $5,000 computer. The decision whether to lease or buy is affected by many factors, including the tax bracket of the computer user, whether the user's business is incorporated, the tax laws of the state in which the user is doing business, the value of the computer equipment, and the prevailing interest rates. We have not considered the possible advantages in "sale and leaseback" arrangements or the advantages for computer equipment that qualifies for research and development tax credits. If you are considering a major computer purchase or have any questions about

TABLE 3-2
After-Tax Cost of Purchasing and Leasing (income: $85,000)

	Purchase	Lease
Computer user	Johnson	Smith
Price of computer	$5,000	$5,000
After-tax cost		
Cash payments	$2,800–3,300	$3,200
Financed (at 15 percent)	$3,500–4,200	—

whether leasing is the best way to acquire your computer, consult an accountant, tax attorney, or other tax expert. Also keep in mind that total after-tax cost is not the only consideration in deciding whether to lease or buy. As we have seen, there may be cash flow or maintenance advantages that make the leasing alternative attractive.

PROVISIONS OF THE COMPUTER LEASE AGREEMENT

When leasing a large system, the computer user may be able to negotiate the terms of the lease agreement. The drafting of such an agreement is not a task that you should attempt without skilled legal advice. A little later in this chapter we'll discuss some of the factors to be considered before discussing a lease arrangement with an attorney.

Usually, however, the user is not in a position to negotiate the terms of the lease, except perhaps the cost. When you lease a computer you generally will be asked to sign a lease agreement form provided by the leasing company (which may be a computer retail store that leases as well as sells computers, a company that specializes in the leasing of computers, or a company that leases computers along with other kinds of equipment). Let's briefly examine the most important provisions of a typical lease agreement. (The appendix contains an example of a complete computer lease agreement.)

LEASE PERIOD

Computers are generally leased for a minimum of thirty-six months. The lease period may be for any number of years greater than three, although a lease of computer equipment for more than five years is unusual, given the short useful life of equipment in the rapidly changing computer industry. The lease agreement may provide for renewal of the lease period at the option of the computer user, either for an additional year or on a month-to-month basis.

OWNERSHIP

The lease states that the title to the equipment remains with the leasing com pany (the lessor). If title passes to the user (the lessee), then the arrangement is not a lease but a sale. In that case you, as the user, will lose any tax advantages that you thought you were getting from the lease. Make sure that you aren't making a mistake on this important issue.

LOCATION OF USE

The leasing company needs to keep track of its equipment for repair and main-tenance and, possibly, repossession. The lease agreement usually specifies where the equipment is to be used and requires that the user seek permission before moving it. Ordinarily the leasing company will be flexible enough to accommodate the user's business needs; the important thing is to avoid misun-derstandings by making sure that the leasing company knows the computer's whereabouts.

REPAIRS AND MAINTENANCE

One of the most important terms of the lease involves responsibility for main-taining and repairing the computer. The user will be responsible for damage to the computer from mishandling and neglect, but the obligation to repair prob-lems resulting from ordinary wear and tear may be placed on either the user or the leasing company. The user should make sure he or she knows who's re-sponsible for repairs before signing the lease. A mistake on this point could greatly increase the total cost to the user over the life of the lease.

DISCLAIMER OF WARRANTIES AND CONSEQUENTIAL DAMAGES

In recent years, courts in most states have applied the provisions of the Uni-form Commercial Code to equipment leases as well as to sales. This means that the implied warranties of merchantability and fitness for a particular purpose become part of the lease unless disclaimed by the leasing company. Predict-ably, most lease agreements disclaim the implied warranties. There may not be any express warranties given by the leasing company, although the lease agree-ment may assign the manufacturer's express warranty to the user if the equip-ment is new (see Chapter 2 for a detailed discussion of warranties). The lease agreement also disclaims any liability on the part of the leasing company for consequential damages. These include such damages as business losses from inability to use the computer after a breakdown.

ASSIGNMENT TO THIRD PARTY

The lease agreement probably will prevent the user from allowing another person or company to operate the computer without the permission of the leasing company. If the user intends to transfer use of the computer either temporarily or permanently, he or she should work this out with the leasing company before the lease is signed. The leasing company probably will be happy to accommodate any reasonable use of the computer.

OTHER PROVISIONS

The lease agreement contains many provisions other than those we have discussed. For example, in some leases there may be provisions for renewal of the lease. With a renewal clause, the user can keep the computer and continue making monthly payments rather than return the computer at the end of the lease period. There may be provisions for additional fees in the event of late payments as well as for acceleration of payments in the event of failure to pay. Acceleration means that the leasing company may demand immediate payment of all lease payments that are scheduled through the end of the lease. Of course, after paying the full amount, the user can keep using the computer through the end of the lease period. The user may also be required to obtain insurance if the leased equipment is not already covered by the user's office insurance policies. Finally, there probably will be an integration clause to invalidate any oral statements made to the user concerning the capabilities and performance of the computer.

You will want to review the sample computer lease agreement in the appendix before talking to a representative of the leasing company. Be sure to ask the representative to explain anything you don't understand. If you feel that the leasing company would be receptive to the idea, you might suggest changes to the lease agreement to protect your interests.

NEGOTIATING THE TERMS OF A COMPUTER LEASE AGREEMENT

Negotiating a computer lease agreement is more feasible if a large computer system is involved or if the user is a large company or has an established working relationship with the leasing company. When you have the opportunity to negotiate, consider the following points.

Place the responsibility for repairing any problems with the computer on the leasing company. To provide for continued operation while repairs are being made, require that the leasing company supply replacement equipment when repairs take more than a few days.

Establish that the leasing company will support the computer. This should include initial instruction on how to operate the computer and continued access to advice on operation of the equipment.

Provide for freedom in locating and using the computer. The user should try to obtain the right of assignment or sublease of the equipment. The leasing company should have the right to require notice of but not permission for, such actions.

Don't let the leasing company disclaim all warranties. Include an express warranty that the computer will be free of defects for a period of one year (or longer, if possible). If the leasing company assures you that the computer is appropriate for your particular needs, put that promise down in writing, and give yourself the right to cancel the lease if the computer can't do the job. Don't let the leasing company disclaim all consequential damages (business losses). Put into the lease agreement a summary of the business tasks that the computer is to perform. This will give the leasing company notice of what the consequences to your business could be if the computer is defective or if the company fails to make prompt repairs.

Write into the lease agreement the clauses necessary to take advantage of the investment tax credit or other favorable tax provisions. Consult an accountant or another tax expert about structuring the lease arrangement to obtain the most favorable tax treatment. Talk with your attorney about other changes in lease terms that might enhance your legal rights.

COMPUTER SERVICES

We have discussed in this chapter how renting can provide you with temporary access to a computer and save the expense of buying a machine that might be underutilized. An even less expensive means of obtaining temporary computing power is to purchase computer services. One such service is computer time-sharing, in which the user pays by the hour or fraction of an hour for access to a computer and related peripheral equipment. A business can also take advantage of the efficiency of computers by sending work such as customer billing and other bookkeeping functions to firms that do the work on their own computers. A business that uses these services may prepare its own data entry forms to speed the processing of the work.

When contracting for computer time-sharing or data processing services for your business, take care to understand any agreements you're asked to sign. The usual commercial law protections may not apply, since contracts for data processing services aren't included in the same legal category as the sale of goods. If there's anything you don't understand about the arrangement, ask an attorney to review the contract. Try to avoid any long-term commitments that you can't cancel at your option if you're not satisfied.

PART TWO
Acquiring Computer Software

═══════════════════════════════

Buying Packaged Software
4

In the early days of computer use in the office and home, computer users were plagued by a shortage of useful software. If you wanted programs for your computer, you either had to program it yourself or hire someone to program for you. Now there's a large number of software packages for standard business applications such as word processing, information management, inventory control, and financial planning. This wider availability of off-the-shelf software has dramatically reduced the cost. It has also created some new and interesting legal issues. This chapter explains these issues as they affect the computer user.

Even today, not all computer applications can be accommodated by buying a standard software package. Some applications are unique, or so complex that no program on the market is appropriate. In these cases you will have to have company employees develop the needed programs or else hire an outside programmer to do the work. Sometimes a packaged program will meet some of your needs but will still not be completely satisfactory. Then the decision whether to develop your own program or buy packaged software will depend on many factors, such as the relative cost of the packaged and custom-made programs, the in-house programming resources available, and the length of time it will take to develop the software. If you decide you need outside help to create a specialized program, refer to Chapter 5, which discusses the legal aspects of hiring a computer programmer to develop custom software.

In this chapter we deal with the issues involved in the procurement of packaged software from the point of view of the consumer. Some of these subjects, such as software licensing agreements and copyright law as it relates to computer software, are approached differently when the interests of the software author or publisher are considered. That's the job of Part III of this book. Software writers should read those chapters in addition to this one to get a complete picture of the law concerning ownership, protection, and marketing of computer software.

SOURCES OF PACKAGED SOFTWARE

The software that's available in packaged form may have been developed by a computer manufacturer, a software company, or even by an individual programmer working at night in a basement recreation room. Whoever developed the program, the computer user can obtain the software from four main sources.

Many programs with basic applications are sold through computer manufacturers and the retail outlets that handle their products. Personal computers and some larger systems are often sold as part of a business system, with a few software packages bundled with the computer. Typically these packages can be used for basic office applications such as word processing and information management. Some manufacturers target professionals such as architects and engineers and provide computer systems complete with software for computer-aided design and other programs for the specific needs of those users.

The most common source for software packages is the direct-sales vendor that sells the software separately. Such vendors include retail stores that sell only software; stores that sell both hardware and software; and firms (including the software development houses themselves) that market to businesses through field representatives, seminars, and other means. Some software vendors carry hundreds or even thousands of packages for business, education, entertainment, and other computing uses.

A third major source of packaged software is the mail-order company. Buying software from this source appeals to users because mail-order houses can usually offer a lower price than a retail vendor for the same package. Mail-order firms are also more likely to carry the less popular packages that direct-sales vendors avoid because of limited shelf space. Later in this chapter we will discuss the particular legal problems involved in mail-order sales.

A less well-known source of software, but one useful to some computer users, is the user computer network or bulletin board. A computer network can be set up to service a group of business professionals, programmers, or other users who need to communicate or work with common information. Network members are provided with phone numbers by which they can access data bases and other services such as electronic mail. The network may charge a registration fee and hourly access fees. Bulletin boards are more informal than networks, requiring only a system operator who devotes a computer to handling phone contacts from users. Bulletin boards are often organized by groups of users who own the same type of computer and want to obtain information and programs for their particular model. One important feature of both networks and bulletin boards is the ability to transfer public domain software to users. These computer programs do not come in fancy packages and are not accompanied by written documentation; they simply are transferred over the phone lines to your computer. In some cases these communications networks (which can be located through computer magazines or word of mouth) can be a useful source of inexpensive, even free, software.

THE TYPICAL SOFTWARE BUYER

Let's take a look at a couple of typical computer users as they acquire packaged software. As we work through these examples we will examine the devices that software developers and vendors use to protect their legal rights and their financial investment in the software. We will see that the needs and desires of the computer user sometimes conflict with the wishes of the software developer, and we will learn how to avoid disputes that might arise over the use of software.

Our first prospective software buyer is Susan, a manager at a company called Acme Bearing. The Acme marketing department wants to obtain computer software that will enable the company to keep track of sales orders, forecast future sales, and assist in preparing schedules for manufacturing of engine bearings. Susan has been discussing Acme's needs with a small firm that markets a package called "Sales-Link" for $3,000. Sales-Link, which is compatible with the Acme office computer, can receive orders directly from Acme's sales representatives anywhere in the country. The salesperson just sends an order from a computer terminal over a modem into the Sales-Link program, which records it and produces reports that Acme can use to plan the manufacture of bearings. Susan has seen a demonstration of Sales-Link and likes the program. She was given a document entitled "Software License Agreement" and asked to sign it to close the deal. While she is back at her office trying to make a final decision about whether to buy Sales-Link, she receives a call from her friend Roger, who seems to be having a bit of trouble.

Roger is a manager at United Valve, a company on the other side of town. Roger has never been as cautious as Susan and is always looking for a way to cut costs. So rather than try out the Sales-Link program, Roger went to the

Software Store several months before and bought "Sales-Manager," a popular package that sells for $500. Sales-Manager doesn't have the remote linkup capability of Sales-Link. With Sales-Manager, Roger's staff has to enter sales orders into the computer manually after receiving them over the phone. Still, the system generates good reports, and the salesperson at the Software Store promised that it would cut the time spent on recording and projecting sales by 50 percent.

When Roger got Sales-Manager running at the United Valve offices, he found that it saved some staff time but nowhere near the 50 percent promised by the salesperson at the Software Store. In the first week of operation, Roger decided that he wanted to make a backup copy of the program in case something happened to the original disk. It was then that he discovered that the program was "locked." When he tried to copy the program onto another disk, the computer wouldn't respond. Roger called a friend who knew a lot about computers. The friend dropped by on his lunch hour and explained to Roger that the program was copy protected by the software publisher to keep people from making illegal copies. The friend figured out how to bypass the copy protection and made four copies of Sales-Manager. Roger kept one copy in the office as a backup for the original, mailed two copies to branch offices of United Valve in other states, and gave the fourth copy to the friend for helping out.

Unfortunately for Roger, there was an inherent programming design problem with Sales-Manager. The program was designed to hold only a limited number of sales orders in the computer's memory. If the memory filled up, the program didn't give any warning but instead just erased the oldest sales orders as new ones were entered. That happened one day when United Valve had a lot of orders coming in. An order for one thousand valves from a truck manufacturer was erased, and as a result, a large defense contract project was delayed two weeks. The truck manufacturer is now suing United for failing to deliver the valves.

That wasn't Roger's only problem with the software. Two months after he bought Sales-Manager, while Roger was trying to print out a sales report form, he discovered that the original disk had a defect that prevented printing of the report. He sent the disk back to the software publisher for a replacement while the staff worked overtime to extract the sales information from the computer and prepare a manual report. Roger figures that the defective disk cost United $2,000 in lost work time.

Roger is now thoroughly disillusioned with Sales-Manager and has called Susan to tell her of his misfortunes. He asks her whether he can get back the money he spent on the program. Can he hold the company that publishes Sales-Manager responsible for the construction project delay or the extra time that

Hagelshaw: The Computer User's Legal Guide (Chilton)

ACQUIRING COMPUTER SOFTWARE

United spent making the manual sales report? What about the promise that the Software Store salesperson made concerning the 50-percent time savings? Will Roger have problems because he made copies of the Sales-Manager program? Susan tells him that she doesn't know the answer to these questions and suggests that he buy a copy of *The Computer User's Legal Guide* to find out.

In order to answer Roger's questions, we first have to look at the software license agreement that came with the Sales-Manager program.

SOFTWARE LICENSE AGREEMENTS

Figure 4–1 shows Sales-Manager Corporation's software license agreement, a condensed version of the typical agreement that accompanies packaged software. (The appendix contains two complete examples of software license agreements.) Your license agreement will be found either inside the software package or on the outer box cover or wrapping. The external forms are known as "box-top," "shrink-wrap," or "tear-open" license agreements, and they will be discussed later in this chapter. The terms of the agreements vary among publishers, but the agreement in Figure 4–1 covers the main provisions. We'll see how these agreements work by answering the questions that Roger has asked about his problems with the Sales-Manager program.

MAKING COPIES OF THE PROGRAM

Roger is worried about whether it was proper to make copies of Sales-Manager. The right to make copies of computer software is severely limited. The restrictions on copying are the result of two legal devices: copyright law and the license agreement.

The great majority of computer programs offered for sale are copyright protected. If you find a program that has not been copyrighted, either the company offering the program is inexperienced or it has found some advantage in waiving copyright protection. Some software authors are experimenting with giving away their programs or selling them for only the cost of the disk that contains them, in the hope that users will be willing to pay a voluntary registration fee to receive documentation and support for the program. These adventurous publishers actually encourage copying of their programs so that they can reach as many prospective voluntary registrants as possible. These authors figure that they will make more money this way than by selling fewer copies at a price that encourages illegal copying. But most programs are copyrighted, and the publishers do not want users to make copies.

The copyright for a computer program works in much the same way as the

FIG. 4–1
A Typical Software License Agreement

SALES-MANAGER CORPORATION—SOFTWARE LICENSE AGREEMENT

Important: The Sales-Manager program contained in this package is licensed to customers for their use only, on the terms set forth below. Please sign the registration card attached to this agreement and return it to Sales-Manager Corporation (SMC). The registration card acknowledges that you have read this agreement and agree to its terms. Only upon return of the registration card will you be entitled to use the software.

1. License: SMC hereby grants to you, upon your return of the signed registration card to SMC, a nonexclusive license to use this Sales-Manager program, subject to the terms and restrictions set forth in this agreement.

2. Copyright: The Sales-Manager program and its documentation are copyrighted. You may not copy or otherwise reproduce any part of the program or its documentation, except that you may make a backup copy for your own use.

3. Restrictions on Use and Transfer: The original and any backup copies of the Sales-Manager program are to be used only in connection with a single computer at any one time. You may not distribute copies to others, either in disk form or electronically. You may transfer this license together with the original and all backup copies of the program, provided that the transferee completes and returns a signed copy of this agreement.

4. Limited Warranty: SMC warrants the diskette on which the Sales-Manager software is recorded to be free of defects in materials and workmanship for a period of ninety (90) days after the date of original purchase. If a defect should occur within this ninety-day period, SMC will replace the defective diskette free of charge. Replacement of the diskette is your sole remedy in the event of a defect. The program and its documentation are licensed "as is," and there are no warranties as to their performance, merchantability, or fitness for a particular purpose.

5. Limitation of Liability: SMC and its agents shall not be liable for any direct, incidental, or consequential damages, including loss of anticipated profits, arising out of the use of the program or the breach of any warranty. Some states do not allow limitations on implied warranties or liability for incidental or consequential damages, so the above may not apply to you.

6. This License Agreement is the complete agreement between us and supersedes any prior oral or written agreement or statement concerning the Sales-Manager program.

Hagelshaw: The Computer User's Legal Guide (Chilton)

copyright for the book that you are reading at this moment. You can copy all or part of this book for certain purposes, such as backup (e.g., in order to take a chapter home from the office for further study), without violating the copyright laws. In the case of computer software, a 1980 amendment to the copyright laws forbids the duplication of computer programs except to make backup copies. But you can't make copies of either this book or a computer program to give to your friends. The author or the publisher of a book probably won't expend the time and money necessary to stop you from making illicit copies in small quantities. The main barrier to making such copies is economic. Since the cost of buying a second book is not much more than the cost of photocopying the first book, making copies to give to your friends hardly seems worth the trouble. In the case of a computer program, however, copying is easy and can be done at just a fraction of the cost of buying another original. This makes copying very attractive, both in order to have backup copies and to give away or sell copies to other users. Making copies for distribution to others is a violation of the copyright laws and may subject you to substantial damages and legal costs.

The license agreement is another device for legally forbidding copying of computer programs. When you pay a software vendor and receive a package containing computer disks and written documentation, you have not actually purchased those items. Instead, you have merely paid for a license to use the software. Had you bought all ownership rights to the program, you could copy it or do with it as you pleased. But under the license arrangement, you have only as much right to use the software as is specified in the license agreement. In Roger's case, he is permitted to make a backup copy of the Sales-Manager program for his own use. Some license agreements do not permit copying even for backup. In those instances the publishers usually provide a backup copy in the software package or will send another copy when they receive a registration card or copy of the license agreement signed by the user. There may be an additional fee for the backup copy.

With the possible exception of a backup copy, no copies of a computer program are permitted under copyright law and the license agreement. Roger violated the agreement and the copyright law when he sent two copies to the United Valve branch offices. This is true even though the software was purchased by the company. The license agreement limits use of the program not just to a single purchaser, such as a corporation, but to a single *computer*. The branch offices of Roger's company have separate computers, and the company would have to buy an original Sales-Manager program for each office, or even for each computer within the same office if the computers cannot be linked together to use one program at the same time. Some software publishers accommodate businesses that require more than one copy for use on several computers. The business might be allowed to make and use extra copies upon payment of additional fees. Of course, this arrangement depends a great deal on the honesty of the user, since there is no way for the publisher to know how many copies are being used.

Since Roger was justified in making only one copy for backup, he clearly violated the copyright law and the license agreement when he gave a copy to the friend who helped him break the copy protection. If the publisher of Sales-Manager had found out about the violation, Roger could have been sued and forced to pay damages for copyright infringement. However, unless to make an example of him to deter other infringers, the publisher would probably not take Roger to court because the expense and bother are too much for just a few copies. Because of this, and because it is so difficult for the software publisher to identify people who make illegal copies, thousands of illegal copies of computer programs are made every day, and nothing is done about it. This situation will continue as long as there is such a great difference between the cost of the original software (often hundreds or even thousands of dollars) and the cost of making a bootleg copy (a few dollars for blank disks). Of course, pirates who try to copy and sell computer software in large quantities will find themselves the targets of civil and criminal prosecution. But about the only thing that the publisher can do to discourage small-scale copying is to provide incentives of convenience to legitimate, registered users. Usually only one copy of the user's manual is provided with the software, and the publisher generally will not sell extra manuals. The legitimate user may have access to vendor support (the opportunity to ask questions and resolve problems concerning the operation of the software) and may receive periodic updates to the program and the user manual. These extras are very important to some users, especially businesses.

DEFECTIVE DISKS

Roger's original Sales-Manager disk was defective. It wouldn't print one of the reports that it was supposed to produce. Because of this and the other problems that the Sale-Manager program has caused him, Roger wants to know if he can get his money back. In a typical sales transaction, you can rescind the sales contract and receive a refund if the product proves to be defective. But under Roger's software license agreement, his remedy is limited to replacement of the disk if he discoveres the defect within ninety days. He discovered the problem after only two months, so he can get a new disk from the publisher. But he can't get his money back. If he hadn't discovered the defect until more than ninety days after purchase, he couldn't have received a replacement disk but would have had to buy a new one. Some software publishers offer a longer warranty on their disks. Others will replace them even after the warranty period expires upon payment of an additional fee.

Later in this chapter we will examine the question of whether the purchase of software is a transfer of a license, as it purports to be, or really a sale of goods that is subject to broader protections and remedies in favor of the purchaser. The law in some states does not permit limitations on warranties that are implied in sales transactions. You should consult an attorney in your state if you are not satisfied with simply receiving a replacement of a defective disk.

SOFTWARE DESIGN FLAWS

One of Roger's biggest problems with the Sales-Manager program was the program's propensity to erase data from the computer without warning. Although this type of problem is extreme and rarely occurs, a lot of the software now being sold contains design flaws of various sorts. Most of these problems are minor and although they may be irritating, they don't prevent the programs from running. (Sometimes there is no problem with the program, but the instruction manual is so poorly written that the user can't figure out how to use the program effectively.) Is there anything the user can do about imperfect software?

Normally, when a product is poorly designed and doesn't perform as expected, the purchaser can pursue legal remedies against the seller. For example, if you buy a lawn mower that is designed badly and won't cut the grass unless you push it over the same area twice, the lawn mower is not of salable quality. The manufacturer and the retail store have broken the implied warranty of merchantability that comes with the sale of every product. You can return the lawn mower and get your money back.

Unfortunately for the computer user, the purchase of software, as we have seen, does not fit neatly into the category of a sale of goods since the arrangement has been characterized by software publishers as the granting of a license. For this reason, the implied warranty protections may not apply (we will discuss shortly whether the courts may begin to view the transaction as a sale to which the warranties apply). In an effort to make sure that the software purchaser cannot take advantage of any warranties, the license agreement disclaims them. For example, Roger's Sales-Manager agreement stated that the software was licensed as is, without warranties for performance, merchantability, or fitness for a particular purpose. Roger cannot get his money back because of the design flaw in the Sales-Manager program. There may still be some legal remedies available in the case of serious programming errors that the software publisher knew about when the program was sold. This could be viewed by a court as fraudulent conduct, which would be grounds for recovery of the purchase price and other damages by the purchaser.

CONSEQUENTIAL DAMAGES

The erasure of a sales order by the poorly designed Sales-Manager program has created an angry customer for United Valve. And the defective disk that balked at producing the needed sales report required additional work time and expense for Roger's staff. Can Roger place the responsibility for these troubles and expenses on Sales-Manager Corporation?

If there were no disclaimer of consequential or indirect damages, the software publisher might be held liable for any foreseeable damages resulting from its negligent actions or for breach of warranties. Sales-Manager Corporation certainly knows that purchasers of the program will use it to record sales orders and prepare reports. If the orders are lost or the reports can't be printed, it is foreseeable that the user may suffer serious business losses. To protect itself against claims of lost profits or extra expenses, the software publisher inserts clauses in the license agreement to limit its liability. Roger's Sales-Manager agreement disclaims any liability for "direct, incidental, or consequential damages, including loss of anticipated profits." Unless the law in Roger's state does not permit such limitations on consequential damages, United Valve will not be able to recover any money from Sales-Manager Corporation for the business problems caused by the program. Some states will not fully honor these limitations of liability clauses. If a program or disk problem causes you a substantial business loss, you should consult an attorney in your state to see if any legal remedies are available. The computer user can minimize exposure to these problems by maintaining good manual records to back up the computer when important information is involved.

SALESPEOPLE'S PROMISES

When Roger bought the Sales-Manager package, the salesperson told him that the program would reduce his staff time by 50 percent. That didn't happen, as is often the case with optimistic statements made by software salespeople. Many such promises can be regarded as idle sales pitches that are not to be taken literally. The claim about the 50-percent time saving is probably in that category. Roger shouldn't have attached much weight to that claim. But sometimes salespeople make specific statements about the capabilities and performance of software that the typical purchaser would tend to accept at face value. For example, the salesperson might have told Roger that Sales-Manager would

Hagelshaw: The Computer User's Legal Guide (Chilton)

ACQUIRING COMPUTER SOFTWARE

not only keep track of sales orders but also manage the company's inventory of valves. An inexperienced software buyer like Roger may be inclined to believe the salesperson's statements, since the people at Software Store are supposed to be experts on software. If it turned out that the program did not manage inventory, can Roger take any legal action against Software Store or against the software publisher?

If the salesperson knew that the statement was untrue when he or she made it, Roger might be able to sue for damages on the grounds of fraud. But in most cases in which software salespeople give false information, they are not doing it intentionally but are just unfamiliar with the product. Still, the purchaser might be able to rescind the sales contract and get his or her money back if the false promise concerns an important aspect of the program. The difficulty is in proving that the false statement was made and that you relied on the statement in making the purchase. If a salesperson's promise about the performance of the software is an important factor in your decision to buy, write the promise on a piece of paper, ask the salesperson to sign and date it, and attach the paper to the sales contact or receipt. Also attach any advertisements or brochures containing statements that you relied on in making your purchase decision. These precautions will help a great deal in proving your case if a dispute occurs.

The software publisher also might make promises about the capabilities of the software, in the form of advertisements or statements made by a salesperson as a representative of the publisher. Unless you can prove fraud, it will be difficult to hold the publisher to these promises. The software license agreement, as we saw, contains an integration clause invalidating any promises not contained in the agreement. So Roger would have no success if he asked for his money back from the publisher on the basis of the false promise of a 50-percent time savings.

By now Roger has read all the way through the software license agreement for the Sales-Manager program. The program has caused him a lot of headaches, but the license agreement seems to restrict most of his legal rights against Sales-Manager Corporation. Roger never read or even saw the license agreement until after he had bought the software and opened it back at the office. Can they really enforce all those restrictions against him?

ENFORCEABILITY OF SOFTWARE LICENSE AGREEMENTS

Software publishers want to characterize the purchase of computer software as involving only the transfer of a license, under the terms specified in the license agreement. This license arrangement was pioneered by IBM Corporation and has been adopted by most software publishers. There have been almost no court decisions on the validity of the standard license agreements in the case of packaged computer software, and there is some doubt as to whether the arrangement is really that of a license or of a sale of goods. The distinction is important, because a sale of goods is subject in every state to the provisions of the Uniform Commercial Code (UCC). Among other things, the UCC gives the purchaser of the product the protection of implied warranties (these were discussed in detail in Chapter 2). The code also prohibits terms of sale that are unconscionable, or unfair, to the purchaser. Such unconscionable terms might include attempts to limit remedies or to disclaim all liability for defects in the product. More important, if the arrangement is classified as a sale, the validity of the entire license agreement is called into question. Some courts might refuse to enforce any of its restrictive terms against the purchaser.

When software is sold together with a computer as part of an integrated system, the UCC applies to the purchase of the software (Chatlos Systems, Inc., v. National Cash Register Corp., 479 F. Supp. 738 [D.N.J. 1979], aff'd 670 F.2d 1304 [3rd Cir. 1982]. A computer user who buys an integrated system (for example, a computerized cash register and inventory control system) might be able to challenge the enforcement of a license agreement that comes with the software. But a system doesn't qualify as integrated simply because some software packages were included in the deal when the computer was bought; that situation is really a purchase of software apart from the hardware—they just happen to have been bought at the same time.

Even when the software is purchased separately from the hardware, there's still reason to believe that the transaction is a sale of goods. When Roger bought Sales-Manager, he was given a sales receipt for the software package that was the same as those used for the sale of floppy disks or any other product in the store. Roger wasn't told by the salesperson that he was only acquiring a license to use the software. He didn't even see the license agreement until he took the package back to the office and opened it. These procedures and events are more consistent with a sale than with a transfer of a license. As time goes on some courts may agree that the user has actually purchased a copy of the computer progran and its documentation—not just obtained a license to use the program. This conclusion would give the user the free right to transfer ownership of his or her copy (but not the right to make additional copies), would extend UCC protection to the purchase, and would cast doubt upon or even invalidate the terms of the software license agreement. However, under the current law, the user only holds a license.

Even if the purchase of software continues to be regarded as a transfer of a license, the software publisher may still have trouble enforcing all of the terms of the license agreement. Very often the purchaser has no opportunity to negotiate the terms of the agreement. The agreement is presented to the buyer as a preprinted form, often tucked away inside a sealed package. Courts tend to disfavor these standardized form agreements, which are refered to as contracts of "adhesion" because they adhere to the product so that you can't buy the product without accepting the form. Knowing that the purchaser never really agreed to the terms, courts may begin to refuse to enforce some of the limitations imposed upon the purchaser by the license agreements. Of course, even if some terms of the license agreement, such as limitations on legal remedies and liability for business losses, are not enforced, the user of the program is still prevented from making copies of the program by the copyright laws. Copyright law operates independently of any license agreement between the software publisher and the user of the program.

BOX-TOP AND SHRINK-WRAP LICENSE AGREEMENTS

In order to shore up the validity of their license agreements, software publishers have begun to put the license agreement on the outside of the package containing the software. The agreement may either be printed on the box (the "box-top" agreement) or held in place by the transparent plastic package wrapping (the "shrink-wrap" agreement). Publishers have been advised by their attorneys that they should give the purchaser as much notice as possible, prior to purchase and use of the program, of the existence and terms of the license agreement.

Typically box-top and shrink-wrap agreements warn the purchaser in large letters that the only right being acquired is a license to use the program and that upon opening the package the purchaser accepts the terms of the license agreement. This arrangement is more likely to create a valid license than if the agreement were hidden inside the box. The purchaser now knows about the agreement and its terms, or at least has the opportunity to know about them, before purchase and use of the software. This increases the likelihood that courts will see the transaction as the granting of a license and not as a sale and that they will enforce the terms of the license agreements against computer users. However, even when the purchaser knows about the license agreement before purchase, it is presented to him or her as a take-it-or-leave-it contract of adhesion. There's still room to argue (although such arguments are only sometimes successful) that certain terms are unfair and shouldn't be enforced.

In the case of mail-order sales, the purchaser usually doesn't have a chance to see a box-top license agreement because he or she does not even see the box prior to sale. For this reason the mail-order purchaser may have a better chance of avoiding the enforcement of the license agreement provisions than does the user who bought the software in a store. But overall, there are important legal advantages to software publishers in using the box-top and shrink-wrap license agreements, and we can expect that they will soon become the standard for packaged software. (For an example of a complete shrink-wrap software license agreement, see the appendix.)

NEGOTIATING THE TERMS OF A SOFTWARE LICENSE AGREEMENT

By now, Roger has explained all of his software problems to his friend Susan at Acme Bearing. Susan has decided to buy the Sales-Link package for $3,000 but hasn't yet signed any contracts. Roger tells her not to buy anything without first reading the license agreement. Susan always knew that Roger's carefree ways would get him into trouble, but she's glad to have the benefit of his experience. She now wants to talk with the Sales-Link representative about making changes in the standard software license agreement to avoid some of the problems and restrictions that Roger encountered.

As we've said many times before, there's no contract or agreement that cannot be modified by consent of the two parties who are signing it. In the case of lower-cost, packaged software bought at a software store, there is probably little opportunity for the purchaser to influence the terms of the license agreement. The software store as well as the software publisher would likely refuse to sell the program rather than modify the agreement. But the situation may be different when the computer user is paying a higher price for more specialized software such as Susan's Sales-Link program. In such cases the user often receives a demonstration of the program and has a chance to talk at length with the sales representative. The situation is more conducive to bargaining over the terms of the license agreement. What considerations should Susan raise with the Sales-Link people?

The software license agreement should be used to define the quality and level of support that the user expects for the software. The agreement should state the user's needs and the expected capabilities of the software and explain the responsibilities of both the user and the company selling the software (the vendor). The user shouldn't feel that he or she is imposing on the vendor or showing distrust by asking to add or modify clauses in the agreement. A complete, clearly written agreement that addresses the specific needs of the user will help to prevent disputes and to avoid the later involvement of attorneys and courts. Now we'll examine some important provisions that the user should try to insert into the license agreement. The vendor will probably not give in to all of these items, but they are goals to shoot for.

USER NEEDS AND SOFTWARE CAPABILITY

A few short paragraphs should be added to the agreement to summarize the specific purpose for which you are acquiring the software and your expectations about the software's capabilities. For example, Susan should try to include an explanation of Acme Bearing's need for a computerized sales management system. The agreement should state that the user understands that the Sales-Link program has the capability of receiving sales orders directly from Acme's sales representatives through remote computer terminals, of recording the sales orders, and of producing reports that Acme can use to plan the manufacture of engine bearings. This description of needs and expected capabilities should be detailed enough to support a comparison with the software's actual performance once it is in use. Susan should also define the remedies available to her if the software does not perform according to the stated expectations. She should have the right to get a full refund of her $3,000 if the vendor cannot correct the deficiency within a reasonable period of time.

COPIES

The user should have the right to make backup copies of disks and documentation as needed to protect against loss or damage to the originals. If the software is to be used on more than one computer in the same office, or in different office locations of the same company, the user should get the right to make copies for the other computers. Such a use will probably require the payment of additional license fees, but it would be a cheaper solution than buying a new software package for each computer.

FREE RIGHT TO USE AND TRANSFER SOFTWARE

You should try to get the right to use the software without restriction, as dictated by your computing needs. This includes the right to use the software on another computer or system than the one originally specified, to integrate it with other software, and to disclose the software and documentation to any employees or consultants who need to work with it. The user should also be able to transfer the software to other locations or divisions within the same company or to sell the original (but not copies) to another user without having to obtain permission of the vendor.

SOFTWARE MAINTENANCE

It's not enough that the software works well when first used. You also want to make sure that it keeps on working despite changes that can occur over time. For example, Acme Bearing might get the Sales-Link program running but later change the operating procedures of their sales department enough so that a modification of the software is necessary to accommodate the new procedures. Or the company might buy a new computer and wish to modify the program to work with the new hardware. Or after learning the program, Susan might encounter problems with some of the more obscure applications because of poor documentation. The license agreement should make the vendor responsible for correcting the program and documentation when the problem is inherent in the software. If the software needs modifications because of the user's changing requirements (new hardware or new office procedures), the user should have the right to make the modifications without restriction. You should be assured access to the source code for the software so that your programmers will be able to make the necessary modifications.

Some software vendors offer separate maintenance service agreements. For an extra fee you can have access to advice on how to operate the program, and the services of a vendor representative to help work out problems. Of course, the user should try to get this maintenance commitment from the vendor in the license agreement for no additional charge. But if you're considering buying a separate maintenance contract, decide whether you'll get enough use out of it to justify the price of the contract. Also remember that there may be independent service companies that you can call on for technical support—a less expensive alternative than a maintenance contract.

ACCEPTANCE TESTING

It's not always easy to find the right software for your needs. Salespeople, as we've noted, often aren't completely familiar with the software they're selling, let alone the user's unique requirements. To avoid paying for software that can't help you, include provisions in the license agreement for an acceptance test. The acceptance test gives you a period of time, generally thirty or sixty days, within which to try out the software to see if it performs as promised. If the software is unacceptable, you can have the option of returning it or asking the vendor to replace it with something more appropriate. You should not have to make payment, or at least not full payment, until you accept the software after testing. The license agreement should specify what the test will be. For example, Susan's agreement should state that she will test the Sales-Link program to make sure that it can handle orders from remote computer terminals and can produce the promised reports. The acceptance test device is not meant to give the user an easy excuse for backing out of the sale. It simply ensures that you will not have to pay for software that does not perform the way the salesperson said it would.

CONSEQUENTIAL DAMAGES

Remember the problems that Roger and United Valve had because of defects in the Sales-Manager program? Those problems resulted in costly business losses, but Roger's license agreement disclaimed any liability on the part of the software publisher for such consequential damages. If you know that your business will be placing great reliance on the quality and dependability of the software, try to avoid having a disclaimer of consequential damages in the license agreement. After all, if a supplier of materials fails to deliver on time, you can sue the supplier for breach of contract and all resulting damages, including lost profits that were foreseeable. If a software problem causes your business to lose money, why shouldn't the vendor of the software be held responsible too? The vendor may not agree to leaving a disclaimer of consequential damages out of the license agreement. But in any case, you should include in the agreement a short description of how the software will be used in your business. This will put the vendor on notice that a software defect or failure could result in lost profits, which will strengthen your legal position should a dispute arise.

WARRANTIES

The user should try to include as many useful warranties in the license agreement as possible. A warranty of title will guarantee that the vendor, and not some other person or company, owns all rights in the software. If a third party tries to stop you from using the software (e.g., in the event of a legal contest over the right to the software), the agreement should obligate the vendor to pay all costs of defending lawsuits and permit you to recover the purchase price from the vendor.

The user should negotiate for an extended warranty against defects in the program, the disks that contain it, and the written documentation. This warranty will provide added protection after the acceptance test period. The warranty should be for a period of at least six months to a year, to give you sufficient time to discover any problems. The user should have the right to receive a replacement software package or a full refund, at the user's option, should a defect be discovered. You should also try to avoid any clauses in the license agreement that disclaim or limit the scope or duration of implied warranties.

In addition to the standard clauses just discussed, you should include in the license agreement other provisions that are appropriate for your particular situation. For example, if the salesperson promises that the software will save 50 percent of your staff time, put that promise in writing in the agreement. Also attach to the agreement any advertising literature that contains statements about the capabilities of the software and add a clause that says that the attachments are part of the agreement. The agreement should say that if these promises are not met, you have the right to return the software and get your money back.

In the few cases involving software that have been decided so far, the courts have tended to favor the user when the question involved an interpretation of the license agreement. But they have usually limited the liability of the vendor to what was stated in the agreement. Therefore it's important to specify throughout the agreement the remedies available to you if the vendor fails to meet its obligations. An attorney can provide additional assistance in rewriting the license agreement to protect your interests as user of the software.

MAIL-ORDER SOFTWARE

Mail-order companies are a popular source of computer software, primarily because of their lower prices. From the user's point of view there is little difference between buying from a software store and buying through the mail, except for the accessibility of the vendor (although, as we discussed earlier, the software publisher may have more difficulty in enforcing the terms of the license agreement against a mail-order purchaser). If the mail-order company sends you the wrong program or makes a false promise about the software through advertising or over the phone, you may find yourself involved in a long-distance legal dispute. You will have more trouble getting satisfaction for your problem than you would with a local vendor. Make sure that the price saving from the mail-order purchase is worth the added risk of a long-distance transaction, especially when you're buying an unfamiliar product.

SOFTWARE RENTALS

In the late 1970s a new phenomenon appeared on the computer scene, the software rental business. Rental companies rent software packages by the week or month, with weekly rental fees as high as 15 to 20 percent of the purchase price. The rental companies advertise that renting gives you the opportunity to try the software before deciding whether to purchase it. It's true that by renting software you can eliminate some of the risk of buying an unfamiliar program. But the user also has the opportunity to copy the rented software, return the original, and keep the copy for his or her own use. Software publishers claim that this is exactly what is happening to the majority of rented programs. They regard the whole software rental business as little more than organized piracy.

In 1983, MicroPro International Corporation, a major software publisher, sued a leading software rental company, United Computer Corporation. MicroPro claimed that United Computer was facilitating the illegal copying of its popular Wordstar program by renting it out to computer users on a short-term basis. MicroPro's lawyers argued that these rentals violated the copyright laws because United Computer knew that users were renting programs primarily in order to copy them. MicroPro also felt that their software license agreements were being broken, because the agreements prohibited the transfer of use of the software.

The lawsuit against United Computer was delayed, perhaps indefinitely, when United Computer filed for bankruptcy in mid-1984. The future of software rental companies is still undecided. A few software publishers have arranged to have rental companies pay them a royalty fee for each program that is rented. These publishers figure that they probably can't stop the illegal copying, so they might as well make some money out of it. Other publishers refuse to work with the rental companies, and more lawsuits will undoubtedly be filed. Regardless of whether the rental companies are found to be in violation of copyright law or the license agreements, a user who rents a program and copies it is clearly doing so illegally. The user of rented software is not a party to the license agreement and is not bound by it, but he or she is still subject to the copyright laws. No matter where the software comes from, copyright law doesn't permit the copying of a computer program except to make backup copies.

LOCKED COMPUTER PROGRAMS

Very often a computer user is unable to copy a program (legitimate or otherwise) because the program is locked. A locked, or copy-protected, program contains programming instructions that prevent the computer from making a copy. A user with specialized programming knowledge can get around the copy protection, but the typical user cannot. The protection is designed to stop illegal copying of software. But it has created problems for users who want to make legitimate backup copies, without thwarting the knowledgeable software pirate.

Software publishers have usually chosen one of two options for dealing with this dilemma. Some have abandoned copy protection altogether in order to keep their customers happy, relying on copyright law and other legal protections to stop the illegal copiers. Other publishers continue to copy-protect their disks and provide the user with one or more backup disks, either in the original package or mailed separately upon receipt of a signed software registration card (which acknowledges that the user has read and agrees to the terms of the license agreement). We can expect that many publishers will continue to use and improve copy protection systems in the years ahead.

There's probably nothing illegal about simply "breaking the lock" on a computer program. If you modify the program so that it can be copied, you probably haven't violated any law. The software license agreement may contain a prohibition against modifying the program, but it's questionable whether that restriction is enforceable. A lot of programs must be modified in order to run on the computer system: for example, you may need to add additional instructions so that the program knows what kind of printer you have. It's unlikely that a modification for that purpose or for other reasonable purposes—such as making backup copies—can be prohibited by the license agreement. Whether your actions in copying a program are legal depends not on whether you broke a copy protection but on the reason why you broke it. If you're trying to make a backup copy for your own use, you haven't violated the copyright laws. A copy for any other purpose isn't permitted.

Contracting for Customized Software

5

The rapidly expanding use of computers in business has created a growing market for standardized, mass-produced software packages. But not every application can be satisfied by a standard program. Sometimes a company has unique needs for which an off-the-shelf package is incomplete or otherwise inappropriate. Buying packaged software can be a lot like buying a suit off the rack; you take it home only to find that the sleeves are too long. The packaged software just doesn't quite fit the application you had in mind. In these cases you will have to hire a programmer to "customize" the software.

Some companies employ in-house programmers to modify or originate the needed program, but more typically the user must retain outside programming talent. These programmers charge for their services at a healthy hourly rate, and a software development project can cost many thousands of dollars. When you become involved in these projects, you need to protect your rights and carefully define your relationship with the software developer. All too often, perhaps because they feel that they are ignorant about computers, users rely on the superior expertise of the programmers and simply sign the contract that they are offered. Sometimes the parties, in a naive reliance on their mutual good faith, start work without any written contract at all, with disastrous results.

A lack of computer knowledge should not stop any businessperson from exercising prudent business judgment. Every important software development project should be based on a comprehensive written contract. The computer user should never underestimate the problems that can arise from an ill-defined arrangement, regardless of the high reputation of the people involved or the personal trust between them. The following hypothetical case illustrates the way in which legal and business problems can surface in the absence of a complete written contract.

DANGERS OF HIRING WITHOUT A WRITTEN CONTRACT

Fred, president of Fred's Wholesalers, Inc., of Casper, Wyoming, decided that he wanted to save costs through increased computerization of his food products wholesaling business. Fred already had been using his company computer to do his payroll and to keep track of the company cash flow and accounts receivable. He now wanted to expand the operation to include processing of customer orders, inventory control, and automatic reordering from suppliers. He needed to find a good programmer to develop this new system.

Fred didn't know any programmers, but he had heard a lot about a local outfit, Yellowstone Expert Programmers, Inc. (YEP). He called YEP and set up a meeting with Stan, the chief programmer. Fred didn't understand what programmers do, but he knew his own business well. When Stan arrived for the meeting, Fred was able to explain to him exactly what tasks he wanted the computer to perform. They spoke at length about the program specifications and the cost for YEP's services. Stan took notes as they talked and seemed to have all the answers to Fred's questions. Fred was impressed and agreed to pay $50 an hour for the programming work. When Fred asked if Stan could finish by the end of the following month, Stan simply replied, "Yep."

Fred didn't see the need to put everything down in writing ("That's why I left the big city," he used to say). YEP was the expert in the field, and there was no reason to think the company wouldn't do a good job. Besides, this just didn't seem the same as a deal with his suppliers, in which Fred was always careful to get a good contract signed before he did anything else. YEP mailed Fred a copy of its "Standard Retainer Agreement," which Fred signed and returned with his check after a cursory review. No other agreements were signed.

YEP sent two of its best programmers to work on Fred's project. By the end of the second month the work wasn't quite finished and the programming time had already exceeded Stan's estimates by 20 percent. Fred had discussed the completion date and estimated cost with Stan at their meeting, but now he realized that they had forgotten to talk about what would happen if those limits were exceeded. In any case, the program was close to completion, so Fred decided he would just pay the extra money and wait a little longer.

By midmonth Fred's new procedure was fully operational, and he was anticipating enhanced year-end profits. Those plans were shattered at the end of the month when his cost control people stormed his office waving reams of supply orders. They said that the computer wasn't printing out the promised end-of-month summary of orders by type and total cost and that they had to do the calculations manually from the individual order forms. They said that it had been easier the old way, because they had kept running totals on the books. Fred was certain that he had requested the report feature. But when he called YEP, Stan told him, "You couldn't have specified it, or my boys would have put it in. Besides, you could have asked for a performance test if you wanted one." After that Fred thought that he really might have forgotten to specify the monthly summary report feature. He sheepishly asked Stan to send someone over to make the addition, at Fred's extra expense.

Fred's problems were just beginning. He received an order for sixty gallons of ice cream from a local caterer who was servicing the annual Firemen's picnic. The day of the picnic the caterer arrived to pick up the ice cream, only to find sixty cases of anchovies awaiting him on Fred's loading dock. There was no ice cream in stock, and the picnic was ruined. The caterer, who had handled the picnic for the past ten years, was told by the firemen that he "might as well forget about next year." The caterer told Fred to "get a good lawyer." Fred demanded that Stan himself come and uncover the problem. Stan found that the entry codes for ice cream and anchovies had inadvertently been reversed by the programmer. "Sorry about that Fred," he said, "but you know all of our work is accepted 'as is.' Besides, our retainer agreement says we have no legal responsibility for errors other than to correct the problem."

Fred told Stan he didn't want anyone from YEP ever touching his computer again. With the help of another programming consultant, the last bugs were eliminated from the program. Within a few months the procedure was running so smoothly that Fred began to brag about it at regional wholesalers' meetings. Other companies expressed an interest in buying the computer program, along with Fred's forms and procedures, as a package. One of the YEP programmers had left at Fred's a printout of the source code for the program, and Fred's new consultant said there would be no problem implementing the program at other locations.

Fred reviewed the Standard Retainer Agreement once more and noticed that it said the user holds only a "license" and that "the program, as written, belongs to YEP, Inc., exclusively." Fred's program had been modified several times by now, and the agreement didn't mention modifications, so Fred figured he was safe. He began to market his package to other wholesalers. When Stan discovered this, he called Fred to demand compliance with the retainer agreement and return of the source code, which he said had been left at Fred's by accident. Stan told Fred to "get a good lawyer." Fred slumped into his office chair, yearning for the "good old precomputer days."

VALUE OF A WRITTEN CONTRACT

The prospective user of customized software shouldn't take too much comfort in the fictional nature of Fred's problems. Real businesspeople also get involved in disputes over software development projects. Projects are often begun with the best of intentions and the greatest trust between the parties but with insufficient attention to the need for a carefully worded document embodying the agreement of the parties. There is no substitute for anticipating and avoiding problems through a written contract.

Even attorneys may fail to protect their interests in a software development situation. One Tennessee law firm decided to retain programmers to develop a time management and billing program for its office computer. The programmers estimated that the job would take seventy-five hours and cost a total of $3,000. The attorneys never drew up a written contract. The programmers took over a year to finish their work, and the final bill totaled more than $12,000. When the program was finally operational, the attorneys formed a separate corporation to market the package to other law firms. The programmers refused to deliver the source code, since it was their understanding that the program belonged to them and that the lawyers only held a license to use it at their offices. The dispute ended up in court, with a trial and an appeal (Computer Billings Services v. Boles [Tennessee, unreported]).

The message is clear: Answer your questions and spell out your rights *in writing* before the work begins. Use a comprehensive written contract to avoid costly, time-consuming problems later. (See the appendix for an example of a software development contract—the contract Fred should have signed with YEP.)

PROVISIONS OF A SOFTWARE DEVELOPMENT CONTRACT

At this point it will be useful to examine the issues that the computer user should consider when contracting for custom programming. The same considerations are important whether the project is to develop a program from scratch or to modify an off-the-shelf program, and whether the outside programmers are hired to do the entire job or only to consult with staff programmers. The subject is approached in this chapter from the point of view of the program user, but the programmer too should consider these topics before entering into a contract. (Some ways in which software consultants and programmers can limit their liability are described in Chapter 10.)

Not all projects warrant the same legal treatment. For some minor emergency troubleshooting work, there is no time and probably no need for a formal contract. However, certain major projects require expert legal advice and should never be undertaken by the businessperson solely on the basis of knowledge gleaned from this or any other book. But if you understand what provisions should be contained in a software development contract, you will be able to assist your attorney in drafting a contract designed to protect your interests. You also will be in a better position to understand any contract proposed by the programmer and to suggest appropriate modifications. In some cases you may wish to draft your own contract, either alone or with the programmer. For recurring needs, you can shape the basic provisions into your own "form" contract, using the form given in the appendix as a guide. In all instances, good business judgment should be used to determine the best approach.

Be wary of any contract drafted by the programmer or the programmer's attorney. Programmers may be the experts in computer matters, but in legal affairs they, like any other businesspeople, are primarily concerned with protecting their own interests. You or your attorney should review any proposed agreement before signing it. Remember that any contract term is negotiable, including those contained in preprinted forms. Always be sure that the following issues are addressed to your satisfaction before closing the deal.

SPECIFICATIONS

You must protect yourself by putting in writing at the start exactly what the program is to do and how it is to do it. Often the specifications are contained in a proposal written by the firm hired to do the programming, by the user, or by an outside consultant. Larger projects frequently require a detailed book of specifications to be written after the initial proposal. The more detailed the written specifications, the better the position of the user, since he or she will then be in a position to point to specific inadequacies in the final product.

The written specifications should include both technical specifications and expectation for performance. The technical specifications include such items as hardware requirements, programming language and operating system, and program logic flowcharts. This portion of the specifications should provide as much detail as you feel necessary on how the software is to make your computer produce the desired results.

The expectation specifications spell out precisely what the desired results are. You should describe, in detail, the nature of the business problems the program is meant to solve; the content of reports the computer will generate; the type and quantity of information to be stored and the manner of its retrieval; the way in which the program and its output will blend with established office functions; and the details of clerical staff involvement with the computer and its new software, including training and use of operating instructions contained within the program or in the written documentation. In short, you should communicate to the programmer *exactly* what you expect the new software to do for you. It is always easier to write these specifications when you already have a well-defined and smoothly functioning manual system. When you can explain clearly to the programmer how the tasks are being performed manually, he or she will save programming time and money and will probably end up with a computerized procedure that performs the same tasks faster and better.

In some cases the task of making specifications, especially technical ones, requires a considerable amount of work by the programmer. The parties may be faced with the choice of starting work on the specifications without signing a contract or signing a contract with uncertainty as to how the final product will look. This problem can be solved by writing two separate contracts or one two-part contract. The first contract requires the programmer to draw up technical specifications and to work with you to help document your expectations for the project. The specifications are then detailed in the second contract, which requires the programmer to perform the programming work in accordance with the specifications.

Remember that specifications for the project, even if written, are not automatically binding on the parties. The specifications must be *incorporated into the contract* to have legal effect. It's not necessary to retype all of the terms into the contract. They may be incorporated by reference, with language such as "The parties agree that all work will be performed in accordance with the specifications contained in the document entitled 'Project Proposal No. 007,' which is hereby incorporated by reference into this contract."

The contract also should indicate who is responsible if the end product does not meet the written specifications. The problems resulting from a failure to produce the specified program could range from the mere expense of correcting the program to serious damage to the user's business or to third persons (as we saw in Fred's case). If the user wants the programmer to be responsible for any or all of the problems, he or she should say so in the contract. (We'll discuss the subjects of warranties and liability to third parties in more depth later in the chapter.)

COMPLETION DATE AND PRICE

The contract should specify the time frame within which the project is to be completed and the programmer's fees. If possible, the user will want to establish a total price for the project. A prime source of legal disputes in software development is cost overruns. The user who can negotiate a fixed price at the start of the project need not suffer the surprise and cost of a final bill greatly exceeding the original estimate. Of course, the programmer may resist establishing a total price. Programmers, as is true with many professionals, prefer to charge at an hourly rate, because of the uncertainties involved in estimating the time needed to compelte a project. If you can't achieve the protection of a fixed total price, you should negotiate for a contract cost ceiling, for a lower hourly rate after a specified number of hours billed, or for some other concession in return for hourly billing. After all, an expert programmer should have some idea of the time needed for a project.

The contract should always include a firm date for completion. On more complex projects the parties can agree to a series of dates for completion of various stages of the work. This keeps the work flowing and allows the user to check for conformance with specifications at each stage. Such an arrangement might call for payment in stages as well, with a withholding of the final payment until the software has been completed and accepted. If you must have the program in operation by a certain date, you should communicate the reasons to the programmer. The company that complains of lost customers or added expense because of delays in completion of a software project is on firmer legal ground if those possibilities were spelled out in the contract to bring them to the programmer's attention.

PROPRIETARY RIGHTS

One of the fastest-growing areas in the new field of computer law is litigation over the ownership of computer software. A major computer program is rarely developed by one person working entirely alone. When several people or companies are involved in the development of a program, they frequently contend for the fruits of their efforts. The computer user can avoid these costly disputes by clarifying his or her rights in the written software contract.

Common sense dictates that the person paying for the software development should own the software. Unfortunately, legal ownership rights are not settled so easily, and you must take additional steps to protect your investment. Failure to do so could result in loss of a profitable opportunity to copy and market the program or to save expenses with in-house modifications. In certain cases the programmer will bring to the user an existing program for adaptation to the user's system. The programmer would then insist upon retaining ownership while extending only a license to the user. If the program is truly a customized job, however, the user is paying for development of a new program, and the contract should indicate clearly that the user owns the final product.

The contract should state that the program is a "work made for hire," to be owned by the user. Under the Computer Software Copyright Act of 1980, a program "made for hire" belongs to the employer or other person for whom the program was written. The contract should further state that "in the event that the program does not constitute a 'work made for hire' within the meaning of federal copyright law, (the programmer) hereby assigns all his copyright and other proprietary interest in the program to (the user), effective upon final payment." These two provisions will ensure that the ownership rights accrue to the user and not to the programmer, regardless of whether the programmer is classified as an employee or an independent contractor.

At times the user has no particular need to own the program he or she has paid to develop. The user may not intend to market the program to other users and may be content to rely on the program's author for modifications and copies. Proprietary rights in software are readily transferable by agreement, and the development contract itself can provide that the programmer owns the software. If the ownership of the software is of value to the programmer, the user should negotiate an adjustment in price or other terms in exchange for relinquishing his or her proprietary interest. If the user is to own the program, the contract should also provide for delivery of all documentation and other materials essential to the full enjoyment of ownership rights. This includes the source code and all work papers needed to maintain, modify, and reproduce the program. Software ownership rights lose much of their value without the tools necessary to understand the program. (The subject of software ownership is covered in greater detail in Part III.)

LICENSING FOR USE

If the programmer retains ownership of the software, the user will hold a license to use the program for his or her benefit. The scope and nature of the license can vary according to the wishes of the parties. The license may be for an indefinite or a limited period. The user may pay royalties in exchange for the license or pay nothing because he or she has already paid for development of the software. If the user wants to be able to sell his or her software license to a third party, the contract should state that the license is "transferable."

As in the case when the user owns the software, full use under a license requires delivery of all supporting documentation needed to operate, maintain, and modify the program. The user should obtain the right to make backup copies of the program, although he or she will be prohibited from distributing copies to third parties. (For a more extensive discussion of software licensing, including examples of license agreements, see Chapters 4 and 8.)

ACCEPTANCE TEST

Just as a careful consumer never buys a car without first taking it for a test drive, a purchaser of customized software should not agree to accept the finished product without ensuring that it does the job it is supposed to do. The contract should give you the right to test the program for a period of time (typically thirty to sixty days) before making the decision to accept or reject it. Rejection cannot be based on subjective evaluation; the program must fail to meet the specifications incorporated into the contract. The programmer cannot be faulted for the results of a programming job that complied with the specifications that you agreed to. You can be liable for breach of contract if you reject a program without adequate justification.

The contract may include varying payment arrangements to adjust for a possible failure of the program during testing. For example, the contract might provide that the programmer keep certain advance payments as compensation for his or her good-faith efforts, even if the programmer fails to make the program work as promised. He or she should always be given an opportunity to cure the defects before rejection. Remember that both the programmer and the user share the same goal: creating a program that satisfies the user's computing needs. The software contract should be drafted to further that goal with the maximum amount of goodwill and the minimum amount of friction between the parties.

TRAINING AND MAINTENANCE

If the new software requires special training for the user's staff, the contract should explain the terms and conditions of such training. Usually the need becomes obvious at the initial planning stage of the project and is included in the program specifications as a matter of course. The user should never underestimate the need for additional operator training even after testing and acceptance of the software. Questions arise later that can best be answered by the programmer. The contract should provide for access to consultation for an extended period of time beyond the completion date. This type of provision is easiest to obtain at the initial contract stage. An adjustment later, after problems have arisen, usually costs more.

As with operator training, software maintenance is best provided for when the contract is first drafted. The user can hire outside maintenance services, but the original programmer can often do it more effectively because he or she knows the software. The user should not minimize the need for a maintenance arrangement. Even with good specifications and proper acceptance testing, problems invariably show up during later operation. Don't rely on a performance warranty to protect against these problems. Warranties only indicate who is legally responsible for a program failure. A maintenance clause in the contract ensures that someone will come to fix the problem.

WARRANTIES

A warranty is a promise that a particular statement is true. If it turns out not to be true, the warranty has been breached. For example, if a manufacturer warrants that a computer will be free of defects, the manufacturer breaches the warranty if the user discovers a defect. The user then may pursue the remedies specified in the contract for breach of warranty. There are several types of warranties that the user should consider for inclusion in the software development contract. The remedies for breach of the warranties or other contract promises are discussed later in this chapter.

PERFORMANCE WARRANTIES

A performance warranty is a promise that the software will do the job it is supposed to do. Programmers often resist this warranty, especially if the particular results that the program is to achieve are not specified in adequate detail or are overly optimistic. Before agreeing to the warranty, the programmer will insist on a detailed description of the desired results as well as of standards for determining whether the failure was inherent in the program or caused by the user. Whenever possible, however, you should seek the added protection of a performance warranty. Sometimes the shortcomings in the program do not appear during testing, or for some reason a testing period is not possible. The performance warranty ensures that the user will obtain the results that have been paid for.

WARRANTY OF ORIGINAL DEVELOPMENT

The programmer should warrant that the program is an original effort, free from any copyright or proprietary rights infringement. This is especially important when any portion of the software has been developed before the project in question. This warranty should include a statement that the programmer will indemnify the user if any third party sues the user over rights in the software. "Indemnify" means that the programmer will ultimately be responsible for any damages you must pay to a third party for infringement of proprietary rights. In addition to indemnity, you will want to provide a remedy enabling you to recover from the programmer's attorneys' fees and damages for business losses suffered as a result of a dispute with a third party over rights to the software.

OTHER WARRANTIES

The contract can include other warranties appropriate to the project. If you intend to expand your hardware or software system in the future, you may wish to have the programmer warrant that the software being developed has this growth potential and will not be made obsolete by the later changes. If you suspect that the programming firm does not have substantial experience, you may desire a warranty that the programmers are qualified for the job. This warranty improves your legal position in any future dispute over failure of the software. You may also require a warranty that the programmer is carrying a certain minimum amount of professional liability insurance, to provide a source of funds in the event of damage caused by programming errors. The inclusion of additional warranties in the contract should be guided by good business judgment, balancing the need to establish a healthy working relationship with the programmer with the need for maximum legal protection of the user's interests.

BUSINESS LOSSES AND LIABILITY TO THIRD PARTIES

As we've discussed, users can protect themselves against liability to a third party for infringement of proprietary rights through a warranty of original development with an indemnity clause. A potentially more serious problem involves possible business losses to the user and harm to third persons, especially customers or clients, from an improperly designed or malfunctioning computer program. Computer software failure has been responsible for, among other problems, lost profits and even bankruptcy as well as lost clients. In the example at the beginning of the chapter, the picnic caterer who received anchovies instead of ice cream sought to hold Fred responsible for what was really a mistake by the programmer. In these instances, the user will want to place the ultimate responsibility upon the programmer.

If the programmer writes a program that complies with the contract specifications, he or she has not breached the contract and cannot be held liable for business losses resulting from operation of the program. In our example, Fred's office staff spent extra time manually processing customer orders after they discovered that the program would not produce a sales report. This problem cost Fred some money, but he couldn't hold the programmers responsible because he wasn't able to prove that he had contracted for the report feature. If that feature had been included in the program specifications, a court might have found the programmer liable for Fred's business losses (assuming that the programmer could have foreseen that such losses would result). For self-protection, the programmer will try to include in the contract a clause that disclaims liability for consequential or incidental damages (business losses). If possible, the user should avoid any such disclaimer. At the very least, the contract specifications should be detailed enough to give the programmer notice of the possible impact on the user's business of the software's failure to perform as expected.

In the case of third party losses (problems caused to customers or clients), the programmer ordinarily won't be liable unless there's a contract provision to that effect. The programmer has no direct business relationship with the third parties (i.e., is not in "privity of contract" with them), and product liability laws don't cover custom software, which is a service and not a sale of goods (although the programmer might be liable to the user or to third parties on the grounds of negligence or professional malpractice; see Chapter 10 for a discussion of these issues). Therefore, the user should seek to hold the programmer responsible for damage resulting to customers or clients through a special provision in the contract. Of course, programmers resist any contract term that extends this liability to them, because it's difficult to foresee all the problems that may arise and not always clear when a problem is a result of software failure or user error. But if the user's bargaining position is strong enough to permit transfer of liability to the programmer, the user should seek to do so. The contract should detail as much as possible the uses to which the program will be put, so as to provide clear notice to the programmer of potential third-party losses. The contract should also contain a warranty that the programmer is insured against such losses.

SOFTWARE MODIFICATIONS

A unique characteristic of computer software is its ability to be modified and reshaped into a form substantially different from the original product. Instructions can be added or deleted, and the program can be rewritten to run on different computers as necessary to meet the user's changing needs. These modifications and improvements can create problems with the legal rights specified in the software contract and lead to many disputes over the effect of the changes. For example, a user who alters the software may void a performance warranty, since the programmer only warrants that the original program will perform as specified. The programmer also may escape liability for business losses or third-party damages caused by program defects if the program has been altered. The software contract should explain clearly the effect of future modifications to the software. Will modifications by the user be permitted at all when the programmer owns the software? If so, will the programmer own the modifications as well? How will modifications affect the maintenance obligations of the programmer? Do modifications by the user void performance warranties or affect liability for business losses or damge to third parties?

If the user is allowed a free hand in altering the software, the programmer will probably not agree to accept responsibility for events occurring after the changes. The programmer will more readily accept postmodification liability when he or she, and not the user, makes the alterations. If the programmer is making the changes, the contract should indicate that such modifications do not affect any of the contract obligations. If modifications by the user are permitted, the user still should seek a contract clause holding the programmer responsible for software problems not related to the alterations.

CONFIDENTIALITY AND SECURITY

Computer users often have a need to protect their work from unauthorized disclosure to competitors or others with adverse interests. The software contract should contain provisions for ensuring adequate security and confidentiality of trade secrets. The user may seek to limit or screen the staff of the programming firm when appropriate and require their compliance with company security safeguards. The programmer should agree not to disclose to anyone the information obtained from the user concerning his or her operations and products, including the intended application of the software being developed. The user should keep in mind that his or her products and ideas can lose the protection of trade secret law if information about them is disclosed to persons not bound by an agreement to maintain their confidentiality. (Trade secret protection for software itself is discussed in Chapter 7.)

TAXES

A customized software project typically is not subject to sales tax, since it involves the provision of services and not the sale of goods. However, if the project includes off-the-shelf software such as a word processing package, that component might be taxable. Sales tax also can be levied when the software is sold as part of an integrated hardware-software system, and supplies such as disks and manuals can be taxed when delivered with the programming services. The user should check the law in his or her particular state concerning sales and use taxes. The contract should specify whether such taxes are included in the contract price and, if not, who is responsible for paying them. Taxes levied on the programmer that are not specifically related to the project must be the responsibility of the programmer. The contract should clarify whether the programmer has the status of an independent contractor or an employee, for the purposes of income tax, Social Security tax, and employment tax. If the programmer is considered an employee, the user must collect these employment-related taxes. (Other tax issues of interest to the computer user are discussed in Chapter 9.)

LEGAL REMEDIES

Once the user and the programmer have established their respective obligations under the contract, they must determine what will happen if the obligations are not met. The remedies clause in the contract contains this information. The legal remedies available to the user for a contract breach by the programmer depend on the type of breach and whether it occurs before or after acceptance of the software.

BREACH BEFORE ACCEPTANCE

The user should ensure that he or she has the option of rescinding (canceling) the contract if a breach of an important contract term occurs prior to completion of the project and acceptance of the software. For example, you might discover that the completion date of the project will be delayed six months or that the expected results cannot be achieved without a drastic increase in cost. The option of recision permits you to avoid further payments under the contract without breaching the contract by your failure to pay. The contract should always allow an opportunity for the programmer to "cure," or correct, any deficiency. Terminating the contract may be an expensive option for the user, since he or she has invested money and effort in the project that could be wasted if it has to be begun anew. The contract should be flexible enough to allow the parties to work out their problems and continue the project if at all possible.

BREACH AFTER ACCEPTANCE

The contract should always require that the programmer correct any problems with the software that arise. If the bugs can't be corrected, the remedy should be payment to compensate for the software's decrease in value that has resulted from the problems. There should also be remedies for breach of the waranties concerning ownership rights. For example, if a third party claiming to own an interest in the software sues the user, the programmer should be required to pay any damages awarded against the user in court, as well as attorneys' fees and other costs of litigation. The programmer will resist remedy provisions for lost profits of the user or damage to third parties due to software defects, but you should include these terms if possible. Be certain that the contract describes the intended uses of the software so that the programmer has notice of potential business or third-party losses from a program defect.

OTHER CONTRACT PROVISIONS

The contract may contain additional provisions as appropriate. Here are some examples.

NO SUBCONTRACTING WITHOUT CONSENT

This gives the user control over the programmers who will work with the computer, in order to ensure high-quality work and to protect the security and confidentiality of the user's operations.

BANKRUPTCY OR DISSOLUTION OF THE PROGRAMMER'S BUSINESS

The user should have the option of terminating the contract if the programmer loses his or her business viability. Without this option, you might be required to continue the contract with other programmers or maintenance personnel selected by a bankruptcy trustee. The contract should be made enforceable against the "heirs and assigns" of the programmer, to ensure recourse against someone in case the original programmer is not available.

ARBITRATION

An increasingly attractive alternative to court trials is dispute resolution using an arbitrator. Arbitration is normally faster and less expensive than going to court. Parties to a contract may agree that any dispute concerning performance of the agreement be resolved by one or more arbitrators. The contract can provide that the arbitration be binding or nonbinding. The arbitrator may be named in the contract, and the parties may agree on rules or standards to be used at any arbitration hearing.

NOTICES

The contract should include a procedure for giving notice of important occurrences such as program failures or alterations by the user. Specify whether these notices may be oral or must be in writing.

SUBSEQUENT CONTRACT AMENDMENTS

The contract may contain a clause stating that amendments to the contract must be made in a written document signed by all parties. This prevents later confusion over claims of oral changes in rights and obligations.

All of these issues should be considered before any software development contract is written or signed. By considering all of these points, the computer user will focus attention on the protection of his or her most important interests. Of course, some complex projects dictate a broader expanse of legal considerations that are beyond the scope of this book. When these questions arise, you should seek appropriate legal advice. For further reference, the appendix contains a sample software development contract.

Even a good software contract doesn't guarantee that no legal disputes will occur. Sometimes the failure of a software project is so complete or the relationship of the parties has deteriorated so much that the courtroom is inevitable. One Minnesota auto supply wholesaler contracted for a computer system that included software for inventory control. The programmers told the auto supplier that the only way they could automate the inventory control system was to automate the entire accounting system. In fact, the extra work was not necessary, and the programmers were trying to overcharge. In court the programmers admitted that their statement was not true but defended themselves on the ground that the statement was "so patently unbelievable that no reasonable reliance could be placed on it." Not surprisingly, the auto supplier won a sizable judgment in the case (Clements Auto Company v. Service Bureau Corp., 444 F.2d 169 [8th Cir. 1971]).

No document, no matter how well drafted, can prevent all possible legal disputes. But if computer users take care to clarify their interests and protect their rights by establishing a complete, written contract at the outset of their software development projects, they can avoid the needless troubles that arise from misunderstandings, faulty memories, and lack of communication.

PART THREE
Legal Protection and Marketing of Computer Software

================================

Ownership of Software
6

The computer software industry is new and lucrative. Computer programs often require a great deal of time and expense to develop, but a good program can be very profitable, whether developed by a software company, the programming staff of a university or private business, or an individual programmer. Because there is so much at stake, a host of legal conflicts and problems have arisen over the ownership, distribution, and use of computer programs. Programmers, both amateur and professional, are asking questions about developing and selling software. Is a programmer ever free to use for personal gain ideas generated while he or she is programming for an employer? What steps should a software author take to protect his or her ownership rights during the development stage? What should the author know about software distribution agreements before approaching a publisher to market a program? What should the author know about user license agreements? If you are an employer, what should you do to make sure that employees don't disclose information about your software to potential competitors?

In this chapter the legal aspects of computer software ownership will be discussed. In Chapter 7 we will discuss the various legal methods of protecting proprietary (ownership) rights in software, including trade secret law, copyrights, patents, and other means of protection. Chapter 8 examines the legal aspects of dealing with a software publisher for the evaluation and marketing of your programs. Chapter 8 also discusses license agreements and preventing unauthorized use of software. You should understand from the start that legal protections, even when coupled with technological safeguards, are never completely effective in preventing illicit copying of programs and theft of ideas. It's a little like walking outdoors in a heavy rainstorm; you're going to get wet no matter what you do, but you won't get completely soaked if you take along an umbrella. An understanding of the "umbrella" of legal protection discussed in Chapters 6, 7, and 8 can help the software author avoid the serious blunders that permit the program to slip into the public domain. The reader will discover that the law provides a significant amount of protection that, even though it can't eliminate all piracy, might make the difference between profitability and wasted effort.

As is true of other sections of this book, the chapters on legally protecting computer software and dealing with publishers are not intended to turn computer users into experts capable of handling all their own legal affairs and representing themselves in court. As the old saying goes, "He who acts as his own lawyer has a fool for a client." If you think your software is valuable, then you should seek the advice of an attorney before signing any agreements or taking other actions that affect your rights. But the knowledge gained from reading these chapters can help you avoid mistakes that may undermine your rights and lead to disputes with employers, employees, or competitors. You'll also have the ability to ask intelligent questions and give useful information to your attorney.

THE LEGAL DEFINITION OF COMPUTER SOFTWARE

When computer users hear the term *software*, they know what it means. Software means WordStar, Lotus 1-2-3, or any other program that makes your computer work for you. We think of software both in terms of its physical components—floppy disks and user's manuals—and in a more abstract sense, as the force that causes the machine to run. Programmers regard software as the end product of their efforts, the final package that will be given to the boss or sold to consumers.

In legal affairs, these general conceptions of software are not sufficient. Lawyers have tried to define the phrase "computer software" more precisely in order to fit this new technology into the existing system of law. Software has been given different, and sometimes conflicting, definitions by various organizations, including the Internal Revenue Service and state tax authorities (in determining income and sales tax issues); the U.S. Copyright and Patent Offices (in considering applications); the U.S. State Department (in attempting to limit exports of high technology to certain countries); and the courts (in deciding questions of contract interpretation and ownership of computer programs). These definitions have changed over time, leading to a great deal of confusion in the courts and among software writers and users. It will be useful now to describe more precisely what software is, in order to understand the legal concepts of ownership and the protection methods discussed in Chapter 7.

We often think of computer software and computer programs as being the same thing. In a general sense they are the same thing: the means by which the computer is able to perform the desired tasks. But in trying to understand the intricacies of legal protection of computer software, we should distinguish the two terms. Computer *programs* are sets of instructions that operate the computer. For example, a program to balance your checkbook is a set of instructions that takes the computer through a logical process of adding deposits and subtracting the amount of the checks to arrive at your final account balance. A computer program can be completely without recognizable form or substance, existing only in the mind of the programmer or the internal memory of the computer.

Computer *software* is the collection of materials that contains, expresses, and explains a computer program. This includes a machine-readable program written in magnetic form on floppy disks or tapes, printouts containing the source code or object code for the program, the programmer's notes and work papers, and the operator's manual explaining how to use the program. The term *software* evolved as a counterpart to the term *hardware* (the computer, monitor, keyboard, and other equipment). The only software that the end user normally sees consists of floppy disks and documentation (operator's manuals), although software can include other materials used and produced by the programmer.

The first step in the creation of software is the writing of flowcharts and other program specifications. From these materials the programmer writes instructions for the computer, usually in a "high-level" (similar to English) computer language such as BASIC or Pascal. These instructions are known as the *source code* of the program. Using a program or a series of programs called *assemblers* or *compilers*, the computer translates the source code into *object code*. Object code may be in machine-readable form, either in the form of high- and low-voltage electrical signals inside the computer or on a magnetic tape or disk. Object code can also be printed out to be "read" by people as a series of ones and zeros. The importance, from a legal standpoint, of the distinction between source code and object code will become clear when we discuss copyrights in Chapter 7.

It's easy to see that computer software has somewhat elusive and abstract aspects (e.g., the thought processes and techniques that make up the program, and the electrical impulses running through the computer) as well as more concrete aspects (e.g., the floppy disks on which the programs are stored in magnetic form, the papers containing the programmer's source code, and the operator's manuals). The unique nature of software has caused endless problems for courts and lawyers, who can't decide whether software is "tangible," "intangible," or something in between. Some lawyers have argued that software is intangible and therefore not subject to sales taxes applying to tangible property. Others claim that software is tangible and therefore covered by the Uniform Commercial Code, which governs the sale of tangible goods. The courts have defined software as tangible for some purposes and intangible for others, with different courts sometimes adopting conflicting positions. Many commentators feel that the computer *program* should be regarded as intangible and the computer *software* (the materials used by the programmer or sold to the end user) as tangible.

Another source of confusion for software authors and their attorneys has been the issue of whether software is an "artistic" creation, like a book or technical paper, or a product of an engineering process. A computer program can be written in source code on paper. But writing the source code is not like writing a novel or some other artistic or even scientific creation. It's really more of an engineering process of defining a problem and then designing the solution, which can often be done through hardware design as well as software design. Courts have had trouble deciding how to regard the process of software development, which has led to much debate and confusion over copyright and patent protection of software. (We'll discuss the views on defining software, and its treatment under the copyright and patent laws, in Chapter 7.)

We now have a better idea of what computer software is: the collection of materials that contains, expresses, and explains computer programs. We also know that lawyers and courts have trouble fitting this new technology into the existing framework of laws and regulations. In Chapter 7 we will see the effect of these debates over the definition of software on computer users who are interested in legal protection of software. But before taking action to protect your software, you have to make sure that it belongs to you. We now turn to the topic of software ownership.

SOFTWARE OWNERSHIP

Computer software is regarded by the law as property that can be owned and transferred like a computer, an automobile, or any other product. Software falls into the category of "intellectual property," since it's created primarily through mental effort rather than manufactured like an automobile. This difference is important when considering the methods of protecting ownership rights. For example, copyright protection is available only for intellectual property. But when it comes to owning, buying, or selling software, the rules are basically the same as for any type of property. If you own the software, you can transfer ownership in return for a lump sum payment or royalties, or you can license the use of the software. If you don't own the software, you cannot use it or profit from it until you acquire the appropriate rights: either a license that permits you to use the software, or ownership rights that allow you to sell or license the software yourself.

Sometimes it's easy to determine who owns a particular piece of software. If you're unemployed and develop a program at home entirely by yourself, it's clear that you own all rights in the software. If your neighbor is helping you with the programming, it's less clear that you're the sole owner. Serious ownership problems can arise when you are a staff programmer and use company computers to work on personal projects or when you use your home computer to work simultaneously on related company and personal projects. Programming concepts and ideas for marketable products jump around easily, with many people contributing their time and thoughts. When the dust clears, ownership of the final product may be very much in doubt. This can lead to legal disputes over the right to license or sell the software. Most of these problems are avoidable if proper attention is paid to clarifying the rights of everyone involved in the software development before the project begins. We now look at three common software development situations in which ownership rights are created: software development by staff programmers; software development by independent programmers or consultants hired for a specific project; and software development by self-employed or spare-time programmers.

SOFTWARE DEVELOPMENT BY STAFF PROGRAMMERS

When a company hires employees, it normally expects to own the fruits of their labor. The employee receives a salary or wages, and the employer owns and controls all that is produced in the course of employment. For example, Alice, a staff programmer with a stockbrokerage firm, has been working on a project that the firm calls "Stocktrace." Stocktrace is a program that tracks the daily performance of securities and signals the firm's brokers when a stock price moves outside a specified range. The broker can then advise clients to buy or sell. Alice developed Stocktrace with the help of other staff programmers, working entirely on the firm's computers at the office.

Even if there were no employment contract or other agreement between Alice and the brokerage firm, the firm owns all rights in Stocktrace. Alice cannot claim that she owns some interest in the software on the basis of her contribution of labor to develop it. The law recognizes that Alice received her salary, and nothing more, as payment for her efforts. The same is true for Bill, a staff programmer at a software development company. Bill worked on creating "Businessplan," an integrated office productivity package. When the project was finished, Bill had his paycheck, and the software company owned all rights in Businessplan.

Even though a contract isn't needed to make the employer the owner of the software in a staff employment situation, it's still advisable to have the employee sign a contract. The contracts that are typically signed by programmer-employees are called "work made for hire" agreements. A work-made-for-hire agreement is a written understanding that all work (programming, system design, supervision, and so forth) performed by the employee is done for the benefit of the company, which owns all rights in any property (tangible or intangible) that's created. The employer should have all new employees sign a work-made-for-hire agreement on their first day on the job, if not before. These agreements are important not only for companies that intend to develop and sell software but also for any company with staff members who do computer-related work. Figure 6–1 contains an agreement between Alice and her employer, a stockbrokerage firm.

A work-made-for-hire agreement serves two basic purposes. First, it clarifies the legal status of the work performed by the employee. The phrase "work made for hire" is used because those particular words create ownership rights for the employer under the copyright laws. If the programmer is a staff employee, as opposed to an independent programmer hired for a specific project, any work created by him or her is automatically a work made for hire belonging to the employer. Still, a written agreement removes any room for argument about the status of the work, thereby minimizing the chances of a legal contest over ownership of the software.

A work-made-for-hire agreement also serves to notify employees, before they have begun work, that anything they produce will belong to the employer. Some employees may mistakenly believe that they have some ownership rights in the software they develop. For example, programmers who write or maintain programs solely for internal use at a university may believe that the employer has no commercial interest in the programs. Such employees may feel free to try to sell or license programs that they have written at work. In fact, colleges and universities often share their programs openly without seeking a profit from them. But in some instances they may want to make money by licensing a program. A work-made-for-hire agreement with the programmer will prevent

FIG. 6—1
Work-Made-For-Hire Agreement with Staff Programmer

ACME BROKERS, INC.—WORK-MADE-FOR-HIRE AGREEMENT

Alice *(Employee)* hereby agrees, in consideration of the payments specified in paragraph 3 of this agreement, that

1. All work performed in the course of employment with ACME Brokers, Inc. *(Company)* is done exclusively for the benefit of the Company, and the product of such work shall be "works made for hire." The Company shall own all rights to such works and may make any use or nonuse of such works without further payment or obligation to Employee.

2. Employee understands that all ideas and information concerning her work are trade secrets of the Company and are not to be discussed with or revealed to any third party without the permission of the Company.

3. The salary agreed upon between Employee and the Company is the sole payment for all services provided by Employee. Employee is not entitled to the payment of royalties or other compensation for works developed in the course of employment.

4. This agreement does not create any right to employment with the Company and is in addition to other agreements that may have been signed by Employee and the Company. Except as specified herein, this agreement does not limit any rights of Employee or the Company created by other contracts or laws.

Signed: _____   _____
　　　　　　　　Alice   President
　　　　　　　　　　　　　　　　　　　ACME Brokers, Inc.

---

actions that could cause the employer to lose the right to sell or license the software.

The use of work-made-for-hire agreements will become increasingly important as more employees engage in "telecommuting," or working at home and communicating with the employer via computers and telephone lines. In the work-at-home situation, the line between work done in the course of employment and work done for oneself can become very blurred. Imagine Alice working at home on the Stocktrace project. As she is working, she begins to get ideas for an advanced version of the program. She puts another disk into the second disk drive of the computer and periodically makes notes on it. Alice eventually creates a better stock-tracing program, working at home with the notes. If Alice tries to sell the new program, can her employer claim any ownership interest in it?

Looking at Alice's agreement in Figure 6–1, we see that she has agreed that all programming and other work performed "in the course of employment" belongs to the employer. Other agreements use similar phrases, giving the employer ownership of all works created "during employment" or in the "scope of employment." When you work at the office it's generally understood by both the employer and the employee that everything done there is done in the "course of employment." When you work at home, it can no longer be assumed that everything is done for the employer. When are you on the job, and when does your spare time begin? Even if the hours are designated, can't you be flexible about it and take a few minutes to work on personal matters when the urge strikes?

The work-made-for-hire agreement in the work-at-home situation has to be more carefully written. Of course, the employer can't expect an employee to sign an agreement that says that all programming work done at home belongs to the employer. Even if the employee signed such an agreement, the courts would probably not enforce it. The best approach would be to make the agreement project or subject matter specific. For example, if Alice is working at home, the agreement can specify that all programming work related to monitoring stock market activity will belong to the employer. This would give the company all rights in the Stocktrace program and in any spin-offs from that project. If Alice designed a video game, it would be hers to keep, regardless of whether she did the work on Tuesday afternoons or Saturday mornings.

As an extra safeguard against employees using company ideas for their own gain, the employer can ask employees to sign a "covenant not to compete." These are discussed in detail in Chapter 7.

SOFTWARE DEVELOPMENT BY INDEPENDENT PROGRAMMERS

As an alternative to hiring staff programmers, outside programmers are often retained to develop software. Normally these programmers are hired to develop or consult on one particular project, after which they stop working for the hiring company or organization. For example, Calvin is a free-lance programmer who was hired by a local school district to develop a computer program to keep track of school enrollment and attendance. The program would accept daily entry of attendance figures from all the schools in the district; print weekly summaries to send to the state education department; and analyze the efect on attendance of such factors as weather, flu epidemics, and nearby rock concerts. Calvin estimated the length of time it would take to complete the project and agreed to do the work for $20,000. He signed a contract with the school district providing for a completion date, acceptance testing, and maintenance of the software.

When the school attendance software was finished, it worked like a charm. Calvin thought that he might like to sell copies to other school districts around the state, since they all have to send the same reports to the education department and they would probably be interested in the analysis of factors affecting attendance. Is Calvin free to sell or license the software? He is not a full-time employee of the school district. As a free-lance programmer, Calvin works on many jobs for different companies and schools as well as for the government. There is no one employer who can claim to own all of what Calvin produces. In this situation, ownership of the school attendance software will be decided by the contract between Calvin and the school district.

In one respect, development of software by an independent programmer (whether an individual or a programming company) is similar to development by a staff programmer: in both cases the software is written at the request of a person or organization that pays the programmer for his or her efforts. But there is a crucial difference from the standpoint of proprietary rights in the software. Everything that employees develop in the course of their employment belongs to the employer (that is, everything is recognized by the law as a work made for hire), even in the absence of a written work-made-for-hire agreement. But the same isn't true when an independent programmer develops the software. The school attendance software will not constitute a work made for hire belonging to the school district unless there is an agreement with the programmer to that effect. If there is no agreement, the software is not a work made for hire, and Calvin owns it and may sell or license it to other users.

It makes sense that work-made-for-hire status isn't automatic if the programmer is not an employee. Sometimes the user of the software has no interest in obtaining proprietary rights. For example, the school district might only want to get the school attendance software working on their computers and might not care if Calvin sells it to other districts. If fact, the district might expressly disclaim any ownership rights when negotiating the cost of the software development with Calvin. Calvin might develop the software for less money if he has the prospect of selling it or licensing it to other users.

Regardless of who is to own the software, the decision should be clearly stated in a written contract. Users sometimes change their minds about what they want to do with software once they see how nicely it works. A written contract clause specifying ownership rights forces everyone to think about the issue and resolve it before a dispute arises. If the user is to own the software, he or she should have the programmer sign a work-made-for-hire agreement similar to the one in Figure 6-2. If the programmer is to own the software, the software development contract should state that the software is not a work made for hire and that all proprietary rights belong to the programmer (see Chapter 5 for a detailed discussion of contracts for the development of customized software).

Until now we have assumed that all aspects of the software (the computer program and documentation) were written by the programmer. This is often not the case. Frequently the programmer writes the program that makes the computer run, but someone else writes an operator's manual describing, in English, how to use the program. Programmers don't always write clear, concise manuals. A professional writer who has learned how to use the program often has a better idea than the programmer of the questions and problems that users will have. In our example, the school district will want an operator's manual for the school attendance program to facilitate use of the program. The school district may assign an employee to write the manual, or may hire a freelance writer. Even software development companies farm out a lot of their manual writing, in order to save their programmers' time and to get a fresh perspective on explaining the program.

The rules for proprietary rights in the operator's manual are the same as those for the program itself. If the work is done by a staff writer, the employer owns the manual (although it's still a good idea to have a work-made-for-hire agreement with the writer). If an independent writer is hired, he or she should be asked to sign a work-made-for-hire agreement. The agreement in Figure 6-2 can serve as a guide, with appropriate changes to reflect that the job involves writing rather than programming. If no agreement is signed, the writer will hold the copyright and will have the right to sell the manual or license its use.

We have now seen how employers or individuals who hire independent programmers or manual writers can, by following a few simple steps, secure ownership rights in software that they paid to have developed. By now the message should be clear to the programmer. You may be able to earn a good salary by developing software for someone else, but if you expect to earn profits from royalties or outright sale, you need to own the software. Other than by contracting for the rights or buying them after development, the only effective way to have them is to write the software on your own time, and preferably on your own computer, at home or in your own office. We now look at the situation in which individual programmers develop software independently, and we'll discuss the rights that go along with the ownership of software.

FIG. 6–2
Work-Made-For-Hire Agreement with Independent Programmer

SCHOOL DISTRICT—WORK-MADE-FOR-HIRE AGREEMENT

Calvin *(Programmer)* hereby agrees, in consideration for the payments specified in paragraph 2 of this agreement, that

1. Programmer will develop for School District a computer program to manage student attendance data, including computer source code and related documentation, according to the attached specifications.

2. Programmer shall receive the sum of $20,000 as compensation for the work described in paragraph 1. Programmer is not entitled to the payment of royalties or other compensation for works developed under this contract.

3. All work performed under this agreement is done exclusively for the benefit of School District and constitutes "works made for hire." School District shall own all rights to such works and may make any use or nonuse of such works without further payment or obligation to Programmer. To the extent that the work does not constitute a "work made for hire," Programmer hereby assigns all proprietary rights in the work to School District.

4. Programmer understands that all ideas and information concerning the work are trade secrets of School District and are not to be discussed with or revealed to any third party without the permission of School District.

Signed: _____   _____
                       Calvin   Superintendent
                                                                                        School District

---

Note: This agreement will be sufficient to secure ownership rights in the software for the company hiring the programmer. However, it is better to include these clauses in a more comprehensive software development contract that covers such topics as acceptance testing, software maintenance, and warranties. See Chapter 5 for a complete discussion of contracting for customized software.

SOFTWARE DEVELOPMENT BY SELF-EMPLOYED AND
SPARE-TIME PROGRAMMERS

When there's no work-made-for-hire situation, proprietary rights belong to the person who develops the software. In other words, if no one is paying you to develop the software or making you sign an agreement, you own the software. If you are an employee or otherwise hire yourself out to write programs, you still own any software that you develop in your spare time away from the workplace. For example, while Calvin was working on the school district project he was also busy with some of his own ideas. Working weekends at home, he wrote a program to teach geometry to high school students. Calvin now wants to market the program. Since the work was entirely his, he holds all proprietary rights and can do with it as he pleases (although he should take steps to protect his rights, as discussed in Chapter 7).

Even self-employed and spare-time programmers get involved in arguments over who owns the software. If more than one programming brain has contributed to the work, ownership can be confused. For example, Dan, who works as a golfing instructor, had an idea for a computer video golfing game. Dan is an amateur programmer and did most of the programming on "Golf-Game" himself. But he ran into some problems and asked Calvin, who is a better programmer, to help him out. Calvin made some useful suggestions and rewrote some of the code. Golf-Game worked nicely, and Dan decided to take it to a publisher. Calvin said that was fine, as long as he got his share of the profits. Until then Dan hadn't been planning to give Calvin a share. Does Calvin have any rights in Golf-Game? Calvin might have an interest if Dan had said something about sharing the profits or had otherwise led Calvin to believe that he wasn't just volunteering his work and ideas. When a joint effort is involved, it's a good idea to write a short agreement to clarify proprietary rights ("Calvin agrees he gets nothing"; or "Calvin gets one-third of all earnings from the program"). At least talk about it before the work starts, in order to avoid a later misunderstanding.

RIGHTS OF SOFTWARE OWNERSHIP

Now that we've determined who owns the software in the three most common development situations, we have to ask what it means to own computer software. That is, what legal rights does the owner have, and what can he or she do with the software?

The owner of computer software has the exclusive right to control and use the software. Any infringement of this right can be stopped through legal action. Of course, you can't make any money from your software unless you're willing to give up some of this control. This is done through one of two legal devices: an assignment of rights or a license for use.

ASSIGNMENT OF RIGHTS

An assignment transfers all rights in the software to someone else. You'll want to make an assignment when you're selling the software outright. For example, Dan may decide to sell his golf video game to a software publisher for $25,000. When Dan makes this assignment, he has no further rights in the software. The publisher can do whatever it wants with the software and doesn't have to pay Dan royalties or ask his permission for any actions it takes. Although an assignment of rights for a fixed price prevents you from receiving the royalties that might be earned from a commercially successful program, it also eliminates the marketing risks. If the program flops, you still keep the money you received when you made the assignment. An assignment can also be made in return for royalties. In this case, the publisher receives all ownership rights, but instead of being paid a lump sum the programmer receives a royalty based on the number of copies of the program that are sold (royalty agreements are explained in more detail in Chapter 8). A simplified version of an assignment of software rights is given in Figure 6–3.

LICENSE FOR USE

We have already examined license agreements from the perspective of the end user, in Chapter 4 (for packaged software) and Chapter 5 (for custom software). Now we'll look at software license agreements from the point of view of the software developer.

Unlike an assignment, a license doesn't transfer all ownership rights in the software—only the rights necessary for a more limited purpose (such as using or marketing the software). Software is generally licensed in two manners. The owner can license it to a software publisher as an alternative to assignment of rights. The publisher then relicenses the software to users, paying royalties to the owner. Or the owner can license the software directly to users. The user may pay a periodic (monthly or yearly) license fee or in the case of packaged software, make a one-time payment (really more of a purchase).

The owner of the software retains all rights not granted by the license. The most important right that remains is the right to receive the royalties or license fees from the marketing of the software. For example, Dan might have licensed Golf-Game to the publisher instead of assigning (selling) all his rights for

FIG. 6–3
Assignment of Software Rights

SOFTPUBLISHING, INC.—ASSIGNMENT OF SOFTWARE RIGHTS

This agreement is signed this 1st day of January, 1985, between Dan *(Seller)* and SoftPublishing, Inc. *(Buyer)*.

In consideration for the payment of $25,000, Seller hereby transfers and assigns to Buyer all copyrights and other rights in Golf-Game. Buyer shall have the right to control, use, or transfer rights in Golf-Game without further obligation to Seller. Seller retains no rights in Golf-Game.

Seller warrants that he has the legal right to make this assignment and that such assignment does not infringe upon the rights of any third parties.

_____	_____
Dan	President
	SoftPublishing, Inc.

$25,000. The publisher would then relicense the game to users, paying Dan a percentage of the revenues in the form of royalties. If Dan wanted to get some money "up front," he could sell his right to receive royalties to his friend Calvin. Dan would pocket the money from Calvin, and the publisher would pay the royalties to Calvin when Golf-Game began to sell. The assignment of rights to Calvin would be done using the type of agreement shown in Figure 6–3. The agreement should indicate that a third party, in this case the publisher, holds a license. The publisher's license is not affected by the assignment of ownership rights to Calvin. In Chapter 8 we will discuss in greater detail the license-royalty arrangement with software publishers and the licensing of software directly to users.

PROTECTION OF OWNERSHIP RIGHTS

Ownership of software carries with it the right to protect against infringement of your rights. This is really more of an obligation than a right, although legally it is a right because no one else is allowed to intervene and do it for you. This could be important when the program is under license to a publisher. For example, if Dan licensed Golf-Game to a publisher and another company obtained copies of the game and tried to market it, the publisher could not go to court on Dan's behalf to stop the illegal infringement of rights. If Dan did nothing, the pirate company would get away with its infringement. For this reason, some publishers insist on an assignment of rights, rather than a license, from the software developer.

Of course, under most circumstances the software owner wants to do everything possible to protect against infringement of his or her rights. *How* to protect yourself effectively is one of the most complex and interesting problems in the field of computer law. Chapter 7 is devoted to understanding the methods and strategies of legal protection of software.

==

Methods of Protecting Software Ownership Rights

7

No one wants to invest a lot of time and money in making a product only to see it carried away by strangers who don't care whether the product's developer ever earns a profit. But that is precisely what happens with great frequency in the computer software industry. Even the large software publishers, with their access to the best legal advice and the latest in copy protection technology, lose millions of dollars to theft of ideas and unauthorized copying of software. The precise amount of revenue lost by the software industry is impossible to determine, but it may be as high as one-quarter to one-half of the total market sales revenue.

Computer software is difficult to protect because it is so easily copied. A $500 television set has to be manufactured from hundreds of parts, but a $500 computer program can multiply faster than rabbits at a very low cost per unit. A program can be transferred from one storage medium (a disk or tape) to another in a matter of seconds. It can be transmitted over cables or telephone lines anywhere in the world at the push of a button. Besides direct copying, a skilled programmer with access to the source code can write another program with a somewhat different appearance that performs the same functions as the first program. In this way an idea can be stolen, leaving the original developer with the difficult task of proving that the second program was derived from his or her work. Operator's manuals are equally easy to photocopy or rewrite.

A programmer who or company that develops software has to protect its

Hagelshaw: The Computer User's Legal Guide (Chilton)

rights against threats from several sources. Users may buy software and then make unauthorized copies for their own use or to give or sell to others. The great difference between the high cost of a legitimate copy and the very low cost of a bootleg copy (perhaps no more than the cost of a blank disk) provides great incentive for illicit copying of programs. Companies that employ staff programmers or hire outside programmers have to be especially careful to prevent them from disclosing proprietary information to outsiders. Former employees are notorious for setting up rival companies and selling software that is "coincidentally" similar to programs developed at their former company. Finally, software developers also have to keep an eye on competitors. Developing computer software can be a long and expensive process, and it is faster and cheaper to use someone else's source code. If a software package looks like a winner, competitors may want to reproduce, or at least imitate, the program. For example, there were many attempts to imitate Atari's popular and profitable Pac-Man video game. One company developed a maze-chase game, known as K. C. Munchkin, that was quite similar to Pac-Man. Atari sued the company producing K. C. Munchkin. The court ruled that K. C. Munchkin gobbled up his dots too much like Pac-Man, and an injunction was issued against the makers of K. C. Munchkin (Atari, Inc., v. North American Philips Consumer Electronics Corp., 672 F.2d 607 [7th Cir. 1982]; U.S. cert. den., 459 U.S. 880).

The law is changing rapidly in the area of protection of software ownership rights. Congress has been considering and passing bills to broaden legal protection of software, most notably with the passage of the Computer Software Copyright Act of 1980. The courts have also expanded protection of software, as have many state legislatures. The lawmakers see the need to help software developers protect the fruits of their efforts, in order to encourage investment of talent and money and the exchange of ideas without fear of theft.

Despite the progress, the legal protections available to software developers are still inadequate. Many of the problems are related to difficulties in detecting infringements and enforcing the laws, not the absence of laws themselves. But the software developer or owner shouldn't give up just because the system of legal protection isn't perfect. You don't stop walking down the street just because the police can't catch every crook who might be hiding in an alley. You put on your hat, walk out the door, and go about your business, taking all reasonable precautions to avoid injury or financial loss.

The same is true with software development. A determined pirate can copy or imitate your program and might get away with it despite your best efforts to protect it. But there's no need to lose some or all of the profits from your work through your own carelessness. You can do many things to protect yourself. Long before marketing your software, and even before beginning to write it, you can develop a strategy for legal protection of your rights. The best strategy to use will depend in part on your particular circumstances—the number of people involved in the development process and the relationship among them, the relative complexity and uniqueness of the software, the way it is to be marketed, and the resources available to the developer.

In this chapter we deal with how you can protect your computer software by making use of the laws concerning trade secrets, unfair competition, copyrights, and patents. We also examine nonlegal protection devices and the selection of protection strategies. We start with the topic that should always be a software developer's first consideration: protecting software ideas as trade secrets.

TRADE SECRET LAW

Trade secret law protects information, devices, and processes that give you a competitive edge over those who don't know what you know. For example, if you develop a soft drink that contains a unique blend of ingredients, you can prevent a competitor from using your recipe by keeping the recipe "secret." Unlike copyright and patent law, the law of trade secrets is not composed of a comprehensive national system of protection. Trade secret law is created by the legislatures and courts of each individual state and varies from state to state (although not greatly). The purpose of trade secret law is to encourage invention and development of products by protecting confidential information.

Every computer software author should be aware of trade secret law and how it works. If the software is being developed for eventual sale or licensing for profit, trade secret protection is a must.

During the developmental stage, and sometimes during the marketing stage, software should remain a trade secret. You may be very excited about the software you are developing and want to tell the whole world about it. But it is both practically and legally smart to tell no one what you are doing. If it is necessary to disclose your ideas, whether to employees, coworkers, consultants, or prospective publishers, do it only after taking care to preserve your work as a trade secret. There may be nothing worthwhile left to copyright or sell if you relinquish the protection of trade secret law and lose your ideas to opportunistic competitors.

TRADE SECRET PROTECTION FOR SOFTWARE

Trade secret protection is not available for every computer program that is written. The program must contain some unique aspects. Software that performs ordinary functions in a manner that is known and used by others cannot be the trade secret of any one company. For example, if you write a simple program to balance your company checkbook, or even if you write a more complicated compiler or operating system, the program may not be novel enough to be considered a trade secret. At the same time, software that performs ordinary functions using commonly known features can still be a trade secret if the features are put together in a unique way and the software gives a competitive advantage to its developer. Almost every complicated program contains at least some unique features of logic and structure, because programmers have different styles and different ideas of how the program should be structured and what users will want to buy. Each of these unique packages of ideas and techniques is protectable as a trade secret.

Consider the example of Calvin, who has written a program for computer instruction of geometry. If Calvin had been the first to develop a geometry instruction program, the fact that he had gotten ahead of the competition would have made the components of his software protectable as trade secrets. Of course, in reality there are many geometry programs written by other programmers. All of these programs may do more or less the same thing, in the sense that they present geometry problems to the user, ask the user to pick the correct answer from among several choices, inform the user when he or she is wrong, and provide an explanation for the right answer. But Calvin's geometry software is a little different from the others. Not only does it provide an explanation for the correct answer, but it also suggests reasons why the user may have picked a wrong answer (such as using the wrong mathematical formula or misplacing a decimal point). Calvin's program also operates faster than most of the other geometry instruction software. This better performance is a result of a combination of programming features that are unique to his software and that give Calvin a competitive advantage over his rivals. These unique aspects can be protected as trade secrets.

Trade secret law protects more than just the computer program you have written. Other aspects of the software, such as the operator's manual (before it is published and distributed) and all printouts of codes and programmer's notes can also be protected as trade secrets. Other business information, including customer lists, information concerning negotiations with publishers, results of product testing, and even the names of programmers who are working on particular projects, is also eligible. In short, any information used in your business that gives you an advantage over competitors (and is not generally known to them) may be a trade secret. Of course, it isn't enough that the information, device, or process is eligible for protection. You have to take steps to protect it and observe certain precautions to keep that protection.

OBTAINING AND KEEPING TRADE SECRET PROTECTION

Trade secret protection is established for software by treating the software as a secret. That may sound simple, but software owners and writers constantly fail to do it. Programmers enjoy discussing their work with other programmers, and this interaction helps them pick up new techniques and improve their skills. But programmers have to be careful to restrain their enthusiasm about their work and not disclose information that they'd be better off keeping confidential. This is especially important in the developmental stage, when the program doesn't yet have the benefit of any other type of legal protection such as copyright or license agreements. For example, consider Calvin's geometry program, when it is half finished. He is working from a programmer's flowchart and other notes, and the program is nothing more than a lot of code contained on a few floppy disks. It has obviously not yet been copyrighted or distributed with a restrictive license agreement, and there has been no signed agreement by those coming into contact with the program not to disclose its substance. If Calvin goes to a meeting of his computer club and talks about the structure of his program and the techniques he is using, anyone can use those ideas to compete with him, and there is nothing he can do about it. At this crucial stage in developing his geometry program, Calvin would be better off keeping quiet.

If you can resist the temptation of telling your friends and colleagues about your latest software ideas, you have gone a long way toward preserving them under trade secret law. But keeping quiet is feasible only when you are working entirely by yourself. Very often, more than one person is involved in the development process. Then some discussion of ideas is essential if the project is to be successful. The fact that ideas are disclosed—whether to coworkers, outside consutlants, or even users—won't result in a loss of trade secret protection. The information doesn't have to be a true secret (in the sense that no one else knows about it but you) to be a trade secret under the law. The important thing is that the individual or group intends to keep the information confidential and takes reasonable precautions to prevent its disclosure to someone who is not working on, or legitimately using, the software. If these precautions are taken, the software developer can prevent use of the information even though the safeguards weren't airtight and some information leaked out.

There are certain standard procedures that a company, however large or small, should implement to preserve trade secrets. Some of these involve physical security, such as locking up materials when they are not in use, issuing employee identification passes, implementing sign-out procedures for disks or materials that contain programs or parts of programs, and using passwords to gain access to the computers. Even a solo programmer should look out for the physical security of disks and other materials.

The software developer should also physically identify as confidential all materials containing trade secrets. All copies of the source code, written materials, and disk covers should be stamped with a notice worded something like this:

CONFIDENTIAL

This program belongs to ACME, Inc., and contains trade secrets of ACME, Inc. The program and its contents are not to be disclosed to or used by any person who has not received prior authorization from ACME, Inc. Any such disclosure or use may subject the violator to civil and criminal penalties as provided by law.

The purpose of this notice is to inform people who come into contact with the materials that the owner intends that the information remain confidential. Someone who tries to use the materials without permission knows that he or she could be subject to the penalties for trade secret theft.

DISCLOSURE OF TRADE SECRETS

There are times when it is necessary to give permission for someone to use materials that contain trade secrets. This person could be the end user of the software. Even at the marketing stage, however, there may be some aspects of the software (such as the source code) that are not accessible to the user and could still be "secret" enough to be protected under trade secret law. If the software is distributed to a limited number of users, they could be asked to keep secret all aspects of the software, even those that are obvious to them. Chapter 8 discusses the use of license agreements to protect trade secrets disclosed to users.

It is also frequently necessary to disclose trade secrets to employees, consultants, or even friends who want to help without pay. In each of these situations there is the potential for unwanted dispersion of trade secrets. If Calvin, who is working alone on his software, has trouble keeping quiet at his computer club, how is a company with twenty programmers going to keep its information confidential? It's difficult if not impossible to keep all information from leaking out. But the company can stop outsiders from using the leaked information by taking steps to secure trade secret protection. In addition to ensuring physical security of materials and identifying materials containing

FIG. 7–1
Nondisclosure Agreement for Employee

BUSINESSTECH, INC.—NONDISCLOSURE AGREEMENT

1. Bill Smith (*Employee*), in consideration for his employment by Businesstech, Inc. (*Company*), agrees to hold in a fiduciary capacity, and not to disclose to any third parties, any trade secrets or confidential proprietary information of the company.

2. The information encompassed by this agreement includes knowledge about the management, products, product development, marketing activities, and any other device, process, or information considered confidential by Company.

3. Employee agrees not to disclose such information during his term of employment and for a period of three (3) years following his termination. Upon termination of employment, Employee agrees to turn over to Company all materials that contain trade secrets or confidential proprietary information of Company.

_____   _____
Bill Smith   President
                                          Businesstech, Inc.

Note: This agreement can be incorporated into a broader "work made for hire" agreement signed by the employee. "Work made for hire" agreements are discussed in Chapter 6.

trade secrets with a "Confidential" notice, a company should have its employees sign nondisclosure agreements.

A *nondisclosure agreement* tells the employee, consultant, or friend that he or she is not to reveal trade secrets to anyone else. The purpose of the agreement is to create a confidential relationship between the people signing the agreement. In this relationship, the employee or consultant has an obligation not to disclose the trade secrets that he or she learns. A violation of this agreement could furnish the basis for a lawsuit against the employee or consultant, even if he or she is not the one who actually uses the information.

The nondisclosure agreement can be general in scope, forbidding disclosure of all trade secrets of the company. Figure 7–1 is an example of a general employee nondisclosure agreement. The agreement can also be specific, relat-

FIG. 7–2
Nondisclosure Agreement for Consultant

FIFTH NATIONAL BANK—NONDISCLOSURE AGREEMENT

1. Kevin Jones (Consultant), in consideration for payments received under his consulting contract with Fifth National Bank (Bank), agrees to hold in a fiduciary capacity, and to not disclose to any third parties, any trade secrets or confidential proprietary information he learns, develops, or discovers during development of the check-sorting program described in the consulting contract between Consultant and the Bank.

2. All work performed by Consultant under the consulting contract shall be a "work made for hire" belonging exclusively to the Bank.

3. Consultant agrees not to disclose such information through the duration of his contract and for a period of three (3) years thereafter. Upon termination or completion of the contract, Consultant agrees to turn over to the Bank all materials that contain trade secrets or confidential proprietary information of the Bank.

_____   _____
Kevin Jones   President
                                             Fifth National Bank

Note: Normally a nondisclosure agreement for an outside programmer is included as part of a comprehensive software development or maintenance contract. See Chapter 5 for a discussion of contracting for customized software.

ing to a single company project. Figure 7-2 is an example of a specific consultant agreement.

Nondisclosure agreements are advisable even if you completely trust the people you're working with. These agreements can offer assurance to others, such as software publishers, that your ideas are under control and are not circulating freely among potential competitors. Take the example of Dan, who developed his video golf game with the help of his friend Calvin. If Dan tries to publish Golf-Game, the software publisher may have reservations when he learns that Calvin was involved. The publisher does not want to pay Dan and invest money in advertising if he fears that Calvin may have disclosed information about the game to competitors or is using the information himself. Dan will be able to reassure the publisher and will have a better chance of closing his deal if he can show a nondisclosure agreement signed by Calvin. (In Chapter **8** we examine trade secret law in more depth in the context of dealing with publishers.)

SPIN-OFF COMPANIES AND COVENANTS NOT TO COMPETE

Nondisclosure agreements usually are honored while programmers are working for their employers. Generally employees don't intentionally disclose trade secrets, and they do their best to guard against unintentional disclosure. They even protect information that does not rise to the level of a trade secret but that still would help a competitor, because they want their company to do well. What happens after programmers leave the company may be a different story. When they are no longer with their old company, there is less incentive for them to be careful about disclosing confidential information. A former employee may even want to start his or her own company and use information learned from the former employer.

In the sample nondisclosure agreements (Figures 7–1 and 7–2), the employee or consultant agreed not to disclose trade secrets for five years after termination of his or her employment. These agreements are enforceable against a former employee who tries to use or disclose trade secrets belonging to the company before the nondisclosure period is up. For example, while Bill was an employee of Businesstech, Inc., he worked on "Businessplan," an integrated office productivity package. Bill had signed the agreement in Figure 7–1 before he started working at the company. After a year Bill left Businesstech and started a company with several other programmers. Using specific information and techniques from the Businessplan project, Bill's company developed a similar software package, "Companyplan." If Businesstech, Inc., can prove that Bill used and disclosed to his coworkers or to publishers trade secrets of Businesstech, the company can take legal action against Bill for violating his nondisclosure agreement (the specific penalties that can be imposed upon Bill will be discusesd shortly).

The problem that Businesstech may have is in trying to prove that Bill used any of its trade secrets. First, it would have to prove that information Bill learned while working on Businessplan constituted trade secrets—that is, that it was information known to or used by Businesstech only and that it gave Businesstech a competitive advantage. Even if Businesstech can prove that Bill's nondisclosure agreement covered information about Businessplan, it also has to prove that Bill actually used or disclosed the information. Bill will claim that he developed Companyplan using generally known techniques and information and did not use any trade secrets or information obtained during his employment at Businesstech. Businesstech might have a very difficult time proving that it was "ripped off" by Bill.

To get around the difficulty of proving theft of trade secrets by former employees, many companies require employees to sign a *covenant not to compete*. These covenants are promises by the employees that they will not try to develop or sell products or services that compete with those of their employer after their employment ends. For example, Businesstech may be concerned that some of its programmers will leave the company and develop competing products, using knowledge gained at Businesstech. The company doesn't want to serve as a training ground for future competitors. Businesstech can have Bill and the other programmers agree that they will not compete with the company for a period of time after their termination (Figure 7–3 is an example of a covenant not to compete).

There is great advantage to Businesstech in having Bill's signature on a covenant not to compete. Now if Bill's new company develops Companyplan and tries to market it, Businesstech does not have to prove that the software was based on the Businessplan program or that Bill has appropriated their trade secrets. Bill violates the covenant not to compete simply by trying to market Companyplan (an office productivity program) within three years of leaving his job at Businesstech. Businesstech could sue for damages and for an injunction to prevent Bill from selling Companyplan.

Not every noncompetition covenant will be enforced by the courts. The former employer has a right to protect the company's confidential information, but at the same time the former employee has a right to earn a living. These covenants are examined closely by the courts; to be enforceable, they must be limited in scope and duration. The Businesstech covenant would not be enforced, for example, if it prohibited Bill from transacting business not related to his work at Businesstech or prohibited him from competing for a period longer than a few years. Because technology and products change rapidly in the computer software industry, courts may feel that a noncompetition restriction of only a few months is adequate to protect the former employer. A prohibition on use of customer information should be limited to the geographic area in which the former company is selling its products. In other words, the terms of the covenant should impose no more restrictions than are necessary to protect the business of the former employer; anything more may make the entire covenant unenforceable.

If you are a programmer with ideas of starting your own business someday, you should think twice about signing a covenant not to compete. Employers do their best to protect confidential information that gives them an advantage in

FIG. 7–3
Covenant Not to Compete

BUSINESSTECH, INC.—COVENANT NOT TO COMPETE

Bill Smith *(Employee),* in consideration for his employment by Businesstech, Inc. *(Company),* agrees that upon termination of employment with the Company

  1. Employee will not, for a period of three (3) years following his termination, engage anywhere in the world in the business of developing or marketing office productivity software or any other products of the type developed by the Company during Employee's term of employment with the Company.

  2. Employee will not, for a period of three (3) years following his termination, use or reveal to anyone, anywhere in the world, the customer lists or other customer or marketing information of the Company.

  3. The purpose of the agreement is to protect trade secrets and other proprietary information of the Company. The agreement in no way restricts Employee's right to secure other employment. Employee agrees not to reveal trade secrets and other proprietary information of the Company to any third persons during and after his term of employment.

_____   _____

Bill Smith   President
                                                          Businesstech, Inc.

Note: A covenant not to compete is normally included as part of an employment contract specifying salary and other terms of employment. Questions about other aspects of employment contracts can best be answered by an attorney.

the marketplace. But you have to make sure that your future activities are not unnecessarily restricted. If the employer insists that you sign, try to reduce the coverage of the agreement. You want to have a covenant that is as limited in duration and geographic scope as possible. It's also a good idea to have a covenant that narrowly defines the products or services that you are prohibited from selling. You should at most be prevented from competing in areas in which you gained specific knowledge from the employer, not in all areas generally related to the employer's business.

LEGAL REMEDIES FOR THEFT OF TRADE SECRETS

The person who or company that doesn't reveal trade secrets unnecessarily and follows the advice given in this chapter when disclosure is necessary will be able to seek the protection of trade secret law. Even these precautions cannot stop all leaks of confidential information. Many trade "secrets" will not be kept secret. But if the software owner has done a reasonable job of protecting the trade secrets, he or she will be able to take legal action against someone who tries to use the information.

If you can prove that a trade secret theft has occurred, both civil and criminal remedies are available. Civil remedies include recovery of profits made by the person who used the trade secrets, recovery of your own lost profits and other damages, and an injunction against the competitor. It's always better to stop someone from using your trade secrets than to allow their use and later try to prove how much you were damaged. For this reason most companies first seek an injunction to prevent actual or threatened use of their ideas and information. For example, in 1983 IBM sued some of its former employees who had started a company called Cybernex Corporation. Cybernex was making thin film heads used in data storage devices, and IBM claimed that the production process used trade secrets belonging to IBM. A preliminary injunction was issued in March 1984 against Cybernex prohibiting any further manufacturing or marketing of the thin film heads. The case is still pending.

Lawsuits by companies against former employees for theft of computer trade secrets are multiplying. The decisions show that a company that properly protects its trade secrets will be backed by the courts. Your chances of success in court will depend a great deal on the circumstances. You'll have an easier time proving that you're entitled to the court's assistance if the pirate is a former employee or someone else who had special access to your secrets. The court will also look more favorably on your case if the former associate signed a nondisclosure agreement or a covenant not to compete.

To add a little leverage to their claims, some software developers have been protecting their trade secrets by suing violators under the Racketeer Influenced and Corrupt Organizations Act (RICO). RICO was originally intended for use against organized crime and for recovery of money by people whose property or business was damaged by violations of the act. But the act has been broadly defined to cover any two or more acts prohibited by certain laws. Theft of trade secrets can qualify as a violation of RICO. The advantage of suing under RICO is that triple damages, as well as attorneys' fees and costs, are awarded if you win your case (it's not clear yet whether you can get an injunction under the act). Triple damages could well be enough to put the pirate out of business, which makes RICO a significant deterrent to prospective trade secret thieves. However, RICO can't be used in every case. You should consult your attorney about the proper strategy for your particular situation.

Besides civil penalties, theft of trade secrets can be punished by the criminal law. The RICO Act can send a pirate to federal prison, and many states outlaw the theft of trade secrets, specifically computer secrets. The most famous example of the use of criminal law against appropriation of computer secrets involved theft of information from IBM in 1981 and 1982. A government sting operation uncovered an industrial spy ring that appeared to have taken IBM secrets to Japan, and charges were brought against Hitachi, Ltd., Mitsubishi Electric Corp., and twenty-two individual defendants. The companies and most of the people involved pleaded guilty or no contest, paid fines, and agreed to stop using the stolen information. Of course, the government doesn't bring criminal charges in every case of trade secret theft. The criminal law is used only in the larger or more outrageous cases of which the government wants to make an example. But the prospect of going to jail is another deterrent to theft that helps keep your secrets a little more secure.

To summarize: The protection that the law gives to software trade secrets is significant. There is no excuse other than carelessness for not using this protection from the moment you first conceive your software project until the developmental stage is completed (and, in some cases, also the marketing stage). After you have taken all reasonable steps to keep your software secret, then you can consider whether you need to copyright it.

COPYRIGHT LAW

The purpose of copyright law is to stop others from copying or plagiarizing what you have written, drawn, photographed, or otherwise tangibly expressed. Copyright law, unlike trade secret law, is not directly interested in preserving your competitive advantages in the marketplace (although that can be one of the benefits of copyright registration). The U.S. Copyright Office will register any original work, whether it is a brilliant computer program or a sappy eight-line poem you wrote during your lunch hour. Copyrights are handled by the federal government, and there is a national system of registration. It is not necessary to register a work to obtain copyright protection, but registration gives you certain advantages and more complete protection.

Whereas trade secret law protects commercial ideas, regardless of how they are expressed, copyright law protects only expressions of ideas and not the ideas themselves. If that sounds confusing, consider the following example: Calvin and Zelda are computer programmers who are interested in writing educational programs. They both attended a seminar in which a professor urged the programmers in the audience to write more programs to teach geometry to high school students. This sounded like a good idea to Calvin, so he decided to write a geometry instruction program. Before he began writing, he made notes showing the logical structure of the program and also discussed the basic concept with a consultant he hired to help him on the project. He had the consultant sign a nondisclosure agreement, and he stamped the notes "Confidential" and kept them locked in a drawer when he wasn't using them. Frank, another programmer, got Calvin's consultant drunk and pumped him for information about the geometry program. Frank also got his hands on Calvin's notes. Using Calvin's ideas, Frank wrote a geometry instruction program that performed the same functions as Calvin's program, although the source code was different. Calvin could sue Frank under trade secret law to prevent him from selling the program that was based on Calvin's confidential ideas. As trade secrets, Calvin's ideas are protected, regardless of the form in which they were expressed.

After Calvin finished his geometry program, he registered it with the Copyright Office. If Frank obtains a copy of Calvin's program and tries to sell it in the same or a substantially similar form, Calvin could sue Frank for violation of the copyright laws. However, if Frank develops his own program from the basic information he stole from Calvin, that would not be a copyright violation. Copyright law does not protect Calvin's *ideas*, but only Calvin's *final expression of those ideas*. Calvin would have to sue Frank under the trade secret laws.

Copyright law also provides no remedy for Calvin against Zelda, if she leaves the seminar and writes her own geometry instruction program. It doesn't matter that Calvin wrote his program first or that he registered it with the Copyright Office before Zelda registered (or even wrote) her program. Copyright law does not reserve ideas for the exclusive use of any particular person. It only prevents someone from copying (or very closely mimicking) your work. Only patent law protects you if someone who has no knowledge of your work develops a product similar or identical to yours, and that protection is not available for most computer software (patents are discussed later in the chapter).

COPYRIGHTING COMPUTER SOFTWARE

Can all computer software be copyrighted? The answer to this question has only recently become clear. Of course, operator's manuals like any other original written material, can be copyrighted. And under the 1976 copyright act and the amendments made to it in 1980, the computer program itself can be copyrighted (if it meets the threshold requirements we're about to discuss). At first, problems and arguments arose over what constitutes a computer program for the purposes of copyright law. The Copyright Office and the courts recognized that a program written in source code could be copyrighted. Phrases such as "GOTO 140" looked like something that a human being could read and understand if he or she had the necessary training. But the courts got confused when they looked at programs written in object code, or contained in binary magnetic form on tapes or disks, or contained on a ROM chip. A line such as "00010110" is more difficult to pass off as something that human beings are supposed to understand, and a program in magnetic form on a disk can't be read by people at all, only by machines.

Early cases drew a distinction between source code and object code, allowing the former to be copyrighted but not the latter. For example, in the case of Data Cash Systems v. JS&A Group, 480 F.Supp. 1063 [N.D. Ill. 1979]), the court would not sustain the copyright of a program contained in ROM because it was not intelligible to a human being. The distinction between source and object code was eventually broken when Apple Computer, Inc., sued Franklin Computer Corporation to stop Franklin from using Apple's operating system in Franklin's Apple-compatible computers. Franklin argued that the Apple operating system was not a form of expression that could be copyrighted but part of the machine hardware itself, which isn't eligible for copyright. On appeal the court ruled in favor of Apple, finding that there was no legal distinction between source code and object code and that computer programs embedded in ROM chips satisfy the 1980 copyright act's requirement of expression (Apple Computer, Inc., v. Franklin Computer Corp., 714 F.2d 1240 [3d Cir. 1983]). Franklin was forced to stop selling computers containing Apple's operating system.

The decision in the Apple case will likely be extended to other attempts to copyright computer programs in object form. Now the important question for software authors and developers is not whether their software, in whatever form, is eligible for copyright protection, but if copyrighting is the appropriate form of protection for their software. Very shortly we will look at the relationship between copyright and trade secret law and examine the best strategy for protecting software. For now, let's assume that you have decided to copyright your software. First you have to determine whether your software is eligible for copyright registration.

ELIGIBILITY FOR COPYRIGHT

Before software can be copyrighted, it must meet three basic requirements. First, the software must be expressed in some tangible form. Remember, we said earlier that copyright law does not protect mere ideas. Those ideas must be typed or written (as, for example, the printed source code of a program or an operator's manual is) or contained on a magnetic tape or disk. Also, the software cannot be a fragmentary work, such as half a program that doesn't do anything; it has to be able to stand on its own as a complete work.

Second, the software must be the original work of the author. Originality does not mean that the work has to be state-of-the-art or make some new contribution to the software industry. It only means that the author has to have created the software him- or herself and not simply copied or made minor variations in someone else's work. It's all right if your program closely resembles someone else's, as long as it was your original work and you didn't copy from someone. Consider two programs, written by different programmers, for checking the spelling of words in a body of text. These two programs necessarily do the same thing (compare words in text to a file of correctly spelled words in order to identify the incorrectly spelled words). They may even contain very similar logical structure and coding. In a sense, neither is unique. But they are both considered original works as long as the programmers didn't copy from each other or from someone else.

Finally, your software can't be copyrighted if it is part of the public domain. There are two common ways in which software falls into the public domain. It can happen intentionally, as, for example, when a programmer offers a computer users' group open access to a program that he or she has developed. It can also happen through neglect, as it does if a work is published without a copyright notice and nothing is done to correct that omission within five years of publication. The copyright laws offer some room for error and delay, so luckily it is not quite as easy for software to fall into the public domain as it is for trade secrets to be lost.

If you conclude that your software is eligible for a copyright (and think that the Copyright Office will agree with you), you can then take action to secure the copyright.

OBTAINING A COPYRIGHT

It's not hard to obtain copyright protection for your software. In fact, you don't really have to do anything, since copyright law protects your ideas from the moment you express them in a tangible form. But it's best to take some additional action. It's true that when you print out the source code for your program, or compile the object code onto a disk or tape, or type a user's manual, you instantly have a copyright on your work. But unless you observe certain formalities set out in the 1980 copyright act, you could lose your copyright or have difficulty enforcing it against infringers.

There are three actions you have to take to establish full copyright protection: Affix a copyright notice to the work; register it; and deposit the required number of copies with the Copyright Office.

NOTICE

Notice is probably the most familiar requirement. We have all seen the little symbol © printed on the title page of books. Either that little symbol or the word *Copyright* (or the abbreviation *Copr.*) has to appear conspicuously on every copy of a work that an author wants to copyright. After the symbol must follow the year in which the work was first published. "Published" means released to users or to distributors, which may be later than the year in which the software was written or manufactured. The name of the copyright owner must follow the year. The name will be that of the software author, unless the program was a work made for hire, in which case the name of the employer (usually a company) appears. Often the program and the user's manual were written by different people, so there will be separate copyright notices for different aspects of the software. If the copyright is transferred to someone else, the new owner's name will appear. Although it isn't necessary, except to protect rights in certain areas outside North America, the phrase "All rights reserved" is often written after the copyright notice. The complete notice will look like this:

© 1985 Mary Smith
All rights reserved

or like this:

Copyright 1985 Mary Smith
All rights reserved

The purpose of the notice is to inform anyone who looks at your work that it is not part of the public domain but rather is subject to a copyright claim by the person, company or organization named in the notice. If people copy a computer program or user's manual, they might get away with it if they can argue that they didn't know it was copyright protected. It's difficult to make that argument if the work contained a conspicuous copyright notice. To make the notice conspicuous, it should be affixed in several locations. For user's manuals, the notice should be placed on the cover or on a title page near the beginning of the manual. If you are distributing copies of source or object code, put the notice at the beginning and at the end of all printouts.

The notice should also be inserted in the program itself, so that when a disk or tape is used the notice is displayed on the computer terminal. It can either be displayed continuously or when the user first turns on the computer or boots a new disk. It is rather irritating to the user to have a copyright notice constantly displayed on the screen, so most often the notice appears only when the disk is first inserted. For example, the notice might appear at the top of a menu of functions from which the user selects an action to be performed by the computer. The copyright notice should also be affixed to the outside of all disks, tape cassettes, and boxes or packaging for the software. In short, make the notice so conspicuous that it *has* to be seen by anyone handling or using your software.

You should make sure that the copyright notice is accurate. If you leave off the symbol © or the word *Copyright* (or *Copr.*), your product is treated as if there were no notice at all. The same is true if you omit the name of the copyright owner or the date of first publication. You can postdate the notice by one year, but postdating by more than a year will make the notice invalid. If you make revised editions of a program or operator's manual, you can add the new dates of publication, but don't leave out the original year of publication, or the notice may be invalid (for example, the notice can read: © 1984, 1985 Mary Smith). You can predate the notice without any serious consequences. If you first publish in 1984 but the notice reads 1981, it's treated as if the copyright began in 1981. That just knocks three years off the life of your copyright, and the copyright lasts far longer than the useful life of the software anyway (fifty years from the time of the author's death or seventy-five years from the date of publication, if the author is a company).

If you fail to put a valid copyright notice on a few copies of your software, you won't necessarily lose the copyright. (It's not like trade secret protection, which can be lost in a moment of carelessness.) You can preserve the copyright by taking reasonable steps to correct the omission within five years after you discover it. This means putting a notice on all copies that you distribute from then on and sending an updated notice label to all earlier users with instructions to affix it to their diskettes or user's manuals. When you have corrected the defects in the copyright notice, you can sue for damages for any future infringements of the copyright. But if someone copies a program or manual that doesn't contain a notice, he or she might be considered an innocent infringer. You may not be able to get money damages from this person for the infringement. In other words, the user can play dumb and get away with copying your software until you give him or her valid notice of the copyright. And you can lose your copyright if you continue to distribute copies of the software without affixing the notice within a reasonable time after the defective notice is discovered.

REGISTRATION

We have mentioned that you automatically have a copyright as soon as you express your ideas in some tangible form. The reason you can't rely on this automatic protection is that you can't sue anyone for infringement of your copyright unless you have registered it with the Copyright Office. Without registration, you have a copyright that you can't enforce. You can sue an infringer even though the infringement occurred before you registered the copyright, as long as you register before filing the lawsuit. But if you're suing for an infringement that occurred before you registered the copyright, you can only recover actual damages, not the statutory damages and attorneys' fees specified in the 1980 copyright act. The only exception to this is the registration grace period of three months from the date of the first publication of the software. If there is an infringement within this grace period and before you register, you are still entitled to all remedies against the infringer, as long as you eventually register within the three months.

To illustrate, let's assume that Calvin begins to sell (publishes) copies of his geometry instruction software on January 1, 1985. The software contains a valid copyright notice on the documentation (user's manual), the outside of the box, and the diskettes and embedded in the program itself. Frank buys a copy of the software on January 15, 1985, and sees all of these copyright notices, including the notice that appears on his computer screen when he runs the program. But Frank checks the copyright records on January 31 and discovers that Calvin hasn't yet registered his copyright. Thinking that he can't be sued for copyright infringement, Frank makes thirty copies of the software and sells them to high school students on February 15.

On February 28, when he has still not registered, Calvin sues Frank for infringement of his copyright. The lawsuit would not be allowed. You cannot sue for infringement of your copyright unless you have first registered. On March 15, Calvin registers his program and documentation with the Copyright Office. He then sues Frank for infringing his copyright. Because Calvin registered within three months of publication, he is entitled to sue Frank for all remedies allowed by the 1980 copyright act, even though the infringement occurred before registration. If Calvin had registered on April 15 (more than three months after publication), he could sue Frank, but he could recover only actual damages for the February infringement (which can be difficult to prove). Calvin could sue and use all remedies if there were infringements by Frank (or anyone else) after he registered on April 15. The point is this: Don't wait more than three months after initial publication of your software to register the copyright.

Is three months enough time to do everything you need to do to register with the Copyright Office? Yes, because registering is really very easy. All you have to do is fill out the right form and send it, along with a check for $10 and a copy of the object code (or sometimes the source code), to the Copyright Office. The proper form to use for registering copyrights for computer programs and their documentation is form TX. You can obtain any copyright form you need (for free) by calling the Copyright Office hotline at 202-287-9100 or writing to Copyright Office, Library of Congress, Washington, D.C. 20559. If you aren't sure what form to request or have questions about filling out a form, call a Copyright Office information specialist at 202-287-8700.

Form TX is used for all literary works, as well as for computer programs. The form is fairly self-explanatory and relatively easy to fill out. There are a few important points to remember when you use the form. First of all, use a separate form for the program and the documentation (user's manual). These two aspects of your software are distinct works as far as copyright law is concerned. It's like registering two different books, or a book and a music score. You can also register product information sheets and advertising copy, using a separate form TX for each item. Unless you think that someone is copying your advertising, there is usually no need to copyright it. You might even encourage people to copy it, to get wider exposure for your software.

Where form TX asks for "Title of This Work," you should type in the name you plan to use when you market the program. If you register under one name and later change the name of the program, you have to register the program again under the new name. The "Name of Author" should be the name of the person or persons who developed the program. However, if the program was a work made for hire, the name of the person who or company that hired the programmer should be entered as the author. Form TX also asks for the year in which the program was completed and the year in which the program was first published. The year of publication should be the same year contained in the copyright notice that you are putting on copies of the disks, documentation, and packaging. The remainder of the form is self-explanatory. If you have questions about the form, call the Copyright Office or your attorney.

Some computer software, such as games and computer art, has unique visual designs. You can protect not only the written code for the program but also the images that appear on the screen with a copyright. The form to use for copyrighting visual images is form PA. Even if you register with form PA, you should also file form TX to copyright the written code of your program.

DEPOSIT

Once you have filled out the appropriate copyright form (TX; or PA and TX), you have to prepare the copy of your work for deposit with the Copyright Office. The Copyright Office wants two copies of a published literary work. If you are copyrighting the operator's manual or other writings, just send two copies along with your form TX and a check for $10. For the computer program itself, you need to send only one copy of the program, reproduced in a form that can be read without the aid of a computer. This means that you don't send a machine-readable disk—you send a printout of the program code. If you're filing form PA to copyright games or computer art, you need to send a videotape showing the screen images that you want to copyright.

It's this requirement of depositing a copy of the program that makes software developers nervous. The Copyright Office records are open to the public, and an enterprising software pirate might locate your program and try to imitate it. It's true that if someone copies it line for line he or she violates your copyright and can be sued. But if the pirate rearranges some of the code, the program can look quite different from the one you copyrighted while still performing the same functions. You would have a hard time proving that the pirate infringed your copyright. In this way a valuable program can be stolen.

Despite the risk involved in registering your program, it's still advisable to register it when you begin to sell it. Remember, you lose important remedies against infringers if you just rely on the automatic copyright protection without registering. Besides, there are ways to discourage a would-be software pirate from snooping around the copyright records.

First of all, you don't have to send a copy of your source code. You can send a copy of the object code instead. In fact, you may never have to publish your source code at all. If your software is of the relatively low-cost, mass-marketed variety, the user doesn't need to use the source code. You can continue to keep the source code secret during marketing. If your software is custom made or otherwise needs to be modified or maintained regularly by the user, you will have to provide the user with a copy of the source code. But in that case it can be protected by trade secret law, with the user signing a nondisclosure agreement. It's still a good idea to put a copyright notice on all copies of your source code, even if you jsut maintain them as trade secrets without registering the copyright. The notice may deter illegal copying of the code, and you could still register the code if you need to sue an infringer (although you would lose some remedies by not registering earlier).

Depositing a copy of only the object code will make it harder for someone to steal the program by examining the copyright records. Not everyone can make sense of countless pages of a program written in binary or hexadecimal code. To further confound the pirates, you only need to deposit the first twenty-five and the last twenty-five pages of the program (although you have to send two complete copies of a published manual). Some programmers make their programs entirely incomprehensible by inserting superfluous code at the beginning and end of the program and then filing only the first and last twenty-five pages. You do have to make sure that your program is recognizable (even if useless) from the code that you file with the Copyright Office. If you sue someone for infringing your copyright, it is the printout on file with the Copyright Office that is used to verify that your program was registered. As an extra mark of identification, write the program so that your copyright notice appears at the beginning and end of the object code printout.

The Copyright Office has never felt entirely comfortable about accepting object code for registration (apparently they can't read it either). If you file object code, the office will accept it but send you a "rule of doubt" letter. Rule of doubt means that the Copyright Office isn't saying for sure whether the work is copyrightable as a work of original authorship. This isn't anything to worry about, because the courts have been upholding copyrights that were registered by the filing of object code. The courts recognize that object code is just a machine-translated version of the source code (see the discussion of the Apple Computer case on page 114). If you have no reason to keep your source code secret (e.g., if the program is widely known but you still want to prevent direct copying of your version) or can't keep it secret (e.g., as with programs written in BASIC), you can file the first and last twenty-five pages of source code instead of object code. Source code will be accepted by the Copyright Office without question and is easier to identify than object code in the event of an infringement suit.

To summarize: If your work is eligible for copyright, you automatically have the copyright when you express your program or documentation in a tangible form. To make sure that you can protect that copyright against infringement, you have to take the following steps:

1. Place a copyright notice on all parts of the software (disks, manuals, packaging) and within the program itself.
2. Register the software (program and documentation) with the U.S. Copyright Office. To register, you have to send the Copyright Office:
   a. One completed form TX (or both forms PA and TX) for the program, and a form TX for the documentation
   b. The first twenty-five and last twenty-five pages of the object code

(or source code) for the program, and two complete copies of the documentation

   c. A check for $10 for each registered work.

ENFORCING A COPYRIGHT

Registration does not guarantee that you have a valid copyright. If someone challenges your copyright or if you sue an infringer, a court might rule that a copyright does not exist or that it exists but belongs to someone else. But if the court finds that the software is your original work, is not part of the public domain, and is properly registered, you will be entitled to enforce the copyright against infringers.

A copyright lasts a long time. It's good for the life of the author plus fifty years. If the software is a work made for hire, the copyright lasts for seventy-five years from the date of first publication. The copyright owner has the exclusive right to make copies of the software and to sell, rent, or lease copies. The important exception to the copyright owner's exclusive right is the right of the lawful possessor of a copy to make backup copies. A user is permitted to make backup copies for his or her own use; the law requires that all backup copies be destroyed when a user sells the software. The copyright owner also has the right to assign all or part of the copyright to another owner. This might be done as part of an arrangement between the developer of the software and a software publisher (see Chapter 8). An assignment of a copyright should be registered with the Copyright Office by filing a copy of a contract or assignment agreement, accompanied by a check for $10.

If anyone infringes your copyright, you can take him or her to court (*if the copyright is registered*). It is a violation of copyright law to copy software without permission or to sell pirated copies. You can sue the infringer for actual damages, including the profits made by the infringer and your own losses, or for statutory damages, a fixed amount permitted by law. Which type of damages you go after will depend on the amount of actual damages and the difficulty of proving them. For example, Calvin is now suing Frank for making thirty copies of his geometry instruction software. If Frank had not yet sold the software, there really would have been no damage to Calvin. Even after Frank sold the thirty copies, Frank's profits, or the value of lost sales to Calvin, might be minimal. Calvin would want to sue Frank for the statutory damages specified in the 1980 copyright act. These damages range from $100 to $50,000, depending on how deliberate and reprehensible Frank's conduct was. The court can also award costs and attorneys' fees to Calvin.

If instead of thirty copies Frank had copied and sold three thousand, Calvin might want to sue him for actual damages. If the court upholds his copyright, Calvin is entitled to recover all the profits that Frank made from selling the software. In addition, Calvin can recover the value of sales that he lost as a result of Frank's activities. These actual damages are harder to prove than statutory damages. But actual damages can be substantially higher if the pirate has a large-scale operation.

In addition to damages, the court can impound and destroy all illegal copies of the software and issue an injunction against further infringements of the copyright. The pirate can also be fined up to $50,000 and imprisoned for up to two years for a willful copyright infringement. But as with the state trade secrets laws, you shouldn't expect the government to bring criminal charges except in the most serious cases.

In the example just given, we were assuming that Frank made exact copies of Calvin's software that were easily identifiable as illegal, infringing copies. In cases of direct copying, the copyright law is a very effective method of protecting your work. The problem with enforcing copyrights is that bootleg software often is not an exact copy of the original. This makes it hard to prove a copyright infringement.

To prove an infringement, you have to show that the copy is (1) an exact replica of, or substantially similar to, the original and (2) that the infringer had access to the original (which can be inferred from similarity). Frank might have stolen Calvin's geometry program in many different ways. He could have taken the source code and rearranged it to look different or rewritten it in another programming language. Or he could have translated it to object code for use on a different computer. These techniques can make someone else's program seem like the original work of the pirate and make copyright infringement almost impossible to prove. Of course, copyright law still provides valuable protection against direct disk-to-disk copying. That's reason enough to make a timely registration of your software.

THE RELATIONSHIP BETWEEN COPYRIGHT AND TRADE SECRET LAW

Some legal commentators have argued that you can't protect computer software simultaneously under trade secret and copyright law. They feel that copyright registration will result in a loss of trade secret protection. To establish a copyright, you have to publish the software (make it available to users). In a sense, you are admitting publication when you put a copyright notice on disks and documentation. When you register the software, you deposit a copy of it in the public records. It can be argued that publication and registration are inconsistent with keeping the software a trade secret.

This potential problem has caused some software developers to shy away from registering their copyrights. Take, for example, Calvin's situation on page 112. Calvin was writing his geometry instruction program when Frank learned about Calvin's idea. Assume that Calvin later finished the software and registered it with the Copyright Office. Meanwhile, Frank used Calvin's ideas to write his own geometry program. If registration destroys trade secret protection, Calvin is in a fix. Frank has not infringed the copyright, because he used the mere *ideas*, not any copyrighted *expression* of those ideas. And Frank cannot be sued for a trade secret violation if copyright registration eliminated that protection. Frank can use Calvin's ideas with impunity.

Luckily, despite the apparent conflict, you don't have to give up trade secret protection in order to gain copyright protection. First of all, publication of software for copyright purposes, with a copyright notice attached, is not the same thing as disclosure of trade secrets. You can publish software by selling one copy to a user. But if that user signs a nondisclosure agreement, your trade secrets are still preserved. Even wider distribution of the software won't necessarily change its status. Your ideas can be trade secrets as long as they are not generally known in the industry.

Even registration with the Copyright Office doesn't have to destroy trade secrets. We learned earlier that you are allowed to file object code in lieu of source code and need to send only the first twenty-five and last twenty-five pages of code. These techniques permit registration without revealing any significant trade secrets. The act of registering a copyright doesn't eliminate trade secret protection if the trade secrets themselves remain undisclosed. In other words, copyright registration does not, as a matter of law, destroy the confidentiality required for trade secret protection (Warrington Associates, Inc., v. Real-Time Engineering Systems, Inc., 522 F.Supp. 367 [N.D. Ill. 1981]).

The interaction of trade secret law and copyright law is still an unsettled area of computer law. But for now it appears that you don't have to choose between one or the other. If you are careful, you can maintain both trade secret and copyright protection for your software.

TIMING OF YOUR LEGAL ACTIONS

That still leaves the question of the appropriate timing of your legal actions. Unlike copyright protection, you don't have to register or file anything to have your ideas protected under trade secret law. You just need to take the precautions to preserve secrecy that we have already discussed. Software writers or developers should maintain their ideas as trade secrets from the moment they are conceived. Vigilance over these secrets should continue throughout development, evaluation by publishers or in-house analysts, and, as much as possible, marketing.

A lot of software authors feel a need to rush out and register their software with the Copyright Office as soon as it is finished. They feel naked if they haven't done something official to protect their work. But this isn't always the best strategy. While registering software with the Copyright Office enhances your ability to prevent unauthorized copying of your work, it can also be an invitation for a software pirate to inspect the copyright records and try to imitate what you have written. We have seen that a copyright violation is often difficult to prove. So you don't want to register your copyright any earlier than is necessary.

When you start marketing software, it's still desirable in many cases to rely primarily on trade secret protection. You'll remember from our earlier discussion of trade secrets that disclosure of the secrets can result in their loss. By maintaining the physical security of the software and insisting that anyone who works with the software (such as employees and consultants) sign nondisclosure agreements, you can keep a trade secret just that through the developmental stage. If you are marketing the software to a relatively small number of users, you can keep up trade secret protection in the same way. You let users in on the secret, so to speak, by granting them a license to use the software and having them sign nondisclosure agreements. If a user reveals your secrets (whether code or documentation) to others or misuses them in any way, you can sue him or her under the trade secret laws (in Chapter 8 we discuss how to license software to end users).

If you use the license/nondisclosure arrangement with users, you have the option of not registering the object code with the Copyright Office. Whether or not you register it will depend on how you evaluate the risk of public exposure of your object code. Since you need to file only the first and last twenty-five pages of object code, the filed code may be completely useless to a would-be pirate. But if the object code is less than fifty pages long or if valuable information would be revealed in the fifty pages that are filed, you might forgo copyright registration altogether. If you choose not to register, it is still advisable to print a copyright notice on all copies of the disks, operator's manuals, and packaging. Remember, your software still has a copyright, even if it is not registered. If someone infringes the copyright, you can then register and sue for actual damages.

The time to register a copyright is when the software is being distributed in quantities too large to protect with nondisclosure agreements and trade secret law. Except for some programs that are written in BASIC, you can normally keep the source code secret by providing only object code on the magnetic media in your software packages (keep the source code in your safe back at the office). But it's pretty hard to keep the object code secret when you distribute a lot of copies. The program may contain technological protections to prevent the code from being read and copied, but many users can break these protections. There is so much exposure of the object code in mass-marketed software that trade secret protection becomes tenuous. You can't ask large numbers of users to sign nondisclosure agreements. Usually they buy the software over the counter in retail stores and won't read what they are asked to sign. The courts probably would not enforce such agreements against the users anyway. There is nothing to do but copyright the software.

Remember, when you register the copyright, observe the precautions that we've discussed. File the object code only, except when the source code cannot be kept secret, in which case you will file the source code. File only the first and last twenty-five pages of the code. These techniques will minimize the risk of theft of the program and may help maintain the secrecy of your ideas.

TRADEMARKS

Trade secret and copyright law are the principal methods of protecting software from unauthorized copying and appropriation of ideas. You can also stop competitors from profiting from the name or image you have built up for your software and from dealing unfairly with you or the public. This is done through enforcement of trademarks and of the law concerning unfair competition.

DEFINITION OF A TRADEMARK

A trademark is a word or symbol that sets your product apart from the products of other companies. It's easy to confuse a *trademark* (the name or symbol that distinguishes your products) and a *trade name* (the name of your business), since many companies use one word or phrase for both. For example, a company might have the trade name "Willow Tree, Inc.," and market software under the trademark "Willow Tree." The company can protect against appropriation or misuse of both its trademark and its trade name, although the latter is covered only by state law and not by the federal tradmark laws. Of course, your company name does not have to be anything like your trademark. A company can be called "ACME, Inc.," and sell computer software under the name "Lizard," with a drawing of a multicolored iguana on the cover of its packages. Both the name Lizard and the drawing can be protected as trademarks.

Not every word, phrase, or symbol can qualify as a trademark. If you operate a fast-food chain and advertise that you sell hamburgers, you can't have a trademark in the word *hamburger*. *Hamburger* is a word of general use that describes the nature of the product. No fast-food restaurant can claim the word for its own. But if you are MacDonald's, you can sell hamburgers under the name "Big Mac" and use and register that name as your exclusive trademark. Your software trademark can't be too generic or universally descriptive either. For example, Businesstech, Inc., developed a business planning and data management software package. If it markets the package under the name "Spreadsheet," the company probably cannot claim a trademark on the name. If the term *spreadsheet* had never been used in the software industry, it could become a trademark. But by now the term has become generic, almost like *hamburger*, and no one can claim it as a trademark. If Businesstech calls its software package "Businessplan," the company has a stronger claim for a trademark. The word *businessplan* is less generic than the word *spreadsheet*.

However, the word *businessplan* is still generally descriptive. Other software companies might claim that their products are also used for business planning. Giving Businesstech a monopoly on use of the term *businessplan* may unfairly prevent the others from describing their products as "business plans" or for use in "business planning." Businesstech would have an even stronger trademark if it had chosen a name such as "Grapevine" or "Astroplan." *Grapevine* has an ordinary meaning to anyone familiar with fruit, but it is a completely arbitrary word when applied to computer software (much like the word *apple*). *Astroplan* is not a word with any ordinary meaning but rather it would be a word coined solely for use by Businesstech in marketing software. These coined words make the strongest trademarks, since others cannot complain that you are preventing them from adequately describing their own products (as would be the case with *hamburger, spreadsheet,* and possibly *businessplan*).

To establish a trademark, you not only have to select an appropraite name (i.e., not generic or too descriptive), but you also have to make sure that the name isn't already being used by someone else. Duplication of names is permitted in certain instances. For example, Tony developed a computer program to help auto repair shops produce printed repair estimates and automate their billing. He thought it would be clever to market the software under the name "Tony's Garage." When he tried to sell the program in Boston, he found out that there was an auto repair shop there by the name of Tony's Garage. But this won't stop Tony from using "Tony's Garage" as a trademark. Use of the phrase in marketing the software isn't going to interfere with the repair shop business in Boston, and there is no likelihood that anyone will be confused, because the products are in separate industries (auto repair and computer software).

However, you can't select a trademark that is being used by someone else in the same industry. Even if the trademark is very unusual, you have to make sure that someone else isn't using it. You might think up the coined phrase "Silly Fish Software" only to be shocked to discover that another company is already selling products under that name. If you go ahead and use the phrase "Silly Fish" in your marketing activities, you could be infringing on a protected trademark. And the words or symbols you use don't have to be exactly the same as someone else's to infringe on that party's trademark. For example, a software company in Pennsylvania, named Managment and Computer Services, Inc., a division of Pentamation Enterprises, Inc., was using the acronym "MACS" on its products. In September 1984 it sued Apple Computer, Inc., claiming that Apple's use of the nickname "Mac" in selling the Macintosh computer was infringing trademarks belong to MACS, Inc. MACS, Inc., alleged that a year earlier the U.S. Patent Office had denied Apple Computer's application to register the name "Mac" because of the resemblance to the trademark used by MACS, Inc. The suit was settled in December 1984 upon payment by Apple of an undisclosed sum of money. Under the terms of the settlement, Apple is free to use the names Mac, MAC, or Mac's on its hardware and software. MACS, Inc., may continue to use the name MACS on its products.

ESTABLISHING A PROTECTABLE TRADEMARK

Once you have selected an appropriate name or symbol for your trademark, you have to conduct a trademark search. This search involves looking through the trademark records in Washington, D.C., to see if anyone is already using the trademark. You can conduct the search yourself, although most people hire a search firm to do it for them at a reasonable fee.

If the trademark search shows that the mark is available, you are then in a position to use it. The important thing to remember about trademark law is that you can't register a trademark until it is already in use. The government wants to prevent people from registering trademarks without using them, which might be done just to keep someone else from using them (or to get money from someone who wants to use them). If you think up a good trademark but don't use it, someone else can use it and thereby take it away from you (unlike copyrights, trademarks are owned by the user, not the developer). The way to use a trademark is to sell a product, with the trademark attached, in interstate commerce (across state lines). For example, ACME, Inc., needs to sell at least one copy of its software to a buyer in another state, with the name Lizard and the drawing of the iguana on the package and the disk jackets.

After you begin using the trademark, you can register it if you want. You don't have to register it immediately. As long as you were the first to use a trademark, no one can steal it from you. You might decide that you don't like the trademark and want to change it, which will save you the expense of registering twice. But if you think you'll want to keep the trademark, you should register it. Trademark registration is a little more difficult than copyright registration. You have to make the trademark search, and you have to put appropriate drawings or designs on the application. An attorney can register the trademark for you, or you can register it yourself by obtaining forms from the Commissioner of Patents and Trademarks, U.S. Patent and Trademark Office, Washington, D.C. 20231.

The Patent and Trademark Office will examine your application and either place the trademark in their registers or reject it. It will be rejected if something is wrong with the application or if your desired trademark is too similar to someone else's trademark. If the trademark is registered, you can start putting the symbol ® next to it on your products (before it is registered you can use TM, but not ®). Besides the federal registration system, there are trademark registration procedures in many states. You should consult an attorney to determine whether you need to register in any particular states.

Trademarks can be bought and sold like any other kind of property. But if you buy one, it's not enough to pay money to the previous owner: the new owner has to use the trademark. Trademarks cannot be registered until they have been used, and they can be lost if use stops. Any arrangement to purchase or license a trademark should be timed so that there is no interruption in use of the trademark.

If you feel that someone has infringed upon your trademark, you can sue under the federal trademark laws (assuming that the trademark is registered). There may also be remedies available under state laws. You can recover damages caused by the infringement and obtain an injunction to prevent further infringement. Of course, it's not worthwhile to sue for every violation of your trademark. Sometimes the infringer is not aware of your trademark, and the problem can be cleared up by writing a nice letter. Other infringements are technical in nature, such as when someone refers in a book to a trademark name or symbol without indicating in whose name it is registered. You should ask your attorney about what action to take in a particular case.

THE LAW OF UNFAIR COMPETITION

The law of unfair competition is designed to protect honest traders from unscrupulous competitors and to protect the public from deception. There are three main types of conduct that unfair competition law prohibits in the computer software context. The first is misappropriation of ideas or property. This can be a useful legal approach when for some reason it's not possible to sue for a copyright, trademark, or trade secret violation. For example, someone might sell pirated software in such a way that it appears to have been developed by a leading software company, perhaps by using the same name or a similar box cover. Under the law of unfair competition, you don't have to prove that you held a trade secret, trademark, or copyright or that it was infringed. You just have to show that the public was misled or an honest company injured by the intentional similarities in the product's content or appearance.

The law of unfair competition also protects the reputation of a business. For example, if someone passes off an inferior product as having been produced by a reputable company or sells bootleg copies of software without the documentation needed to avoid potential problems, he or she is harming the reputation of the legitimate company. The person engaging in these unfair practices could be sued under the unfair competition laws. Again, these laws should be considered when enforcement of trade secrets, copyrights, or trademarks is not possible.

The law also protects consumers against misrepresentations in the sale of computer products. If consumers are misled about the quality or capability of software, about who produced the product, or about the price, the company that is misrepresenting the product may be violating the unfair competition laws.

Unfair competition is controlled by state law. The laws vary among different states, but the normal remedies are money damages or an injunction to stop further unfair competition. The recoverable damges include lost profits, dimunition in commercial reputation, and punitive damages if fraud or malice is involved.

PATENTS

Of all the protective schemes in the law of intellectual property, patent law provides the best protection. If you hold a patent, no one may use your invention for seventeen years. Unlike copyright or trade secret law, patent law protects against independent development of an invention. It doesn't matter that a competitor knew nothing of your ideas while he or she was working on the product; if the invention infringes your patent, you can successfully sue the competitor without having to prove that he or she copied your ideas. A patent infringer may be liable to pay triple damages plus attorneys' fees when he or she is sued.

If you're a software author, you may think that all this sounds too good to be true. You're right. Most computer programs are not eligible for patent protection. Patent law protects primarily machines, processes, and manufactured items. "Laws of nature" and "mental processes" (such as mathematical formulas) have always been excluded from patent protection. The Patent Office has taken the position that the algorithms contained in computer programs should be treated like mathematical formulas.

For years no computer programs could be patented at all. Some exceptions to that rigid rule have since been made. One company sought a patent on an industrial process for curing rubber. The process involved the use of a computer to monitor temperature and time intervals. Even though the computer program used in the process would have been an unpatentable mathematical algorithm by itself, the U.S. Supreme Court ruled that the program was covered by the patent on the whole process (Diamond v. Diehr, 450 U.S. 175 [1981]). This decision doesn't mean that the patent office will start approving a lot of patent applications for computer programs. It just means that programs are patentable when they are an inseparable part of a process or device that is patentable. If programs are contained on a ROM chip, they stand a chance of being patented. In a sense, the program is then part of the hardware. However, this reasoning is a little suspect, since in many cases a program on a ROM chip can be replaced by a program read from a disk into the computer's memory; the latter program could never be patented. So don't put too much faith in the prospects for patenting programs contained in ROM.

Even if the courts begin to expand the categories of computer programs that are eligible for patent protection, software authors won't necessarily start lining up at the Patent Office. First of all, you can't patent something unless it is "novel" and not "obvious." A lot of computer programs, such as those that automate office functions that were previously done manually, are not novel enough to be patented. Another problem is that the patent application process requires thorough disclosure of the contents of the software. This disclosure, which is much greater than in the case of the copyright application process, would almost surely destroy your trade secret protection. Also, applying for a patent is usually expensive, because an attorney has to spend a lot of time on each application. Finally, the whole process is very slow. It can take one to three years for your application to be processed.

The lesson from all this is that patent protection should only be sought for a very few, specialized programs, primarily those that are an integral part of an industrial process. If you think you have a program that's eligible for a patent, talk it over with a patent attorney. Otherwise, stick to the other (easier) methods of legal protection covered earlier in the chapter.

NONLEGAL PROTECTION OF SOFTWARE

Legal methods of protecting software can take you only so far. This chapter has given you a hint of the shortcomings of legal protection schemes. For example, you can register a copyright, but you can't possibly discover every instance of illegal copying of your software. You can take steps to preserve your trade secrets, but if someone actually steals your ideas, you have to go to the trouble and expense of trying to prove your case. It's obvious that a software author or developer has to do more than just protect his or her legal rights.

Nonlegal protection schemes (i.e., schemes not based on the law) fall into two main categories: technological protection and economic protection. A detailed discussion of all the tricks of the trade is beyond the scope of this book. What follows is just enough to get you thinking and planning along the right track.

TECHNOLOGICAL PROTECTION

A lot of software is being distributed with copy protection written into the program (i.e., the program is locked). If someone tries to copy the disk, the program will not allow the computer to make the copy. Copy protection can be effective against novice users, but experienced users often discover how to break the lock. Another problem with copy protection schemes is the difficulty of obtaining backup copies. This is very frustrating to legitimate users who don't know how to break the copy protection. These problems are causing some publishers to abandon copy protection schemes altogether.

Some more sophisticated techniques are now coming into use to prevent illegal copying of programs. A program can be written to record the serial number or other identifying characteristics of the first computer it runs on and then refuse to run on any other computer. This permits backup copies to be made and run but prevents copies from having any value to other users. You can also write a different serial number into each copy of the software, so that illegal copies can be traced back to the original purchaser. That can make users think twice before selling copies to their friends. Also, a delayed copy protection scheme can be written into the program. The program will allow itself to be copied a limited number of times for backup, then stop permitting copies (or even erase itself) thereafter.

There is a lot of money at stake in preventing illegal copying of software. We will certainly see more technological protection schemes developed in the years ahead, limited only by the imagination of some of the best programmers in the software industry.

ECONOMIC PROTECTION

If you can't stop illicit copying of software with legal or technological means, it may be possible to discourage it a little by providing financial encouragement for legitimate use of the software. Registered users can be given access to support and maintenance of the software, as well as updates on the program or the documentation. These things are very important (i.e., worth paying a higher price for) to some users, who will be less tempted to use a bootleg copy of the software if it means they can't get the maintenance and updates.

Pricing strategies are also important in deterring illegal copying. You may write a great program that is the first of its kind to hit the market and find yourself in a position to charge an exorbitant price. But you should think about how the pirates will react to your price. The higher the price, the greater the incentive to produce and sell illegal copies. A more reasonable price will make users more willing to buy a legitimate copy rather than look for a lower-priced bootleg copy. For example, if the software retails for $50 and it costs $20 just to photocopy the documentation, the user is probably going to buy through normal channels. Ironically, the lower price could result in increased profits.

Remember: You're not going to stop all illegal copying and misuse of your software. But by using a combination of legal protection methods, technological safeguards, and economic disincentives, you can protect your software reasonably well and increase its chances to be profitable.

Legal Aspects of Marketing Software

8

You have written your program, worked out all the bugs, and taken steps to legally protect your work. Now you're ready to sell the software. Will you work with a software publisher or do your own production and marketing? What do you have to know about legal protection of software during the marketing stage? What legal knowledge do you need to deal effectively with a publisher or distributor? If you are selling directly to users, do you know how the licensing arrangement works? In this chapter we explore the answers to these questions, as well as other legal topics involved in the marketing of computer software.

METHODS OF MARKETING SOFTWARE

If you think writing the software was hard, try selling it. You can write a computer program all by yourself at home or with a small company staff at work, but marketing involves a lot more people and probably a lot more money than development. Yet it's marketing that makes or breaks your product.

There are many different approaches to marketing computer software. You want to select the right mixture of marketing channels to maximize your sales. The proper approach will vary depending on the product you're selling, since you need to target the prospective users of your particular software. You should get advice from a marketing consultant before spending a lot of time or money on marketing. We can't analyze all marketing strategies for various types of software here. This chapter simply gives you an overview of marketing arrangements and the principal legal documents involved in them. You can use any combination of the arrangements described in this section to sell your software, as long as you haven't given exclusive distribution rights to anyone.

SELLING THROUGH A SOFTWARE PUBLISHER

The easiest way to sell your software is to find a software publisher and leave everything up to it. If bugs remain in the program, the publisher can help you work them out. It may also suggest changes to make the software more attractive to users. When the software is in final form, the publisher will produce and package the disks and manuals and handle advertising and distribution.

Of course, the software author gives up a lot for all this assistance. Typically, he or she will have to assign all ownership rights to the publisher or give the publisher an exclusive license to produce and sell the software. The author receives a lump sum payment or royalties from sales but not all the profits from a successful package. Still, selling through a publisher is the easiest and cheapest way for you to get your software on the market. Later in the chapter we'll discuss the publisher's evaluation of software, and marketing agreements between software developers and publishers.

SELLING THROUGH A HARDWARE MANUFACTURER

Computer companies often acquire software to sell with their computer systems. They are primarily looking for "productivity" software such as word processing or spreadsheet packages, and programming languages. The manufacturers are less interested in games and educational software. They want general-application software that will complement their hardware and increase its sales. Computer companies normally copy the disks and documentation themselves (or through a contractor), sell it under their own name, and pay royalties to the software developer. Manufacturers often sell in large quantities, so this arrangement can be very profitable.

SELLING THROUGH A WHOLESALE DISTRIBUTOR

If you have the resources, you can produce the disks, print the documentation, and package the software yourself. You can then try to market directly to retailers, but a less expensive alternative is to use a wholesale distributor as an intermediary. Software and computer retail stores get much of their software inventory from distributors, and even large software publishers often sell through distributors. The distributor will (1) buy your software outright and resell it, (2) handle it on a commission basis, or (3) take it on consignment. With a consignment, the wholesaler pays only for packages it sells, returning what it doesn't sell. Some distributors specialize in software for particular computers or operating systems, and others operate only within certain geographic areas. Before you sign an agreement with a distributor, find out where it operates and what promotion it will do for your product. Some distributors do very little promotion or dealer training. If possible, avoid giving them exclusive distribution rights that would preclude your dealing with other distributors or directly with retailers.

SELLING THROUGH RETAIL STORES OR MAIL-ORDER HOUSES

If you prefer, you can bypass the wholesale distributors and sell your software one step closer to the end user: through retailers or mail-order firms. Software retailers range from big chains such as Computerland to small, locally owned computer or software stores. In the years ahead it may become common to find low-cost software in regular bookstores as well. As with wholesale distributors, you can either sell the software to the retailers or let them have it on consignment. In selling directly to retail stores or mail-order firms, you are acting as your own wholesale distributor. This will get you a higher price for the software, but it also requires more work on your part. If you plan to sell outside your immediate locale, you will need sales representatives to visit the retailers or mail-order houses to get your software onto their shelves. Sales representatives can provide training and support for the retailers, but since representatives often handle many different products, they may not have the time to push your software as much as you'd like. To avoid this problem, you can hire a direct sales force, but that's very expensive. Some software developers use an employee sales force to deal with national retail chains and other large-city stores while using outside sales representatives to work with independent retailers in smaller cities.

SELLING DIRECTLY TO USERS

Direct sales to end users will give you the highest sales price of any marketing approach, since you don't have to cut in any middlemen. Of course, if you are selling software designed for the mass market, a direct-to-user approach will not sell many software packages. You usually have to go through the retail distribution network if you want users to be aware of your product.

There are two situations in which selling directly to users makes sense. If you have written a program for the mass market (a game, a programming language, an office productivity or telecommunications package), you may have difficulty getting a publisher interested in it. Or you may produce the software packages yourself but find that distributors and retailers don't want to carry them. If this occurs and you're still convinced that the software will sell, you'll have to peddle it yourself. It's possible to do a modest amount of advertising without spending a lot of money—for example, by putting notices on electronic bulletin boards or placing ads in user-group newsletters.

You may also want to sell directly to users when your software is designed for a highly specialized market segment. For example, if your software helps veterinarians diagnose illnesses in cats, wholesale distributors and retailers won't want to handle it because the potential market is too narrow. You'll probably have to sell it directly to users. You will need to advertise in veterinary magazines and show up at veterinarians' conferences to demonstrate the software. The same is true of software designed for other professional groups and for highly specialized business applications and manufacturing processes. You'll have to develop a marketing strategy—with the proper blend of advertising, sales calls, and appearances at trade shows and conferences—that will reach your targeted user group most effectively.

In this chapter we don't go into techniques of marketing software directly to users. There are marketing consultants who can give advice on the best strategy for your situation. We'll limit ourselves to discussing the most important legal aspect of dealing with users: the user license agreement. But first, let's consider what happens if you decide to take your software to a publisher.

DEALING WITH SOFTWARE PUBLISHERS

Ellen is a computer programmer who has written a program called "Comput-A-Point," a computerized appointment calendar. The program keeps track of business or personal appointments and reminds the user of important events and dates. It runs on a leading personal computer and has the potential to be a successful mass-market package. Ellen knows about the various options for marketing software, but she doesn't have much money or time to get involved in producing and selling the package herself. She wants an established software publisher to handle everything for her. A couple of publishers are interested, but Ellen doesn't know much about them. How does she determine which publisher would be the best to work with?

CHOOSING THE RIGHT PUBLISHER

There are a lot of software publishers in business today. Some are small, specialized publishers (handling, for example, only software for structural engineers), and others are large, general-purpose publishers (handling only games, business software, and other widely used software). Some have been in business a long time, and others are relative newcomers. It's important to find the right publisher. If you select a publisher that turns out to be inappropriate for your software, the financial success of your work is in jeopardy. You don't have to sign the first contract that's offered to you. Make sure that you feel comfortable with the publisher first.

Find out what kind of software the publisher usually handles. There are differences between marketing business productivity software and marketing games, for example. Publishers that normally produce business software may be interested in your computer game. But they may not have the experience to recognize that the game won't sell without certain revisions or know how it should be priced to maximize sales. Don't forget that you will have to give exclusive rights to the publisher you select. If the publisher inadvertently sabotages the marketing of your software, it may be too late to find another publisher. Most are honest, so what you should be concerned about primarily is experience. Look for publishers that have experience with your particular type of software.

You should also seek out publishers that are willing to help, when necessary, in developing your software and adding the final touches before marketing. The more the publisher gets involved with your software, the better the chances for its commercial success. Some publishers rush software onto the market without concern for making it the best possible product. So you need to ask many questions about how the publisher operates. Will the publisher suggest changes to make the software more useful to buyers? Will it help you adapt the software for use with different computers and operating systems? Look at products that the publisher is currently selling to see how they are packaged and presented in the marketplace. You want a publisher that does a good job of making the software visually attractive to the consumer.

Ask the publisher how it would market your software. This may be the most important factor in selecting a publisher. Will the publisher seek a lucrative marketing arrangement with a computer manufacturer? Which wholesale distributors does the publisher use (do they operate regionally, nationally, or worldwide)? Does the publisher have strong links to the leading mail-order and retail outlets for software? Select the publisher in the best position to sell your software.

So far we haven't even mentioned royalty payments for your software. If you're able and willing to sell the software at a fixed price, you'll simply sell it to the highest bidder. But if the arrangement is the more common one of royalty payments, your choice seems more complicated. Some publishers offer a higher royalty percentage than others. Isn't that an important consideration in selecting a software publisher? Surprisingly, it's not as important as the other factors already mentioned. If the publisher can't shape your software into a highly attractive product or can't sell very many copies because of inexpert pricing or distribution arrangements, then high royalties won't do you much good. Of course, you don't want to be cheated. You shouldn't accept royalty percentages that are much lower than what the other publishers are offering. But you should be willing to accept a slightly lower percentage from a publisher you feel will do a better job of marketing your software.

Above all else, choose a publisher that is enthusiastic about your software. Make sure the company wants to *sell* the software. Sometimes publishers take software under contract with no intention of selling it. They may already be selling or developing something similar and want to lock up the rights to your software so you can't take it to a competitor. Look for some excitement among the publisher's staff when you talk to them about your program. The developer and the publisher should both believe that they can make good money on the software. Avoid an arrangement that suggests anything less.

SOFTWARE EVALUATION AGREEMENTS

When you decide which publishers to approach and get them interested enough to consider your software, they'll want to evaluate it. Our programmer Ellen has assessed a number of software publishers and decided to approach two of them with her Comput-A-Point program. She goes to the office of the first publisher, Junkware, Inc. The people at Junkware are anxious to see how Ellen's software works and ask her to leave a copy with them. They don't indicate that they want to sign any agreements and don't make any promises about what they will do with the software. Ellen has some doubts about this arrangement, so she asks for some time to think it over and doesn't leave a copy of her program.

At the second publisher, SoftPublishing, Inc., Ellen gets a different reception. These people also are anxious to try out Comput-A-Point, but they take time to explain to Ellen how they test the software and what they are looking for in a marketable program. They also ask Ellen to sign an evaluation agreement.

The agreement Ellen signed is shown in Figure 8–1. The agreement you

FIG. 8–1
Software Evaluation Agreement

SOFTPUBLISHING, INC.—SOFTWARE EVALUATION AGREEMENT

Ellen *(Developer)* and SoftPublishing, Inc. *(Publisher)* make the following agreement for evaluation of Developer's computer program entitled "Comput-A-Point" *(Program)*:

1. Publisher shall evaluate the Program to determine whether Publisher wishes to produce and market the Program.

2. Neither this agreement nor any statement made by Publisher to Developer shall be considered a promise to market the Program. The decision whether to market the program is entirely within the discretion of Publisher. Such decision will be made within sixty (60) days of the date of this agreement. Should Publisher elect not to market the Program, Publisher shall return all copies of the Program and its documentation within the same sixty-day period.

3. Developer warrants that she is the sole owner of all rights in the Program and that the Program is the independent work of Developer and does not violate any copyrights.

4. Publisher understands that the Program contains trade secrets of Developer. Publisher shall maintain proper security for the Program and shall not disclose information concerning the program to any third persons, unless such persons have first signed a nondisclosure agreement. If the program is not accepted by Publisher, Publisher shall not use for its own benefit any information about the Program obtained during the evaluation.

5. This agreement and the evaluation of the Program by Publisher in no way restrict the right of Publisher to develop or market programs that are similar in nature to Developer's Program. Publisher agrees that any such similar programs must have been obtained independently from the submission and testing of Developer's Program.

6. Publisher agrees not to market the Program unless and until a marketing agreement is signed with Developer.

Date: _____

_____   _____
Ellen   President
                                       SoftPublishing Inc.

sign will probably be more detailed than Ellen's. It may include a description of procedures and standards for the testing of the software, and schedules for submission of more information and completion of the testing. But the agreement in Figure 8–1 contains the most important legal provisions that you will find in the evaluation agreement.

The software evaluation agreement is important to both the publisher and the software author. The agreement protects the interests of both and helps avoid misunderstandings. The developer is assured of getting back all copies of the program if the publisher decides not to market it (paragraph 2 of Ellen's agreement). The agreement protects the trade secrets of the developer from disclosure (paragraph 4).

The evaluation agreement protects the publisher in several ways. It specifies that by agreeing to evaluate the program, the publisher has made no commitment to market it (paragraph 2). The agreement also makes it easier for the publisher to develop or market similar programs. This is potentially a sticky problem for publishers. For example, let's assume that SoftPublishing, Inc., doesn't want to market Ellen's Comput-A-Point program. Four months after turning down Ellen, the company publishes a personal-appointment program (either obtained from another software author or developed in-house) with many of the same features as Comput-A-Point. Had there been no evaluation agreement, it would look very much as though the publisher had stolen Ellen's software. But the evaluation agreement provided for protection of Ellen's trade secrets and return of all copies of Ellen's program. Further, Ellen agreed that the publisher was free to market similar, independently obtained software (paragraph 5). As long as the publisher maintained good physical security of the materials, return all copies of the program to Ellen, and otherwise complied with the evaluation agreement, Ellen would have a hard time proving that the publisher appropriated her trade secrets or lost them to a third person.

To protect themselves further against charges of appropriating the developer's ideas, some publishers won't sign an evaluation agreement that contains a nondisclosure clause. In paragraph 4 of Ellen's agreement, the publisher acknowledges that the program contains trade secrets and promises not to disclose them to third persons or use them for its own benefit if the program isn't accepted for publication. If the agreement didn't contain such a clause, the publisher would be in a better position to defend against a claim of theft when it later publishes a similar program. Ellen couldn't sue the publisher for breaking a nondisclosure commitment. Better yet, the publisher would like a clause that denies the existence of trade secrets. Such a clause might read:

Developer acknowledges that the Program and related materials submitted for evaluation contain no trade secrets or other confidential proprietary information. Publisher need not treat such materials as secret or confidential, and the disclosure of such information to Publisher does not establish a confidential relationship between Publisher and Developer.

This clause really isn't fair to the software developer. If Ellen wants Soft-Publishing, Inc., to handle her program, she will be under a lot of pressure to sign the evaluation agreement presented by the publisher, even if it doesn't protect her interests. In some cases the developer may have to sign such an agreement and trust in the honesty of the publisher. After all, publishers won't be in business long if they make a habit of stealing the ideas of the software developers who approach them. But when possible, don't sign an agreement that doesn't provide full protection of trade secrets. You should also avoid revealing the source code for the program, unless the publisher must have it in order to evaluate the software properly. If the publisher doesn't need the source code, just provide the object code, making sure that a copyright notice appears on all printouts and disk covers (see Chapter 7 for a full discussion of copyrights and trade secrets).

In order to evaluate certain programs, the publisher may need to test them away from the company's offices. For example, without seeing the program operate under actual business conditions, the publisher can't be sure that an inventory control program will really work. In these cases the publisher should be asked to require a nondisclosure agreement from the companies and individuals involved in the field testing. This commitment should be written into the initial evaluation agreement. The business doing the testing should also be required to return all copies of the software after testing is completed. If a free copy is payment for doing the testing, a license agreement should be required (license agreements with users are explained later in the chapter).

Some publishers may ask that the developer not submit a program for evaluation to them and to another publisher at the same time. They may try to insert a clause in the evaluation agreement to this effect. If they are interested in a particular program, they want to feel free to bargain with the developer without having to better another offer. They are also concerned that other publishers that have seen the software might like it and decide to market something similar. Your publishing company would like to think that it won't have to compete with someone else right from the start.

Of course, as the developer, you should try to keep your options open. If possible, don't limit yourself to submitting your work to only one publisher at a time. It may be necessary to show a program to several publishers before it's accepted by one of them. This is especially true if you don't have an established reputation of writing commercially successful software. You'll save a lot of time and increase your chances of success if you can submit your software to more than one publisher at a time. If you get more than one offer, you can choose the best one. But don't submit to too many publishers at once. The more your software is circulating among publishers and outside testers, the greater the chance that your ideas will be stolen. Try to narrow your submissions to the few publishers that seem most promising.

As we have said, an evaluation agreement is a good idea for both the publisher and the developer. Don't be afraid to sign such an agreement. Just make sure that it's written to your satisfaction before signing.

DOCUMENTATION WRITERS

Up to now we haven't said much about where software documentation comes from. Documentation (the operator's manual) is one of the most important aspects of computer software. Poor documentation can sink a good program, because it can prevent users from figuring out how to use all the features of the program.

Most software authors don't have the operator's manual with them when they approach a publisher with their program. Many programmers aren't good documentation writers, and others aren't interested in that aspect of software development. In fact, it may not be a good idea to write a manual before a publisher has accepted your program. The publisher might suggest extensive changes in the program before it reaches final form, which would require rewriting the manual. So once you finish the program, you'd be better off spending your time on your next program rather than on writing the manual for the last one. Of course, the publisher may ask for some written explanation of how the program works. It wouldn't hurt to prepare a detailed outline of the program's operation and features to send with the program.

Some publishers request that you submit your own documentation. A publisher may not have the staff to write a manual or want to commit resources to hiring a writer. In that case, you have to write it yourself. If the manual is to be written by a company employee or if you hire a free-lance writer, that person should sign a work-made-for-hire agreement. Work-made-for-hire agreements ensure that the writer's employer owns the documentation, and they protect trade secrets in the program. These agreements are covered in detail in Chapter 6 (see Figure 6–1 for an example of a work-made-for-hire agreement).

SOFTWARE MARKETING AGREEMENTS

After evaluating your software, the publisher may decide that you have a winner. This is good news, but you still have a long way to go before your software reaches the market. Further development may be necessary, and the publisher may still decide not to use your program. However, you've passed the hardest test, the one of initial acceptance. At this point the publisher will want you to sign a marketing agreement.

A software marketing agreement sets out the rights and obligations of the developer and publisher as the software is produced and sold. These agreements go by different names, depending on the publisher and lawyers used. Besides being called *marketing agreements*, they are also known as *royalty agreements*, *license agreements*, *publishing agreements*, and *distribution agreements* (with the word *contract* often substituted for *agreement*). Whatever the name that's used, this is the most important agreement between a software developer and a publisher. The marketing agreement transfers to the publisher ownership rights or a license for the software so that the publisher can relicense (sell) it to users. The agreement also sets up a royalty schedule, which is how a software developer is normally paid.

The license and royalty provisions are the most important aspects of the marketing agreement. But the agreement will contain many other clauses, and some agreements are quite long and complicated. The purpose of these agreements is to define a relationship between publisher and developer that might last for as long as the software is on the market (ideally, years). It's important to cover all major details so that misunderstandings are avoided. Treat the marketing agreement seriously: if there is anything about it that you don't understand, have a lawyer explain it to you.

In the pages that follow, we will discuss the main provisions of a typical software marketing agreement. The appendix contains a complete marketing agreement for Ellen's Comput-A-Point software. Refer to it for examples of the clauses under discussion.

FURTHER DEVELOPMENT

Your program should be in good working order when you first show it to the publisher. But the publisher will probably still suggest modifications to make the software conform to the company's idea of a saleable product. The publisher may send you back to your office to make the changes before it accepts the software. Or the publisher may accept it, draw up the marketing agreement, and then work with you on the changes as part of a fine-tuning process. The marketing agreement should specify the changes the developer is to make and the expected completion dates. The precise materials that you are to provide should be identified: object code in magnetic form, a printout of the source code (although it's best to keep the source code in escrow, as discussed later in the chapter), and other data and materials as appropriate. If the publisher's staff has to spend a lot of time and money to modify the program, the publisher may want to charge the costs against your future royalties. The adjustment in royalties should also be reflected in the agreement.

MAINTENANCE, ENHANCEMENTS, AND TRAINING

Even after fine tuning with in-house testing and modifications, the software may not be as good as it should be. Sometimes problems turn up a few weeks or even months after marketing has begun. For example, it might be discovered by some users that Ellen's Comput-A-Point program fails to automatically reschedule appointments that occur on the thirty-first of any months. The users had been promised the rescheduling feature, and changes will have to be made so that updated disks can be sent out. If Ellen provided the publisher with the source code, the publisher's programmers can modify the software. But if they only have the object code or if they need to do the work very quickly, they will want to bring in Ellen. After all, she's the expert on Comput-A-Point. The marketing agreement can include a commitment by Ellen to make herself available for consultation to correct bugs and maintain the software. The agreement should specify how fast the developer must respond to a request from the publisher for assistance and who is to pay for the work.

If regular updates or enhancements of the software are anticipated, the agreement should spell out the duties of both the publisher and the developer and the amount of additional compensation, if any. The publisher may also want you to consult on the writing of documentation and to teach some of the staff how to use the program. Even if the publisher doesn't promise you extra money for correcting bugs or other help, you would normally want to help out and do the work, because better software usually means more sales and higher royalties. Both the publisher and the developer should keep in mind the need to establish a continuing relationship for their mutual benefit and shouldn't shy away from making commitments to each other in the marketing agreement.

MARKETING QUESTIONS

FIRM COMMITMENT TO MARKET

When a publisher asks you to sign a marketing agreement, this is not necessarily a guarantee that your software will reach the market. Naturally, you would like a commitment from the publisher to produce the packages, send them to distributors, and advertise. But there are several reasons why the publisher doesn't want to make this kind of commitment in writing. First, the software is often not in it's final form when the marketing agreement is signed. The publisher can never be certain that all the bugs will be worked out, even after extensive fine tuning. It may also be unclear how long the adjustments will take.

Perhaps most important, the publisher doesn't know what similar products will be on the market by the time your software is ready to be sold. This will be a major factor in the final decision to manufacture and advertise the product. For example, Ellen may have written her Comput-A-Point program for a new personal computer. If there are delays in getting Comput-A-Point into its final form, other personal-appointment software packages may become available for that computer in the interim. Ellen's publisher may be less enthusiastic (and less willing to spend money on advertising) when competitive programs are available. Finally, initial sales of the software may be slow, leaving the publisher with doubts as to the desirability of further promotion efforts.

Because of all these uncertainties, the publisher will want the agreement to contain a clause giving the publisher complete control over the final decisions of whether to take the product to market and how much effort and money to spend promoting it. As the developer, you want as much of a firm commitment on these issues as possible. At the very least the publisher should be committed to "best efforts" or a "good-faith effort" to market the software.

In book-publishing contracts, these good-faith commitments are enforced. If at some point it becomes financially unsound for the publisher to start or continue marketing a book, the publisher can drop the project without violating the publishing contract. But publishers can't drop a book just because they realize that it won't be quite as profitable as they had thought or simply because they change their mind about it. The law recognizes that it is no small thing for a writer to sign a contract that gives exclusive publishing rights to the publisher and to produce a book manuscript. If the writer fulfills his or her part of the agreement, the publisher must do its best to publish the book.

As time goes on, the courts will probably interpret marketing agreements for software in much the same way as publishing contracts for books. Software publishers will not have to market software if it's really going to hurt them financially, but they will have to make good-faith efforts to market the product. Of course, if the publishing firm loses its enthusiasm for a product, it can technically comply with the marketing agreement by producing and distributing the software but avoid financial loss by spending very little money for promotion. This treatment can be very damaging to a software developer. The publisher probably holds the exclusive rights to market the product, so if the publisher doesn't promote the software, it won't sell anywhere. There's really no way to force a publisher to budget more advertising money for your software (publishers rarely agree to a commitment of money in the marketing agreement). You'd have been better off not signing an agreement with that publisher. You can avoid these problems with a clause in the agreement that permits you to reacquire all rights if the software is not brought to market or if the publisher decides to stop the marketing efforts after they're under way. This gets the publisher off the hook and gives you the chance to find another way to market the software.

COMPETING PRODUCTS

Try to get the publisher to agree not to market a software package that's similar to yours. Sometimes publishers discover a similar program that they like better, which can cause them to quickly lose interest in your software. Of course, publishers resist any clause in the marketing agreement that limits their flexibility in product development or marketing. But sometimes the developer is successful in obtaining such a commitment. Software Arts Inc., the company that developed the popular spreadsheet program "VisiCalc," signed a marketing agreement with VisiCorp under which VisiCorp was given an exclusive license to sell VisiCalc but was not to sell competing products. Software Arts later claimed that VisiCorp violated the agreement by promoting sales of other products that competed with VisiCalc. Software Arts terminated the agreement and started selling VisiCalc itself. VisiCorp sued Software Arts in October 1983. A September 1984 settlement provided that the agreement was terminated and that Software Arts holds the copyright and trademark on VisiCalc. You can try to secure the publisher's exclusive attention to your product through a similar clause in your contract. After all, the publisher is expecting you to give it the exclusive right to market your software. Why shouldn't it show the same loyalty to you?

You should be careful when asking the publisher not to sell competing products. The publisher may want to market a group of products that complement one another, such as a series of financial management packages at various levels of performance and price. The other products may actually help the sales of your software by promoting the whole market for that type of software. So show some deference to the publisher's marketing abilities and ideas.

THE SOFTWARE LICENSE

We learned in Chapter 6 that software belongs to whoever developed it, unless it was developed under a work-made-for-hire agreement, in which case it's owned by the employer of the person or persons who developed it. Ownership of software carries with it the exclusive right to sell or license use of the software. So the software publisher cannot do anything with your software unless you give your permission.

This permission is known as a license. A license can permit almost any kind of use of the software that you want to allow. You can give a license to one person to use your software on one specified computer. You can give someone a license to make copies of the software for use on many computers belonging to the same company. You can also give someone a license to make hundreds or thousands of copies and sell them to anyone who wants to buy them. The last type of license is what you give the software publisher in your marketing agreement.

Sometimes the license is unlimited in scope. You can give the publisher a license to sell your software anywhere in the world, using any method of marketing, for use on any type of computer. Of course, the license can be much more limited than this, too. If the publisher plans to sell only within the United States, you can reserve overseas rights. Another publisher may be interested in selling the software abroad, and you might later be sorry if you gave away the foreign rights in a careless moment. The license can also be limited to certain marketing channels. For example, you could give the publisher a license to sell through retail stores, while retaining the right to sell copies yourself by direct mail. You can also grant a license to sell software only for certain computers or operating systems. For example, you might market one version of the software through a computer manufacturer, while giving the publisher a license to sell a version that runs on other models of computer.

You can expect the publisher to resist any limitations, such as those just mentioned, on the scope of the license. The publisher wants complete control over distribution of the software. But all aspects of the marketing agreement are negotiable, and you should try to retain any rights that you think the publisher doesn't really need or that you can put to better use elsewhere. Pay attention if the publisher asks for the right to "sublicense" the software to other publishers. There's nothing wrong with allowing other publishers to produce and sell the software, as long as the sublicense carries the same limitations as the primary license and you don't lose any right to receive royalties.

The license can be either exclusive or nonexlusive. An exclusive license means that no one else will be allowed to market the software (within the scope of the license) except the publisher holding the license. A nonexclusive license permits you to give licenses to other publishers as well. Even an exclusive license can be limited in scope. For example, the publisher can be given an exclusive license to market within the United States but have no right to market abroad. By contrast, the publisher could be given a nonexclusive license for worldwide marketing. It could sell the software anywhere, but so could others if you give them a license too. So remember, it's not enough to have a clause saying that the license is "exclusive." You also have to define its scope (geographic, marketing methods, hardware compatibility). Exclusivity deals with *who* can operate under a license, and scope refers to *what* they are allowed to do.

It may be important to limit the duration as well as the scope of the license. There can be a time limit on the license. A short duration may be in the devloper's best interest. For example, Ellen might give SoftPublishing, Inc., a two-year license. If the publisher isn't doing a good job of marketing Comput-A-Point after two years, Ellen can try to find another publisher. If the package is selling well, Ellen can renew the license on better terms. Ellen could negotiate other conditions for continuation of the license, such as a minimum number of copies sold per year. If the conditions aren't met, the license terminates, and all rights revert back to Ellen.

Although it's generally a good idea to put limits on the license, because you retain more rights, these limitations can backfire on you. If the publisher doesn't know how long it will have the license, or if the license is nonexclusive or very limited in scope, the publisher may hesitate to invest too much time or money promoting the software. The marketing agreement should be one that both developer and publisher feel comfortable with, so that both will work hard toward the common goal of selling as many copies of the software as possible.

ROYALTY PAYMENTS

Occasionally publishers pay a single, flat fee in return for transfer of ownership of the software. The developer takes the money and has no further financial interest in the success or failure of the product. The flat-fee approach gives developers a guaranteed return for their work, but it's not very popular with either developers or publishers. Publishers prefer developers to take their income in the form of royalties, feeling that if developers have a continuing financial stake in the software, they will be more wiling to help out with maintenance of the software and other problems that arise. The royalty setup also cushions the financial blow to publishers if the program doesn't sell; they may have wasted money in promoting the product, but at least they didn't pay much to the developer. Most developers also want the royalty arrangement, because they feel that it will earn them more money. Unless you are a star in the software industry, it's unlikely that you can do better with an immediate lump-sum payment than with royalties from a successful program.

Royalty payments typically range from 10 to 20 percent of the publisher's net sales revenue. The net sales revenue is the amount paid by the publisher's buyers (usually wholesale distributors or retail outlets), less shipping costs and deductions for copies that were returned. You won't get royalties for some copies that are distributed free, such as dealer demonstration copies. Some marketing agreements allow for royalties on the gross revenue received by the publisher. In that case the royalty percentages are usually set a little lower, so that the amounts you receive under the two different arrangements are roughly the same. The gross or net sales revenue will be somewhere around 50 percent of the retail price. So if you're receiving royalties of 14 percent of the net sales price, you're getting about 7 percent of the price paid by the end user. That may not sound like much, but you have to realize that advertising, distribution, and retailing costs eat up most of the retail price. And those small percentages can add up to a lot of money if your software sells well.

You can ask the publisher for a graduated scale of royalties, with the percentages rising with sales. For example, the royalties might be 10 percent for the first 2,500 programs sold; 12 percent for the next 2,500; and 15 percent for all copies thereafter. The publisher's cost per unit declines as more copies are produced and sold, so the profits usually go up with sales. The publisher should be willing to share some of that extra money with you. Try to get an advance on royalties at the time when the marketing agreement is signed. Normally the publisher wants to pay a modest advance when the agreement is signed, as monetary consideration to bind you to the contract. Don't be afraid to ask for a little more than the publisher offers. Sometimes you have to wait a long time to earn royalties from sales of the software. The agreement should specify whether the advance is refundable or nonrefundable if you don't earn enough royalties to cover the advance.

Always keep in mind that the royalty provisions of the marketing agreement (like all other clauses) are negotiable. You should get the best deal possible. The most obvious candidate for negotiation is the royalty percentage. You can also ask for a fixed number of royalties per unit sold, rather than a percentage of the sales revenue. This gives you some control over the price charged by the publisher. For example, instead of receiving 15 percent of the net sales revenue, you could ask for $15 for each copy sold. The publisher would have to charge a high enough price to pay you the $15 and still make a profit. An alternative is to ask for a percentage of the sales price, with a guaranteed minimum payment per copy. The publisher would then have an incentive not to drop the price too low. Of course, you don't want to tamper too much with the publisher's pricing structure. If you don't let the company choose the price that will make its efforts profitable, it may lose interest in selling the software.

You can also negotiate with the publisher about when royalty payments are to be made. The publisher likes to pay infrequently, because it reduces bookkeeping chores and lets the company hold onto your money longer. You should ask for frequent payments, on a quarterly basis at the minimum. If you feel that your software is going to be a big commercial success, don't be afraid to hire a lawyer or other agent to negotiate some of these points for you before you sign the marketing agreement.

OTHER PROVISIONS

ASSIGNMENT AND REGISTRATION OF COPYRIGHT

There are times when a publisher asks for an assignment of all ownership rights, rather than merely a license to copy and sell the software. This occurs most frequently when a single, flat fee is paid instead of royalties. The publisher becomes the new owner of the software; the developer has the money but no further interest in the software.

It's also possible to transfer ownership of the software to the publisher while still receiving royalties. This may be a more common procedure in the future. Publishers are becoming increasingly concerned about copyright infringements, and they worry that developers, if they remain the copyright owners, won't vigorously defend the copyright against infringers. So the publisher might prefer to hold the copyright itself. This is fine as long as you don't have any plans for the software after the marketing agreement terminates and don't anticipate problems with the relationship. However, it's generally better to keep the copyright yourself. If you need to terminate the marketing agreement, you'll have to own all rights before another publisher will talk to you. If you agree to give the copyright to the publisher, ask for a higher royalty percentage as compensation.

If you do agree to transfer ownership of the software, the marketing agreement should state that the publisher is buying the software (either with a straight payment or royalties) and is responsible for registering and protecting the copyright. If the copyright was previously registered with the Copyright Office, the publisher will need to reregister. This can be done by filing a copy of the marketing agreement, or a shorter copyright assignment form, with with Copyright Office (see Chapter 7 for more information on registering copyrights).

If you are to retain ownership of the software, the publisher will want to make sure that you register the copyright (which is done after "publication," meaning sale of the first copy). The agreement will contain a clause that gives the publisher authority to register the program (or program and operator's manual) in your name. The publisher will also want in the marketing agreement a commitment from you to enforce the copyright against infringers. Sometimes the publisher will agree to pay all legal fees and will just want you to agree to cooperate in any enforcement efforts.

WARRANTIES AND INDEMNIFICATION

The publisher will undoubtedly want you to include a few warranties in the marketing agreement. A warranty is a promise that statements made about a product will turn out to be true. The publisher will want you to warrant that the software you're licensing belongs entirely to you and that you haven't infringed on anyone's copyright or misappropriated trade secrets in writing the software. The firm will also want a warranty that you have not already granted a license to someone else that will conflict with its license. Other standard promises include warranties that you have not previously published the software (which could diminish copyright protection) and that there are no lawsuits pending against you involving the software.

If any of these statements that you have affirmed turns out later to be false, you will have breached that warranty, and the company can terminate the marketing agreement and sue you for any damages it has suffered. So it's best to reveal any ownership problems or other legal problems relating to the software before signing an agreement containing warranties. The agreement probably will also contain indemnification clauses. If another programmer or publisher sues your publisher, claiming violation of copyright or theft of trade secrets, an indemnification clause makes you responsible for attorneys' fees, court costs, and any damages your publisher had to pay in court. Likewise, you should request that the publisher indemnify you by accepting responsibility for paying all cost and judgments if users of the program sue you over problems with the software. It should be the publisher's responsibility to properly test and ensure the quality of the software.

TERMINATION

The marketing agreement should contain a section describing the circumstances under which the agreement can be terminated. You'll want to have the right to end the agreement if the publisher violates a major obligation. Examples would be the publisher's failing to bring the software to market or to continue selling it; operating beyond the scope of the license; or failing to pay royalties. The publisher will also want the right to terminate in the event of any major violations on your part, such as breach of one of the warranties or refusal to help maintain the software. A minor breach of the agreement, such as the publisher's sending a royalty payment a few days late, is not sufficient grounds for termination of the agreement. It's a good idea to require advance notice of intent to terminate the agreement, with a grace period in which the other party can correct the breach.

USER LICENSE AGREEMENTS

Some software isn't suitable for production and distribution by a publisher. The market may be too specialized and limited for a mass-marketing approach. This is the case for a large number of computer programs written for the professions, universities, hospitals, and other institutions and organizations. For example, our friend Calvin from Chapter 6 has written a program for a school district. The program keeps track of school enrollment and attendance, prepares reports for the state education department, and analyzes the effect of various factors on attendance. Calvin has retained all rights to the software and now wants to market it to other school districts in the state. He can't sell it outside the state without extensive changes, because the program is tailored to the reporting requirements of his particular state's education department. Calvin won't get a publisher to package and sell the software, because the total potential market is too small. What Calvin needs to do is visit the school districts himself and give demonstrations of the software.

Calvin tours the state with his software, and it's an instant hit with the school district administrators. The software can save hundreds of labor-hours each year in manual record keeping and reporting. Several administrators want to use the software. Calvin can't leave all of the legal arrangements with users up to a publisher, the way Ellen did with her Comput-A-Point program, so he will have to hire a lawyer to write a software license agreement for him. This won't be a license to produce and relicense (sell) the software, like the one that Ellen gave her publisher; rather, it is a license only to use the software.

In Chapter 4 we discussed user license agreements for mass-marketed software. There are examples of these license agreements in the appendix. If your software is to be mass marketed by a publisher, you can read the agreements in the appendix for an approximation of the statement that your publisher will send to users, attaching it either inside or on the cover of the software package. It's also the type of license agreement that you'll include with your software if you produce it yourself and sell it in large quantities through distributors, retail stores, or direct mail. However, Calvin's license agreement with the school districts will be different from the agreements for mass-marketed software. Calvin's agreement doesn't just impose a few standard restrictions on users whom he has never met. It establishes a working relationship between Calvin, as the developer, and the schools districts, as the users. If you license your software to a limited number of users or even a large number of users who have special maintenance and support requirements, you should use the more detailed, customized type of license agreement that we are about to discuss (see the appendix for an example of a customized license agreement).

Why does Calvin need a license agreement with the school districts that use his software? Can't he just take their money and give them a copy of the program and manual? He could, of course, but he risks losing most of the income from his software. If a copy of computer software is given in exchange for money and no agreements accompany the software, the transaction is a sale. Purchasers might claim that Calvin has transferred to them all of his ownership rights. The purchasers could then make and sell copies to other users. And Calvin would only have received money for the first copy. He would have to ask a court to try to straighten out the mess—and he might lose.

However, if users receive the software under a license, they have no claim to owning the software. They merely hold a nonexclusive license (a grant of permission) to use the software. They can make backup copies for their own use, but they cannot sell or give away copies of the program or manuals. If they sell the original copy of the software, they have to destroy all backup copies. The developer retains all rights of ownership, including the exclusive right to sell or license use of the software. So the main purpose of the license agreement is to protect your ownership rights and prevent users from obtaining copies of the software that they didn't buy from you (unless, of course, they want to become pirates and use or distribute illegal copies).

The software license that Calvin signs with his users also establishes the terms and conditions under which Calvin and the users will work together to meet each other's needs. What the user wants is the ability to use a program that functions well at the start and is maintained in good working order thereafter. Calvin wants protection for his trade secrets and assurances that the user won't infringe Calvin's copyrights or violate the terms of the license.

Calvin also wants his money. The license agreement should state the amount and timing of the payments. The user might make a single payment at the start or a partial payment at the beginning with the balance due after testing and acceptance of the software. Instead of making full payment for a license that will last forever, the user could pay a monthly or annual fee for use of the software. When the user no longer needs the software, he or she can return it and stop making payments. The duration of the license, as well as the method of payment, can be as flexible as needed to satisfy the user's requirements.

Many users will want to test the software before taking a long-term license for it. Demonstrations are often not enough; users want to get their hands on the software and see if it really does the job for them. This desire can be handled by including in the license agreement a temporary license for purposes of testing. For example, Calvin's agreement can give the school district a license to use the software for ninety days, in return for a small payment. If after ninety days, the district decides to keep the software, it makes full payment (or begins regular periodic payments), and the general license provisions of the agreement take effect. If the district decides not to keep the software, it returns the package to Calvin at the end of ninety days and has no further obligations under the agreement.

Users will also want support and maintenance of the software. A guarantee of this assistance in the license agreement may increase sales of the software. Calvin's license agreement should contain a commitment by Calvin to answer questions that the school districts may have about using the software. He should also promise to fix any bugs and otherwise maintain the software. An alternative to maintenance by the developer is to make the source code available and let users do their own maintenance. This may be necessary when there is a large number of users and maintenance is beyond the capability of the original developer. But remember that revealing the source code may result in a loss of trade secrets if certain precautions are not taken. Source code escrows can be useful in these situations; we will discuss escrows shortly.

Some users like to make their own modifications in a program to accommodate changing needs. The license agreement should specify whether this is permitted. There is really no reason not to allow modifications, although they make the software more difficult to maintain. The agreement might specify that the developer has no further maintenance obligations once the software has been modified by the user. The developer will also want to modify and improve the software from time to time. For example, Calvin may intend to modify his school attendance software every time the state education department changes its reporting requirements. He may also write some additional features into the program to make it more versatile. The license agreement should say whether, and at what cost, these modifications and improvements will be made available to current users. Naturally, if Calvin promises to update everyone's program and manual at no extra cost, his software will be more attractive to potential users.

As we mentioned, one of the main purposes of the license agreement is to protect the ownership rights and trade secrets of the software developer. Calvin should use his license agreement to remind users that the software contains trade secrets belonging to Calvin. By signing the agreement, the user agrees not to disclose any information concerning the software to third parties. This commitment is important in preventing appropriation of trade secrets by unauthorized persons. The agreement should also remind the user that the program and manuals are copyrighted, and an appropriate copyright notice should appear on all disk covers and manuals and be embedded in the program (see Chapter 7 for a full discussion of trade secrets and copyrights).

The license agreement can contain restrictions on where the software will be used. Restricting use of the software to one specified location for each user makes it easier to identify bootleg copies. But the agreement should permit the user to change the location after giving written notice. The developer should disclaim any warranties of merchantability or fitness for a particular purpose. The user should take the software "as is." If users were given a period of time to test the software, they shouldn't be allowed to complain later that it isn't what they wanted or expected. The license agreement should also have a termination clause that lists the conditions for ending the license and for demanding return of the software—conditions such as nonpayment, disclosure of trade secrets, or making copies other than for backup.

Your license agreement might cover many other points besides those mentioned. The substance of the agreement will vary with the type of software and the needs of the particular group of users. Because of the complexities, you probably won't want to attempt to draft a license agreement on your own. You really ought to hire a lawyer to do the work. But before talking to your lawyer, read over the sample custom license agreement in the appendix and reread Chapter 7 on legal protection of software. You can save your lawyer time (and thereby save yourself money in legal fees) by having gained some background knowledge and given some thought to what you want in the license agreement before visiting the lawyer's office.

SOURCE-CODE ESCROWS

By now you have learned that you should avoid giving anyone access to the source code for your program. Your ideas are fairly immune from theft when you distribute only the object code, because of the time and difficulty involved in unraveling the code. But a skilled pirate can use the source code to learn how the program is structured and then write a program that performs the same functions (but is different enough in appearance to avoid a copyright violation). Besides making it easier for someone to steal your ideas, distributing the source code (except under controlled conditions with proper nondisclosure agreements) may result in loss of your trade secret protection. If the ideas are stolen and used, you won't have any basis for taking the pirate to court. That's why you file only the object code when you copyright a program and give only the object code to publishers or licensed users.

Despite your best efforts to keep the source code to yourself, you will sometimes have to reveal it. If you sign a marketing agreement with a publisher, the publisher wants to be guaranteed access to the source code so that it can modify and maintain the software. Even if you agree to do the maintenance yourself, the publisher wants access to the code in case you are unavailable or unwilling to work at a later time. Licensed users also want the source code available so that they can perform their own maintenance and modifications, if the license agreement permits, or hedge against your failure to meet promised maintenance or updating obligations.

A good compromise solution is to put a copy of the source code in escrow. When it is in escrow, the code is held by an impartial third person (called an "agent" or "custodian") until certain conditions are met that permit its release. These conditions include death or incapacity of the developer, failure of the developer to meet maintenance or updating obligations, and any other condition that is agreed upon. When one of these events occurs, the custodian releases a copy of the source code to the publisher or user who is seeking access. The escrow agreement should require that (1) all released copies contain proper copyright notices, (2) the publisher or users agree not to disclose information about the code to outside persons, and (3) the copies of the code be returned or destroyed when they are no longer needed.

There can be problems with the use of an escrow arrangement. It's sometimes difficult for the custodian to know when one of the conditions for release has been met. You may feel that you are maintaining the software properly whereas a user may claim that you aren't and demand access to the source code. The custodian will have to make tough decisions about when to release the code, so hire someone whose judgment everyone respects. The custodian should also be a good negotiator who can solve disagreements before they end up in court. An experienced attorney, a bank trust officer, or a programmer with no business connections to you is a good candidate. Because of the uncertainties about when it's proper to release the code, the custodian may want guarantees against liability for a wrongful release. You may have to agree to pay the custodian's legal fees, other costs, and any judgments resulting from lawsuits against him or her.

Another problem with escrows is the cost. Custodians have to be paid for their services. If a publisher is requesting guaranteed access to your source code, ask the publisher to pay for the escrow. You can also try to charge users a small fee each time they request release of a copy of the code.

Despite the problems, the source-code escrow is a good device for ensuring publishers and users access to your source code and at the same time limiting disclosure to circumstances in which it is essential. Figure 8–2 contains a sample, simplified escrow agreement between Calvin and the users of his school attendance software. Usually these provisions are not put into a separate agreement, as in Figure 8–2, but are incorporated into the user license agreement. An escrow agreement with a publisher is normally part of the marketing agreement.

GIVING SOFTWARE AWAY

Some software writers are experimenting with an alternative to working with publishers or selling their software through traditional channels. They are giving the software away for nothing—and making money by doing so. Maybe that sounds impossible—but read on. The developer writes a program and makes it available to anyone who wants to copy it. This is often done by listing the program on electronic "bulletin boards" (such as those belonging to users' groups for certain computers) so that it can be copied over the telephone lines by use of a modem. The developer can also send the program through the mail to a user, who pays the cost of the disk and postage. Users are permitted—even encouraged—to give copies to their friends. If a user wishes, he or she can use the program without paying any money to the developer. But the program contains a message requesting a donation from users who like the program. The user who pays the additional fee (usually ranging from $15 to $200) gets certain benefits, including written documentation, updates to the program, and support from the developer. Software distributed in this manner is sometimes referred to as "freeware."

There are many potential advantages to this distribution method. The arrangement is very attractive to users. The software can be tried out with no obligation before "buying." The developer can debug or improve the program as needed and allow users to copy the updated program anytime they want. The prospect of a free program can result in much wider exposure for the software than traditional marketing techniques would provide. In the long run, you might make more money from the voluntary payments than from the

FIG. 8-2
Source Code Escrow Agreement and Custody Agreement

SOURCE-CODE ESCROW AGREEMENT

Calvin *(Developer)* and Pleasantville Unified School District *(User)* agree to the following:

1. Within ten (10) days of the signing by Developer and User of the agreement licensing use of Developer's school attendance program *(Program)*, Developer will place in the custody of Willie Johnson *(Custodian)* a copy, in printed form, of the source code and source-code documentation for the Program.

2. Developer shall maintain and update the escrowed source code for a period of five (5) years after the final licensing of a copy of the Program by Developer to any user.

3. Custodian shall release a copy of the source code and related documentation to User for use in maintaining and modifying the licensed software (as permitted by the license agreement between Devloper and User) within three (3) days of a written request from user, when one or more of the following conditions has been met:

    a. Developer has gone out of business, died, or become incapacitated or is otherwise unable to provide normal maintenance for the Program; or

    b. Developer is unwilling to provide normal maintenance for the Program following a request by User; or

    c. [List other appropriate conditions].

4. User understands that the source code for the Program contains trade secrets and other proprietary information of Developer and agrees not to disclose any information concerning the source code to any third persons.

5. User shall destroy all copies of the source code and related documentation when the maintenance or modifications have been completed.

6. User shall forward a fee of $_____ to Custodian with each request for release of a copy of the source code from escrow.*

Date: _____

_____   _____
Calvin   Superintendent
                                        Pleasantville U.S.D.

---

* This clause is optional.

CUSTODY AGREEMENT

Willie Johnson *(Custodian)* agrees to serve as custodian of the source code and source code documentation for the Program, under the terms of the above agreement. Custodian may make copies of the code and documentation as necessary. Each additional copy shall contain the same copyright notices as the original copy. Custodian understands that the source code contains trade secrets and other proprietary information of Developer and that he is not to disclose such information to any person, except as provided for in the above escrow agreement.

Date: _____

_____   _____
Calvin   Willie Johnson

roughly 15 percent of the wholesale price that a publisher would pay in royalties on a much smaller number of programs. You don't have to package the software or ship it to distributors and retailers, so you can get started with very little capital. Finally, you don't have the legal headaches of traditional marketing schemes. There are no worries about software pirates when you are encouraging wide-open copying. You are also less likely to be held liable for problems users encounter with the software, because no sales contract relationship is established if the software is given away, and payments are strictly voluntary.

But you take chances when you distribute software without requiring prior payment. Your software becomes part of the public domain, so your copyright protection is lost. If the voluntary payment scheme doesn't work, no publisher will touch the software. The wide distribution might be good for your reputation as a software author, but it's not always good for your pocketbook. You may be better off taking your work to a publisher or selling copies yourself. If you think you have a program that might be very popular, you should consult with a software marketing expert about the best method of distribution. At least consider a publisher or other sales arrangement before releasing your software into the public domain.

PART FOUR
Other Legal Issues for the Computer User

======================================

Computers and
Taxes
9

The only sure things in life are death and taxes, but death doesn't get worse
every time Congress meets.

—Will Rogers

Computers and computer software are becoming virtually indispensable to most businesses. As more money is spent on the acquisition of computer technology, the need to know about the tax implications of these expenditures increases. Software developers can also benefit from tax deductions that will make their projects more profitable.

Many of the tax issues involved with the purchase, sale, and development of computer hardware and software aren't dramatically different from those applicable to other products. This is especially true of the acquisition of computer hardware. Still, the growth of the computer hardware and software industries has raised some interesting new issues in the area of taxation. While it's wise to seek the advice of a tax expert when significant sums of money are involved, all computer users should familiarize themselves with the general principles of tax law relating to computer technology. This chapter provides an introduction to those principles.

The first and second parts of the chapter deal with income tax deductions and credits available to business purchasers and home users of computer products, respectively. The final part covers the tax aspects of developing and selling computer software.

This chapter will take you less than an hour to read, but it could help you to save a considerable amount of money on your taxes and to recognize when you need professional tax advice. A word to the wise: tax law is continually changing. Congress revises many aspects of the tax structure every year. Because of this, specific facts and figures relating to tax law rapidly become obsolete. To minimize that problem, this chapter provides few specific figures regarding tax credit percentages, amounts of allowable deductions, and similar details. We'll concentrate on the general principles of tax law relating to computer technology. If you need to determine the amount of a specific deduction or tax, you should ask your accountant for the latest figures. You may also want to ask about state and local income taxes. We'll be discussing sales tax on software in regard to state law, income tax in regard to federal law.

THE TAXPAYING COMPUTER USER

How you use your computer determines whether you can deduct computer expenses from your taxes. Before getting to the specifics of computer tax law, let's introduce a couple of computer users with typical tax questions.

Steve is the principal owner of Sell Direct, Inc., a direct-mail marketing company. He has just purchased a minicomputer for use at the Sell Direct offices. Operating-system software was included at no additional cost. Steve purchased word processing and data management software separately, as well as some blank disks and other supplies. Steve plans to use the computer only at the offices of Sell Direct, exclusively for company business.

Tina, Steve's wife, is a software author. She recently bought a personal computer, the "Banana-PC," for use in her work. Tina started a company called Tina-Ware, Inc., through which she develops and sells her software. Tina operates the company out of their home, using one room of the house for her office and work space. She intends to use the Banana-PC to write software and keep track of her business records, but she also wants to put her Christmas card mailing list on the computer. In addition, Steve and Tina want their eight-year-old son Dennis to learn about computers. So Tina lets Dennis play computer games and run educational software on her computer.

When Steve saw Tina bring her computer home, he decided that he wanted one too. He bought a "Tangerine-PC" and put it in his study. Steve and Tina own some real estate and securities, so Steve plans to use the Tangerine-PC to help manage their personal investments.

Steve and Tina now want to know whether they can deduct any or all of the above expenditures for income tax purposes.

TAX SAVINGS FROM BUSINESS PURCHASES OF COMPUTER PRODUCTS

First, let's take a look at Steve's acquisition of a minicomputer for his business, Sell Direct, Inc., and see if we can answer his questions about possible tax deductions. Like most computer users, Steve purchased (as opposed to leasing or renting) the computer, software, and computer supplies, and he purchased them new. (In Chapter 3 we touched on the tax advantages and disadvantages of alternative means of acquiring a computer: leasing and renting. If you have questions about the tax implications of leasing or renting computers that were not answered in Chapter 3 or questions about buying used computer products, consult an accountant or other tax expert.)

The basis of our discussion is that Steve's purchase is for business: No tax deduction can be taken for a computer-related expenditure that is not made for business purposes. Some people have had the misconception that the cost of a computer can be deducted regardless of what the computer is used for. A few computer manufacturers and dealers have even suggested this in their advertising or sales presentations. Either they don't know the tax laws and regulations or they're trying to mislead people in order to sell more computers. The fact remains that you're not entitled to deduct the cost of a computer that is for personal use. (Computers used at home often serve a combination of personal and business purposes. We'll discuss deductions for such computers later in the chapter.)

COMPUTER HARDWARE

DEDUCTIONS

The tax treatment of computer hardware purchases isn't very different from that of other kinds of business equipment. The purchase price of computer hardware, including peripherals, is always deductible. So Sell Direct, Inc., can take a deduction for the minicomputer that Steve bought for his company. The only questions are *when* the company can take the deduction or deductions, and *how much* it can take.

Normally, a taxpayer wants to deduct as much of the purchase price of the computer as possible, as soon as possible. Because money can earn interest, a tax savings is worth more to you this year than the same amount of money will be worth in the future. So a good place for Steve to start is with Section 179 of the Internal Revenue Code. Section 179 permits Steve's company to take up to $5,000 of the purchase price as a current expense deduction. The deductible amount will rise to $10,000 by 1990.

In many cases, the Section 179 current-expense deduction covers the entire purchase price of the computer. Many personal computers cost less than the $5,000 to $10,000 deduction that Section 179 will permit over the next several years. This means that you could deduct the entire cost of the computer from your taxable income the first year. Other computer hardware, such as Steve's minicomputer, will cost more than the current expense deduction permitted in one year. Sell Direct, Inc., will have to take depreciation deductions on most of the purchase price. Depreciation of computers is handled in roughly the same manner as depreciation of other office equipment. Under depreciation, a portion of the cost is deducted from business income each year for several years. The percentage that can be taken each year depends upon the length of the depreciation period and the method of depreciation used (straight-line or accelerated methods).

INVESTMENT TAX CREDITS

To encourage investment in capital equipment, Section 38 of the Internal Revenue Code allows a tax credit to businesses for the purchase of certain items. A credit is a direct reduction of taxes, rather than a reduction of taxable income. For example, assume that Steve's company is in the 40-percent tax bracket. A tax credit of $5,000 means that the company pays $5,000 less to the government, whereas a deduction of $5,000 from business income will only reduce its taxes by $2,000. Steve should be alert to any tax credits to which his company is entitled, since even small-percentage credits can be worth a lot of money.

Many computer purchases qualify for an investment tax credit under Section 38. To qualify, the item must be "tangible personal property," which includes computers and peripherals. (The word *personal* is used to distinguish the item from *real* property such as land and buildings. But the item must be used in a business, and not for personal or household purposes.) This definition also includes software that's bundled with the computer. (Bundled software is considered part of the computer for figuring depreciation and Section 179 deductions as well.) There are different ways to calculate the investment tax credit; the choices depend on your tax bracket and other factors. You should consult with an accountant if you think you're eligible for an investment tax credit for the purchase of computer hardware.

RESEARCH AND DEVELOPMENT

If you use computers in research and development (R&D) activities, you can receive special tax advantages. These may include a shorter period for depreciation as well as special tax credits. In addition to computer hardware purchases, other expenditures (e.g., for supplies, researchers' salaries, and equipment rentals) might qualify for special tax treatment. Later in the chapter we'll consider whether the creation of computer software can be an R&D activity that would give the developer more favorable tax treatment for his or her expenses.

DISPOSING OF HARDWARE

If Steve decides to sell his company's minicomputer, he may have to make an income tax adjustment. If the amount that Steve receives from the sale of the computer exceeds the adjusted "basis" of the computer (the original value less the depreciation already taken), the company will have to report the difference as additional ordinary income (or, in some situations, as a capital gain). For example, if Sell Direct, Inc., depreciated the computer to a basis of $8,000 after owning it for four years and then sold it for $10,000, the company would have to add $2,000 to its taxable income for the year of the sale. If computer hardware is traded in as part of a new purchase, the adjusted basis of the old hardware is added to the net purchase price of the new to form the basis for the new property. Sell Direct wouldn't have to make a tax adjustment until the new hardware is sold. Actually, given the poor market for used computers, the sales price seldom exceeds the adjusted basis. So additional income won't be reported very often.

COMPUTER SOFTWARE

DEDUCTIONS

The tax treatment of software costs varies with the way in which the software is acquired. We'll consider four different ways in which our friend Steve might have obtained software for Sell Direct, Inc.

As you may recall, when Steve bought the minicomputer for his company, he received operating-system software with it. The Internal Revenue Service treats bundled software as part of the hardware. There's no need to figure out which portion of the purchase price is for the computer and which portion is for the software. You can take the allowable deductions and credits on the whole cost.

Steve also bought a separate data management software package for the company computer. When software is purchased separately (purchased later than the computer, or purchased at the same time but stated as a separate item on the invoice), it is treated as an intangible asset whose cost should be amortized over its useful life. Amortization of software works much like depreciation of the cost of a computer. A portion of the cost is deducted each year for several years. For example, if the useful life of the data management software is five years, Steve's company will deduct part of the cost each year for five years. The useful life of software is typically five years, although a shorter period may be used if you can show that the software will become useless to you sooner.

Steve acquired other software in two additional ways: he obtained a software license, and he also hired someone to write custom software for the business. The main reason that Steve bought the minicomputer was to improve his company's handling of large mailing lists. Steve had heard about a company that licensed software especially designed for direct-mail marketing firms. Steve acquired this software under a license on January 15 and made payments every three months for a renewal of the license. After six months he decided he didn't like the software. He terminated the license and hired a programmer to develop a customized program for his company's minicomputer. The programmer completed the work on December 15.

Steve now can take two different deductions on the company's tax returns for the year. The license fees for the first program are deductible as current operating expenses (the same would be true for leasing or renting computer hardware). The costs of developing the customized program can either be deducted as a business expense in the year they are incurred or amortized over the useful life of the software. Sell Direct can use either method (it would have to use the same method for consistency if it were taking deductions for two or more custom programs).

INVESTMENT TAX CREDITS

The investment tax credits allowed by Section 38 of the Internal Revenue Code are available only for "tangible personal property." Except in very special circumstances, computer software is regarded by the IRS as intangible property, and the purchaser is therefore not eligible for an investment tax credit. However, if the software comes bundled with a computer, the purchaser may be eligible for an investment tax credit.

DISPOSING OF SOFTWARE

If the cost of acquiring software is being amortized, and if the software is sold at a price higher than the adjusted basis, an adjustment to taxable income must be made (as in the case of recapturing depreciation on hardware, discussed earlier). If the software was created by the taxpayer (as the custom program that

Steve's company paid for was), the amount of the selling price in excess of the adjusted basis is treated as ordinary income. For packaged software, any excess can receive more favorable treatment as a capital gain. If a software package is traded in for an updated version, the basis of the old software is carried over as the basis of the new software. Any additional charges for the new software are added to the new basis, but no adjustment to taxable income is made until the new software is sold.

COMPUTER SUPPLIES, SERVICES, AND OTHER EXPENSES

Expenditures for computer supplies used for business purposes are deductible as ordinary business expenses for the tax year in which they are made. The same is true of expenditures for services such as user training and for repair and maintenance of hardware or software. You have to distinguish between repair and maintenance services that simply keep the computer or software functioning as before and those that increase their value. The latter are capital expenditures that have to be depreciated or amortized over the life of the property, rather than taken as current expense deductions. As already noted, payments for software development services can be amortized or taken as current deductions.

Other business-related expenses are also deductible from your federal income taxes. Interest paid in financing the purchase of computer products is deductible, as are state sales or use taxes and state or local property taxes. You have the option of taking investment tax credits and depreciation deductions on these taxes and interest, rather than taking a current expense deduction.

TAX SAVINGS FROM HOME PURCHASES OF COMPUTER PRODUCTS

When a computer is being used at the taxpayer's business offices or workplace, as Steve's minicomputer is being used at the offices of Sell Direct, Inc., its purpose is clearly for business. The IRS might object to the amount of the deduction taken in a given year or the method by which a certain tax credit is calculated, but it probably won't object to the computer's cost being used to reduce business taxes. Even if you play games on the computer during your lunch break, the IRS realizes that you bought the computer for business reasons and will treat it accordingly for tax purposes.

The government is much more skeptical about computers such as Steve's Tangerine-PC and Tina's Banana-PC that are used at home. Many people operate businesses out of their homes, and it's becoming increasingly common for them to use home computers in their work. If they buy computer products to perform business functions at home, they're entitled to all the tax advantages we discussed earlier for users who have business offices apart from their homes. But the IRS insists on treating home computers differently from computers used in traditional business locations. That's because they know that most home computers that taxpayers claim are being used only for business purposes are in fact being used for both business and personal activities. It's a lot less expensive to buy one computer and use separate disks for business and personal data than to buy two computers and switch between them according to the activity. The government doesn't want people taking deductions from their business income for expenses, or portions of expenses, that are not being used to generate income. So they look at computers with the same sharp eye that they focus on another asset that can be switched easily between business and personal use: automobiles.

DEDUCTIONS AND CREDITS

When are you allowed to take tax deductions or credits for home computers, and what procedures do you have to follow to qualify? The best way to answer these questions is to return to Tina, the software author. You'll recall that Tina has a home office from which she runs her software development company, Tina-Ware, Inc. Tina bought a Banana-PC, which she uses to write software and keep business records. She also uses the computer for her personal mailing lists and allows her son Dennis to run games and educational software on it. To what, if any, tax deductions and credits is she entitled?

The tax laws and regulations require Tina to determine what proportion of the computer's use was directed toward generating income and what proportion was for personal consumption. She can then take a tax credit or deduction for the percentage of the cost that is attributable to the business use. Assume, for example, that 80 percent of the computer's operating time is devoted to Tina's business activities and 20 percent to personal use. Tina would be able to claim a deduction (current expense or depreciation) or tax credit on 80 percent of the cost of the computer.

Through the end of the 1984 tax year, the government was not very strict about the apportionment requirement. If Tina claimed a 100-percent business use of her home computer in 1984, the IRS probably would have accepted her word, even though she was only entitled to 80 percent. As long as she could show that she really ran a trade or business out of her home and that the computer was used to help generate business income, the 100-percent claim would have been allowed. The IRS might have inquired whether the computer was being used in a room set aside as an office, rather than in the living room where anyone could use it. It might also have checked to see that Tina's computer was a powerful model of the sort generally used for business, as opposed to a less expensive computer normally used for home entertainment. But the IRS wouldn't have split hairs by forcing Tina to prove that she never used the computer for personal activities or that little Dennis never laid a hand on the keyboard.

TIME LOGS

Beginning in the 1985 tax year, the government began to tighten up. First of all, new tax laws limiting the eligibility of home computer owners for deductions were passed. If you operate a separate business out of your home, even if it's just a sideline to your regular job, you can still deduct all or part of the cost of your computer. But deductions can no longer be taken by employees who buy computers to do work they take home from the office, unless the computer is required by the employer.

The new laws also crack down on mixed business and personal use of home computers. Starting in 1985, you have to keep a log of computing time spent on different activities. Logs can be either kept manually or compiled by the computer. You have to certify in writing that you are keeping the log. If you're audited, the IRS will examine the log, and if everything isn't in order, the deduction could be disallowed and penalties imposed.

So our friend Tina will have to keep a log of her various uses of the Banana-PC. The log will show that 80 percent of the computer time is devoted to business use, and Tina can claim deductions or tax credits for 80 percent of the cost of the computer. If she wanted to claim 100 percent, she would have to do her personal mailing lists and Dennis's computer lessons on another computer. But even if Tina uses the Banana-PC entirely for business, she still has to keep the time log. Remember: The log is the proof that you're entitled to take a business deduction for your home computer. If a deduction is unsupported by a properly maintained log, you may lose the deduction and be subject to penalties.

PERSONAL INVESTMENT MANAGEMENT

Tina's husband Steve also bought a computer for use at home. He purchased a Tangerine-PC to use in managing the couple's investment properties and securities. Prior to 1985 Steve could have deducted the cost of the Tangerine-PC from his investment income. But under the new rules, his tax benefits from purchase of the computer are sharply reduced. Steve can depreciate the computer over a twelve-year period, but he can't take the Section 179 current expense deduction, five-year accelerated depreciation, or investment tax credit that are available for a computer purchased for some other type of business. Personal investment management is no longer on the same level as other income-earning activities for purposes of deducting computer costs.

OTHER COMPUTER-RELATED EXPENSES

So far we've been focusing on tax deductions and credits for computers used at home. The same ideas apply to other business expenses besides the cost of the computer. If you operate a business at home, you can deduct, as current expenses, the cost of printer ribbons, computer repairs, service contracts, and any other expense (computer-related or not) that helps you in your business. You can also deduct the cost of computer software, although software may have to be amortized rather than taken as a current expense (see the earlier discussion of deductions for software).

TAX SAVINGS FOR DEVELOPERS AND SELLERS OF COMPUTER SOFTWARE

By this point Tina has figured out what deductions and credits to take on her purchases of computer products. She now wants to know what additional tax advantages are available to her as a software developer.

RESEARCH AND DEVELOPMENT TAX CREDITS

A special tax credit is available for R&D expenditures. Wages and salaries, supplies, equipment rental costs, and numerous other expenses are eligible for the credit. Of course, these items are deductible expenses in any business, but the R&D tax credit saves more in taxes than would an ordinary deduction. The credit isn't available for all R&D costs but only for expenses for the tax year that exceed those for a given base period. In other words, you're rewarded with tax breaks for increasing your R&D expenditures over the level of earlier years. These credits are especially important, even crucial, for new companies developing their first products.

Software developers can be engaged in R&D work in the same sense as electrical engineers, chemists, physicists, or any other scientists or inventors. But not every software development project qualifies for the special R&D tax treatment. Development of new or significantly improved programs stands a greater chance of qualifying than development of more routine programs. For example, if Tina is developing an innovative program to facilitate architectural design, her development expenses will qualify for the R&D credits. On the other hand, management information software that is developed for in-house use by a company might not qualify. The IRS may feel that this software is not the kind of scientific R&D work that the tax law encompasses.

Recently there have been proposals within the federal government to eliminate the R&D tax credit for most software development costs. The laws and regulations on R&D credits are likely to undergo changes over the next few years. This is an area in which you need up-to-date advice from a tax expert.

TAXABLE INCOME

Tina has already read Chapters 6, 7, and 8, and she's ready to start selling her software. If Tina packages and sells her own software, her taxable income is figured the same way as in any other business. She subtracts her business expenses from her gross business income to arrive at taxable income. Expenses include all of the computer-related costs discussed earlier, as well as other business costs. These include money spent for supplies, taxes, and insurance; wages paid to employees; payments to independent contractors; advertising expenses; and all other costs incurred in developing and selling the software. If Tina receives royalties from a publisher, she subtracts all expenses incurred in earning those royalties to arrive at taxable income.

Since Tina's home is her principal place of business, she can take a deduction for a home office. She can also deduct a portion of the cost of utilities. To be eligible for the deduction, she has to set aside a room or other area of her home for exclusive use in her business activities. But Tina, and everyone else, should be careful when taking a home office deduction. You have to check a special box on your income tax returns when you claim a deduction for a home office. Taking the deduction increases the chance that you'll be audited, so make sure you're really eligible for it.

SALES TAXES

When Tina sells her software, she may have to collect sales tax from the buyers and turn it over to the state government. There has been a lot of legislation, and many lawsuits, over the last several years concerning sales and use taxes (sales taxes are imposed in the state of purchase, use taxes in the state where an item is used). State laws still vary on whether and when to impose sales and use taxes on computer software, although the trend is toward a more uniform treatment of the issue. We will assume that Tina is selling her software in a typical state; consult an attorney to learn the rules in your own state.

Hagelshaw: The Computer User's Legal Guide (Chilton)

Tina has developed software to teach spelling to children. She sells the software as a complete package and provides no services such as installation or training. In most states, Tina will have to collect sales tax when she sells to the end users of the software. If she sells to wholesalers or retailers, sales or other transaction taxes will be collected at some point, and perhaps at each point, in the distribution chain. Off-the-shelf software is taxed like any other tangible personal property in most states.

If Tina develops customized software for a user, the transaction will probably not be taxed. The rationale is that she is providing personal services, which are not subject to sales tax. When she delivers the software, it will include disks and documentation, but those items are a very small part of the program's total cost. They are usually provided as a convenience to the user, and the whole arrangement is viewed as a nontaxable provision of services.

Somewhere between the sale of off-the-shelf software and the writing of customized software lies software that doesn't fit neatly into either category. Tina might sell a package to many users but provide training services at the start and continued maintenance thereafter at no additional charge. It could then be said that part of the purchase price represents services. Some states would regard the whole purchase price as subject to sales tax, whereas others would treat it as nontaxable customized software. Still others would try to separate the "tangible" prepackaged element of the software from the services element and tax only part of the price. Sales and use taxes may influence your pricing and marketing decisions, so you should learn the laws governing your particular type of software.

(*Remember:* Tax law is a very complex and rapidly changing field. You shouldn't make the mistake of assuming that no aspects of it have changed since this chapter was written. Always be sure to get the latest expert advice on any important question or problem concerning your taxes!)

==

The Computer Professional: Limiting Your Liability
10

The ranks of computer professionals—including programmers and software developers, sellers of hardware and software, and consultants—are expanding rapidly. These professionals are being relied on increasingly by clients and customers for expert work and advice in the development of computer software and for the selection and operation of hardware, software, and computer systems. When the software proves defective or the advice wrong, the clients or customers may consider taking legal action against the person or company they have dealt with. If you are a provider of computer products or services, you need to know the circumstances under which you could be exposed to legal liability, and how to limit that exposure.

YOUR POTENTIAL LIABILITY

We have already discussed how purchasers may be able to get their money back if the computer hardware or software that they purchased proves to be defective (Chapters 2 and 4). Giving people their money back when they're dissatisfied with your product or services is a fairly minor concern. A much more serious problem for the computer professional is the possibility of being forced to pay for business losses suffered by a client who was sold defective software or given imprudent advice. Let's look at some examples of what can go wrong.

1. Dave, a software developer, wrote a program that does income tax calculations. Dave did not realize that the program contained an incorrect formula for determining the value of assets for depreciation purposes. Although Dave had tested the program rigorously, the mistake had never turned up. Dave sold some copies of the tax software to Sally, the owner of a computer retail store. Sally demonstrated the software to customers but didn't do any comprehensive testing herself. One day Rick came into the store, and Sally told him that the software would do all his tax calculations and that he would no longer need an accountant. Rick bought a copy and used the program to calculate his company's income taxes. Six months after he filed his tax returns, the IRS charged Rick with taking depreciation deductions that were too large. They demanded that he pay extra taxes, together with interest and penalties.

Rick wants to sue Dave and Sally over his tax losses. Does he have a case?

2. Fred, the president of a food wholesaling business (from Chapter 5), hired some programmers to develop a program to process customer orders and control inventory. The finished program contained an error that caused an order from one of Fred's customers to be mishandled. Not only did Fred lose the customer's account, but the customer is also suing him over the incident.

Will the programmers be held legally responsible for Fred's problems?

3. Terry, a consultant, helps businesses select the best computers, software, and systems for their needs. Ken, the owner of Ken's Auto Repair, hired Terry to assess his computer needs. Terry was used to dealing with large companies, and she recommended that Ken purchase a computer system that included two user terminals. The system came with software that provided comprehensive inventory management and customer-billing capability. Ken had a small shop with only two mechanics, who fixed an average of twelve cars a day, but Terry had convinced him that a computer would increase his profitability. After a few months, Ken realized that he really didn't need the system; it was just as fast to do everything manually.

Ken is now demanding that Terry pay all the financial losses he incurred as a result of following her advice, including the cost of the system and the value of the work time that he wasted in trying to adapt his procedures to the computer. Does Terry have to pay anything?

There are four principal legal theories under which a computer professional might be held liable for a client or customer's financial losses: breach of warranty, breach of contract, ordinary negligence, and professional negligence (malpractice).

BREACH OF WARRANTY

A warranty is a promise that a fact or statement about a product will turn out to be true (see Chapter 2). For example, assume that a consumer is buying a food processing machine for his or her kitchen. The salesperson tells the consumer that the machine will produce pureed vegetables. The salesperson's statement is a warranty—that is, a promise that the machine will in fact puree vegetables. If it turns out that the best the machine can do is break vegetables into large chunks, the warranty has been "breached" (broken). The consumer is entitled to remedies for the breach (in this case, probably return of the purchase price).

Warranties are established by the Uniform Commercial Code (UCC), which has been adopted in almost every state. The UCC applies only to the sale of goods, not to the provision of services. If you have done a consulting job and a client isn't happy with the results, he or she may be able to sue for breach of contract but not for breach of a UCC warranty. However, an unhappy purchaser of off-the-shelf software is entitled to sue under the UCC, since the transaction is a sale of goods. Custom software may or may not fit under the UCC warranties, depending on how closely the transaction resembles a sale of packaged software and on the decisions of the courts of the particular state. Developers of custom software should assume that their work will be regarded as a sale of goods under the UCC (which means that warranties should be disclaimed, as discussed later in the chapter).

There are different types of warranties, and they can lead to serious liability for computer professionals. Warranties can be either express or implied. Express warranties are promises made by the seller about the quality or characteristics of the product. An example of an express warranty was Sally's statement to Rick that the tax software could perform all of his tax calculations and would replace his accountant. The same promises would create an express warranty if they were printed on the outside package of the software or appeared in advertisements. An express warranty can also be created by a demonstration of the product. If Sally had given Rick a demonstration in which the program prepared a complete business income tax return, there would be an express warranty that the copy of the software that Rick purchased would do the same.

For an implied warranty to be created, it's not necessary for the salesperson or developer of the product to make a promise. Under the UCC, every sale of goods creates an implied warranty of merchantability. This warranty requires that the product perform as it would ordinarily be expected to perform. In our example of the income tax calculation program, the program contained an error that resulted in mistakes in figuring depreciation deductions. We would ordinarily expect that a program of this sort would make accurate calculations, and it carries with it an implied warranty to that effect. The warranty is breached because of the flaw in the program.

Another version of the implied warranty is the warranty of fitness for a particular purpose. This warranty is created when a seller recommends a product as suitable for the purchaser's needs. For example, Rick might have explained to Sally the type of business that he had and shown her financial records and previous tax returns for the company. If Sally had then said something like "Buy this tax software written by Dave; it's just what you need," she would have created a warranty that the software is suitable for the particular purpose that Rick has described (preparation of his company's tax returns). If it turns out that the software is for personal rather than business income tax calculations, the warranty of fitness for a particular purpose is breached.

When a warranty has been breached, the purchaser can take legal action against the seller of the product. In the case of off-the-shelf software, the customer normally sues the retail store or mail-order firm that sold him or her the software. However, some courts allow the purchaser to sue the software publisher (or the developer, if the software is self-published). So Rick would probably sue both Sally and Dave. If Rick can prove that one of the warranties is breached, he can recover damages. These damages will include payment for the difference between the current value of the product and the value it would have had if it had performed as promised. In Rick's case, the entire purchase price could be recovered, since the software is worthless to him in its defective condition. He might also recover incidental or consequential damages (business losses). Consequential damages would include the interest and penalties paid to the IRS, fees paid to accountants to straighten out the tax returns, and the value of Rick's lost work time.

As you can imagine, consequential damages can be quite high. Defective software can cause a business to lose sales and customers and expend valuable employee time in correcting errors. The customers and clients of software users can also suffer losses through delayed shipments, billing errors, and other problems. These third persons may sue the software user, who will in turn want to place responsibility on the computer professional who developed or sold the software. The legal liability could run into many thousands of dollars, not counting attorneys' fees. If you are developing or selling software, you can minimize your exposure to this liability through the use of warranty disclaimers (discussed later in the chapter).

BREACH OF CONTRACT

When you're not selling goods, the UCC warranties don't apply. Most custom software development, free-lance programming, and consulting work isn't governed by the UCC. But ordinarily the computer professional and the client have a written contract containing provisions that could form the basis of a lawsuit by a disgruntled client. In our second example, Fred, the food wholesaler, hired programmers to develop software to manage customer orders and inventory. Fred had no contract, but if there had been one it might have been worded: "The program will fully automate the company's inventory system and procedures." If Fred doesn't feel that his inventory system is fully and properly automated when the work is finished, he might consider legal action against the programmers. The programmers could end up in court, even if they felt that the software was satisfactory.

You have to make sure that your programming or consulting contract doesn't contain a lot of vague promises that could be used against you in a dispute. You should describe in detail what results are expected. If you can't be sure of the results, the contract should say that no results are promised. Later in the chapter we'll discuss disclaimers for custom programming and consulting contracts.

ORDINARY NEGLIGENCE

Everyone has to exercise reasonable care in his or her work. Careless mistakes can be the basis of a lawsuit. In our example of Fred the wholesaler in Chapter 5, the programmers carelessly reversed the entry codes for ice cream and anchovies. The error caused a mix-up in customer orders, and Fred lost a valuable account. An obvious blunder like that would enable Fred to sue the programmers for his losses under a negligence theory. Another example of negligence is the recommendation by a consultant or salesperson to purchase a peripheral that isn't compatible with the client's computer. Walter, the veterinarian in Chapter 2, was recommended purchase of an $800 printer that wasn't compatible with his computer.

Of course, most software contains a few bugs. And it's usually possible to find another programmer who can point out ways the program could have been written better. But this doesn't mean that the original programmer was negligent. As long as the computer professional is reasonably careful in his or her work, mistakes will be forgiven. The injured client might have a better chance of winning a lawsuit if he or she sues for professional negligence (also known as malpractice). If that theory is accepted by the court, mistakes will not be so easily overlooked.

PROFESSIONAL NEGLIGENCE (MALPRACTICE)

Professionals such as doctors, lawyers, and architects are required to perform their work at a certain minimum level of quality and expertise. This level of conduct is higher than that expected of the ordinary person. For example, most people know that knives are dangerous and should be used with care. If you are using a knife in the kitchen and the knife accidentally slips and cuts your fellow chef, you won't be held legally responsible as long as you were exercising reasonable care while using the knife. The same isn't true of a surgeon in the operating room. It's not enough for the surgeon to exercise reasonable care; he or she is held to a much higher standard. If the scalpel slips during an operation, the surgeon probably will be held legally responsible for the resulting injury unless the operation was especially difficult and the dangers were disclosed to the patient.

Advice given by certain professionals is also subject to a high standard of care. If you hire a truck driver to decide where a house should be built, don't bother to sue him or her when the house slides down the hill. The truck driver isn't supposed to be an expert on house construction. But if you hire an architect or civil engineer to decide on a site for the house, you're entitled to rely on his or her professional expertise. If the work doesn't meet the standards of the profession and the house slides down the hill, you can sue the person who gave the bad advice for malpractice.

Up to the present time, computer professionals such as programmers and consultants haven't been held to a professional standard of care. They haven't been subject to malpractice liability because courts have found that for the computer professional the two elements necessary to define a "professional" for malpractice purposes are missing. First, the computer profession doesn't have a standardized, well-defined body of knowledge that all members must know. Lawyers have to go to law school and take certain prescribed courses before they can be admitted to the bar. Members of the medical and engineering professions also must learn a standard body of knowledge before they enter their profession. The educational standards for computer professionals, however, are less uniform. Some programmers and consultants have university training, with an undergraduate or graduate degree, but others are basically self-taught.

The second mark of the traditional profession, an examination and licensing procedure, is also missing in the computer profession. Anyone can be hired as a computer programmer or work as a computer consultant as long as he or she can convince employers or clients of his or her ability. No particular degree is needed, no examination administered, and no license issued. Because the computer profession is easier to enter than other professions, courts have usually not imposed a professional standard of conduct and care on programmers and consultants.

This may well change in the future. Colleges and universities are establishing a more standardized curriculum for computer studies. There have been proposals for certification of programmers who demonstrate a certain minimal level of skill and knowledge. This may not lead to actual licensing of programmers, but it's a step in the direction of creating a "profession" for legal purposes. A professional type of relationship may already exist between providers and users of software and computer services. Computer professionals have knowledge and skills that other people don't have. Their customers and clients often know little about computers and software and have to rely on their advice. Under these circumstances, the courts may begin to impose malpractice liability upon computer professionals.

So computer programmers and consultants should assume that they'll be held to a higher standard of care in their work than the ordinary person. The developer of off-the-shelf software could not be sued for malpractice, since there is no direct professional relationship with the end user. But an unhappy customer or client of a computer professional will be able to recover damages caused by errors in custom programming or by imprudent advice about buying and using computer hardware, software, and systems.

This isn't to say that it will be easy to win a malpractice case against a computer professional. Each custom program or system design is unique, and it's not easy to prove that the job should have been handled differently. If you have proper training for the project and do the best job possible under the circumstances, you probably won't be liable for malpractice if something goes wrong. No one is expected to be perfect. However, if you feel that there's a good chance that the program or system you're designing isn't feasible (or isn't even needed), you should warn your client of that possibility. You might be responsible for the user's losses if you didn't provide any warning about the potential problems and give your client a chance to cancel the project. For example, Terry probably should have advised Ken that he didn't need a computer for his auto repair shop. If clients ignore your warnings, they will have trouble suing you for malpractice if problems arise. The court will find them guilty of "contributory negligence" or conclude that they assumed the risk of any problems.

HOW TO LIMIT YOUR LIABILITY

As we've seen, the potential liability from consulting, software design, and programming mistakes is great, and the courts will probably expand the theories of liability in the future. It's crucial that you take steps to reduce your exposure to this liability. Here are some methods that you can use to protect yourself.

QUALITY CONTROL

Obviously, the best way to avoid legal liability is to make sure that nothing goes wrong in the first place. Mass-marketed software should be well tested and debugged before it's released into the distribution channels. All custom programming should be tested and checked against contract specifications before being turned over to the user. If you, in acting as a consultant or salesperson, don't know the answer to a question or a solution to a problem, you should get qualified assistance. You won't have to worry about lawsuits if there are no problems with what you have done.

AVOIDING EXCESSIVE PROMISES

Don't make promises you can't keep. If you make a statement about the results to be expected from your work, it could be interpreted as a contractual obligation. Similarly, if you advertise that your software has certain capabilities, you may be bound by express warranties that you didn't intend to make. Of course, a certain amount of "puffing" is permitted. If you claim that your programmers do the "best work in the entire state," the statement won't be held against you as a literal promise. But the more specific the statement or advertisement, the more likely it is that it will be enforceable as a warranty or contractual obligation. So make sure that the promsies you make about the software you're developing or the computer system you're recommending match its capabilities.

DISCLOSURE OF NECESSARY INFORMATION

Nothing makes a judge more angry than to find that an informed professional has taken advantage of an uninformed consumer. If you're a salesperson and you sense that a purchaser is about to buy the wrong product, don't let him or her do it. Give the customer the information that he or she needs to make an informed decision about what to buy. The same holds true for consultants and software developers. If a client doesn't ask the appropriate questions and you know that he or she doesn't have your level of technical expertise and is relying on you, you should volunteer the information. Don't go ahead with work or recommend a system that the client might not need. You could be sued for malpractice, or even fraud.

USER TESTING

It's generally a good idea to give a user the opportunity to test software or a computer system before purchasing. A software development contract can include a period for user testing (see Chapter 5), as can a license agreement for previously developed software (see Chapter 8). If you're advising a client to buy software or a computer system, always recommend that he or she test the product before making a final decision. If the user is able to test before paying, the customer shares at least some of the responsibility for losses resulting from inappropriate choices or product failures. The user's involvement in making the final decisions can be raised as a defense if you're sued for breach of contract or malpractice.

WARRANTY DISCLAIMERS

You'll recall from our earlier discussion that express warranties are created when a statement (oral or written) is made concerning the capabilities or characteristics of a product. Express warranties are best not made in the first place. Once made, they can be disclaimed. Implied warranties are created with the sale of off-the-shelf software (and possibly with the sale of custom software as well). Implied warranties can also be disclaimed. A disclaimer doesn't guarantee that a buyer can't sue you. The laws of some states place restrictions on warranty disclaimers. And if the matter goes to court, many judges will find that the disclaimer is unfair to the consumer and will invalidate it. But if you can impose an effective disclaimer, you can restrict the legal rights and remedies of the user of your software. You should routinely seek to disclaim any and all warranties as a means of limiting your liability.

To be effective, disclaimers have to be conspicuous. This is especially important in the sale of off-the-shelf software, where there's probably no personal contact between the software developer and the user. If you put the disclaimer on page 79 of the operator's manual, a court would probably consider the disclaimer invalid. Put it where the user can't help but see it, in type large enough to be read easily. The best location is on the outside of the software package. If it's inside the box, it should be on a separate sheet of paper or on the inside cover of the operator's manual. Be aware that disclaimers located anywhere except on the outside of the package are likely to be held invalid. A disclaimer of warranties for packaged software should contain language such as this:

DISCLAIMER OF WARRANTIES

The software enclosed in this package is licensed solely on an "as is" basis. No warranties, either express or implied, are made by the developer, distributor, or dealer with respect to the software, its merchantability, or its fitness for a particular purpose. The entire risk as to quality and performance is with the licensed user of the software.

See Chapter 4 and the appendix for more discussion and for examples of warranty disclaimers in license agreements for packaged software.

If you're developing custom software, it's also wise to disclaim any warranties that might otherwise be present. You don't necessarily have to paste a disclaimer on the operator's manual or software package (assuming there is a package), although that's not a bad idea. You can simply insert a disclaimer clause into the software development contract (discussed in Chapter 5, with an example in the appendix). The disclaimer should contain language similar to that for packaged software. You want to make clear that the software is accepted "as is," without the benefit of any express or implied warranties.

Even software retailers can get into the act of disclaiming warranties. Retailers can be liable for losses caused by the software they sell, either because of express warranties made by salespeople or because of implied warranties created by the sale. A disclaimer on the software package might benefit the retailers as well as the developer and publisher, but the retailers can play it safe and add their own disclaimers. This might be done with a conspicuous message on all sales receipts. The language would be similar to the other disclaimers: The software is accepted as is, with no express or implied warranties attaching.

OTHER DISCLAIMERS

Besides disclaiming warranties, you should disclaim any responsibility for incidental or consequential damages. These damages could include extensive business losses caused by defective software. Even if all warranties are disclaimed, the user could sue you for negligence or malpractice and recover his or her business losses. So an additional disclaimer of incidental or consequential damages may help limit your liability. This disclaimer is usually added to the regular warranty disclaimer on the software package or included in the custom software contract, or printed on the sales receipt. (The software license agreements in the appendix contain examples of language disclaiming liability for incidental and consequential damages.)

Computer consultants should also put disclaimers into their consulting contracts to make it clear that they aren't guaranteeing any particular results (unless you want to make such a guarantee). Your contract should contain a clause saying that nothing in the contract is to be construed as a warranty or guarantee of any kind and that all advice and recommendations are accepted at the risk of the client.

LIMITED WARRANTIES AND LIQUIDATED DAMAGES

Instead of disclaiming warranties and damages altogether, it's sometimes more effective to give some limited remedies to your client or software user. Complete disclaimers are sometimes invalidated by courts because they seem to be unfair. A contract or license clause that allows some remedies is more likely to be upheld.

In the case of off-the-shelf software, the license agreement typically grants a limited warranty to the user. If the magnetic disk containing the program proves to be defective, the user can return it and receive a replacement free of charge. That may be the only remedy given to the user, regardless of the financial losses or inconvenience caused by the defective program. However, in the states that don't permit complete disclaimers of warranties, you may have to give a limited warranty (usually ninety days from the date of purchase) of merchantability. In that case, the user might be able to recover all damages (unless consequential damages are disclaimed) occurring within the warranty period.

Contracts for custom programming or consulting work can contain something similar to the consumer's limited warranty: a *liquidated damages* clause. This clause basically says that you'll pay if your work causes damage to someone, but you'll only pay a predetermined, limited amount. With liquidated damages, you know exactly what you'll have to pay if there's a problem, which eliminates the prospect of a large award of damages. Payment might be limited to the cost of replacing a defective disk, returning all payments made under the contract, or paying a specified sum of money.

INTEGRATION CLAUSES

An integration clause in a license agreement or other contract is designed to eliminate liability based on promises made outside the written agreement. Ordinarily, if a salesperson makes an oral promise about the capabilities of a product, the retailer or developer may be held to that promise. With an integration clause, a lawsuit can't be brought on the promise unless the promise is contained in the written agreement or contract (which, of course, it probably won't be). An integration clause is usually very simple, with language such as "This agreement is the entire agreement between the parties concerning the development and licensing of the software, and there are no rights or obligations among the parties except as specified herein."

ARBITRATION

A method of limiting liability that is growing in popularity is the arbitration clause. This clause can be inserted into any type of contract. It provides that in the event of a legal dispute the matter will be submitted to an arbitrator rather than to a court. Arbitration is usually a much faster and cheaper method of resolving disputes than is a lawsuit, and the legal fees are generally lower. Damage awards are also frequently smaller in arbitration than in court trials. The arbitration clause can specify who the arbitrator or arbitrators will be, the rules that will govern any hearings before the arbitrators, and any other detail of the process that can be agreed upon.

INSURANCE

Sometimes all precautions fail, and you'll have to pay damages to someone injured by your work. In that case, wouldn't it be better to have another company pay the money for you? If that sounds like a good idea, you should consider purchasing professional insurance coverage. Professionals in many fields are able to buy malpractice insurance, also known as "errors and omissions" insurance. A few insurance companies are now offering this coverage to computer professionals, and its availability will continue to grow. If you're insured when someone sues you in a work-related dispute, the insurance company will pay the legal fees for your defense, as well as any judgments rendered against you. Anyone familiar with insurance policies knows that there will be many exclusions to this general coverage. You'll have to talk with insurance brokers and read the different policies to get the details. Even if you find a good policy, you may not want to buy it. That decision depends on the cost of the policy and your perception of the financial risk of working without insurance.

=====================================

Starting Your Own Company: Organizing It and Raising Capital

11

Thousands of new businesses are started in the United States each year. Most of these new companies won't create great wealth for their owners; many will fail or be abandoned within a few years of their creation. But those with good ideas and proper management will prosper. Starting your own business has its risks, but the rewards from a successful venture can be well worth it.

The computer and computer software industries produce more than their share of new businesses. Employees of high-technology firms regularly leave to set up their own companies, often to compete with their former employers. Software writers start companies to develop and sell their products. And programmers, consultants, and other computer professionals set up businesses to market their services. In this chapter we will learn about the various forms of business organizations, how to decide which form to use, the steps to take to legally create a business, and the legal aspects of raising capital for a business.

Starting your own business doesn't necessarily require millions of dollars and a large staff of employees. The great majority of businesses are run by one person or a small group of people. Many businesses are operated from inexpensive offices or out of the owner's home. If you plan to develop and sell any product or service, you'll have to form a business to do it. You may be able to form the company on your own, or you may want to have an attorney do the work. However you approach the task, this chapter gives you the information you need to get started.

TYPES OF BUSINESS ORGANIZATIONS

There are four basic forms of organization of a profit-making enterprise: (1) individual proprietorship, (2) general partnership, (3) limited partnership, and (4) corporation.

INDIVIDUAL PROPRIETORSHIP

Most small businesses are individual proprietorships. Anyone from the corner grocer to a computer software writer can start a business on his or her own. You don't have to take any legal action or draw up any agreements to create and run a business as a sole proprietor; you just start working. However, if you're operating under a name other than your own, you have to file a fictitious business name statement in the county where you have your principal place of business. For example, if John Smith is operating a business called "Texas Software," he has to file a statement indicating that he's the proprietor of Texas Software. If he doesn't file a fictitious business name statement, he may be precluded from suing to enforce contracts and from taking other legal action. A sole proprietor also has to comply with certain tax-reporting obligations. A separate form has to be prepared for business income, and estimated tax payments must be made. State or local governments may impose other registration, licensing, or tax requirements on sole proprietors. You should check with an attorney to be sure you're complying with all the applicable laws.

GENERAL PARTNERSHIP

If you want to share ownership of your business with other people, you'll have to form either a partnership or corporation. A general partnership is formed by two or more people, who are legally known as "general partners." The general partners share in the operation of the business, as well as in the profits and losses. Unlike a limited partnership, a general partnership can't have outside investors with limited liability. All partners must share the responsibility for losses and are personally liable if the business has insufficient assets to cover financial obligations. The partners split profits and losses, and operate the business, according to the terms of their partnership agreement.

LIMITED PARTNERSHIP

A limited partnership contains at least one general partner, as well as one or more "limited partners." The general partner or partners operate the business, and the limited partners serve as passive investors, somewhat like shareholders in a corporation. The limited partners normally receive either a set return on their investment (much like interest on a loan) or a percentage of the profits. If the business fails, the limited partners lose only the amount of their investment, with no additional personal liability. This promise of limited liability helps the partnership attract investors and capital and is the primary advantage of a limited over a general partnership. But although the limited partners are afforded limited liability, they're forbidden to participate in the operation of the partnership. If they become involved in the operations, they may gain the status of general partners, who are personally liable to creditors should the business fail.

Limited partnerships are frequently used to attract capital from investors who are looking for special tax advantages. Limited partnerships are most common in real estate and research and development situations. In many instances, the corporate form is an appropriate alternative to a limited partnership. Later in the chapter we'll consider the criteria for choosing between the partnership and corporate forms and outline the steps in the creation of partnerships and corporations.

CORPORATION

The word *corporation* conjures up the image of a large business enterprise like General Motors or IBM. But the great majority of corporations are very small. In fact, even if you're working alone, you can choose to operate in the corporate rather than the sole proprietorship form of business. Many states allow a corporation to be formed by one person. When two are required, a spouse or a friend can serve as an uninvolved officer to meet the legal demands for incorporation. So if incorporation would be advantageous to your business, don't pass up the opportunity just because you have a small operation.

A corporation is almost like an artificial person, a legal entity with a life all its own. It's the most flexible form of business organization. Unlike a partnership, a corporation is legally distinct from the people who own it. The shareholders and officers have no personal liability for financial obligations of the corporation (except in certain circumstances where the corporate form is being abused). In theory, a corporation can last forever. Unless it's dissolved, it will survive the deaths of its founders and changes in ownership. It can have one shareholder or millions of shareholders. The stock can be held entirely by one person, family, or group of owners or can be publicly traded to anyone who wants to buy it. Larger corporations are run in a quasidemocratic fashion. The shareholders elect a board of directors, which in turn hires officers to operate the company. In smaller corporations the shareholders, directors, and officers are usually the same few people.

DECIDING WHETHER TO INCORPORATE

Many businesses start out as individual proprietorships or partnerships. At some point the owners have to decide whether or not to incorporate the business. You've probably heard a lot of advice about when a business should be incorporated. "You save taxes when you incorporate," or "Your company can't grow unless you incorporate": these are a few of the standard comments offered by nonexperts. But the decision is much more complicated than that. There are times when it's easier and more financially sound to remain in a noncorporate form. The decision depends on the size and nature of your business and the relative importance to you of a number of often conflicting factors. The analysis is usually very complex, and each situation has its unique features. Before making a decision, consult an attorney or accountant (or both). To help you with some preliminary planning before you talk to an expert, we'll look now at the most important considerations that go into the decision of whether to incorporate a business.

EASE OF SETUP AND OPERATION

The individual proprietorship is the easiest form of business to start and operate. As already mentioned, as long as you're operating under your own name, all you really have to do is start working. A partnership requires a little more trouble to set up, since you usually draft a partnership agreement and have more complex tax-reporting obligations.

A corporation is the most expensive type of business to create. There are incorporation fees and taxes to pay, and you'll have to pay a lawyer to draft the necessary documents, if you don't want to do the work yourself. Also, the formalities of maintaining the corporate form, such as holding shareholders' and directors' meetings, amending the bylaws, and obtaining approval from directors or shareholders for certain actions, take time away from the day-to-day operation of the business. Of course, these inconveniences are usually outweighed by the importance of other factors, such as the tax advantages of incorporation and its usefulness for raising capital.

RAISING CAPITAL: LIMITED LIABILITY

The differences between the forms of organization become very important when the business needs to raise money. An individual proprietorship or general partnership can't have outside investors. The ability of those enterprises to raise money depends primarily on the personal resources and credit of the principals. The same might be true of a limited partnership or corporation in its early stages. But the latter two organizations have additional, built-in methods of raising capital. The limited partnership and corporation offer limited liability to potential limited partners and shareholders, respectively. Comparing the two, a limited partnership can often be set up to raise money without the complexities of creating a corporation and issuing stock. A public (or large private) offering of stock is an especially complicated process, with significant information disclosure requirements. Some of these difficulties can be avoided through private placement of limited partnership shares (although large placements may be subject to the same disclosure requirements as the sale of stock). However, there may be restrictions on how many limited partners can be taken into the partnership. There are no such restrictions on a corporation, which can sell stock to any number of investors. Shares can be sold early in the life of the company to raise money to get started. This is normally done through a limited, private offering of stock. When the company matures, a larger public offering can be made to fuel expansion (and put money in the founders' bank accounts).

The choice between a limited partnership and a corporation may depend on how much money needs to be raised, the timing of the offerings, and the tax advantages available to investors. As you can see, these matters are very complex. You can think about them yourself and do some initial planning, but you'll probably need to get the expert advice of an accountant or attorney before deciding on the best form of business for purposes of raising capital.

BUSINESS TAX CONSIDERATIONS

Aside from the tax advantages to potential investors, the type of business organization you select can affect the tax obligations of the company itself. The income tax rate for a business operated as a partnership may be different from the rate for the same business operated as a corporation. Be careful here: there is no easy solution to the problem of keeping taxes low. When a company is small and has few profits, the corporate tax rate might result in higher taxes than the tax rate applied to individuals and partnerships. This doesn't mean you shouldn't incorporate such a business. The IRS permits small corporations to pay taxes at the individual rate of the owners (known as "Subchapter S" status). So you can have the legal advantages of a corporation (such as limited liability) while paying taxes as if there were no corporation. At higher levels of income, the corporate tax structure might result in lower overall income taxes. A lot depends on whether a substantial portion of the earnings will be distributed to shareholders. If there are large distributions, there will be "double taxation" of the corporate earnings and the shareholders' dividends. This can result in a larger total tax burden than if the company remained unincorporated.

Besides the rate of taxation, there are other tax considerations that may make the corporate form more attractive. The availability of tax-deductible deferred compensation arrangements, such as pension and profit-sharing plans, has traditionally been regarded as one of the primary motivations to incorporate. However, recent changes in the tax laws have given businesses operated in noncorporate forms many of the same pension and profit-sharing advantages. These changes, along with the availability of Subchapter S taxpayer status, have gone a long way toward eliminating the tax differences between the corporate and noncorporate forms of business organization. By the same token, non-tax factors such as limited liability, ease of obtaining investment capital, and paperwork and reporting requirements have become more important in the decision whether to incorporate. But tax considerations are still a large part of the equation, and you should have an accountant examine the finances of your business to help you decide which form of organization is best for you.

CONTINUITY

A general partnership ordinarily terminates upon the retirement or death of a partner. A final accounting is then required, and the business often ceases to operate (unless the partnership agreement provides for a continuation). A limited partnership is unaffected when a limited partner sells out his or her interest or dies, but if a general partner can't continue in the business the effect is the same as in a general partnership. However, a corporation has the advantage of perpetual existence. It continues to exist regardless of retirements or deaths among the principals. Directors and officers can be replaced as needed (the exception to this is a corporation run by one person, which may be dissolved when the owner dies or retires). Title to property is unaffected by changes in personnel, and ownership transfers can be accomplished quickly and with little disruption by a simple sale of stock. The corporate form is well suited for continuing a business beyond the retirement or personal misfortunes of the founders.

TRANSFERABILITY OF OWNERSHIP

As your business grows, you may want to transfer all or part of your ownership interest to others. The only way to do this in an individual proprietorship is to sell the entire business. Participants in a general partnership can effectively transfer a portion of the ownership by replacing current partners or bringing in additional partners, but no ownership interest can be held by someone outside the partnership. A limited partnership agreement can allow for transfer of the interests of the limited partners, much like the selling of corporate stock, but allowing for unrestricted transfer of limited partnership shares may cause the partnership to be taxed as a corporation. Of course, ownership in a corporation can be transferred most easily, through the sale of stock. The articles of incorporation can permit open transfer of stock or place some restrictions on transfer, such as by giving current shareholders the first chance to buy any stock offered for sale.

ATTRACTING KEY PERSONNEL

In the computer and software industries, the best talent is scarce and expensive. If your company wants to acquire top engineers or programmers, you might have to offer them some ownership interest in the company in addition to a salary. It's difficult to make such an offer in a partnership, short of taking in the new personnel as partners. More flexible compensation arrangements are available in corporations. A new employee can be offered stock or stock options as an added enticement to join the company. This is one important reason why most rapidly growing "high tech" companies choose the corporate form of organization.

COMPANY IMAGE

When you're selling products and services, you have to think about what reaction customers will have when they see your company name. If you're incorporated, you can use the word *corporation* or the abbreviation *Inc.* in the company name. Some customers feel more secure about buying from an incorporated business than from one that isn't incorporated. They believe, perhaps somewhat irrationally, that corporations are better established than other types of businesses. Of course, not every potential customer or client pays attention to such details. But you should think about the question as you develop your business image.

HOW TO FORM A PARTNERSHIP

GENERAL PARTNERSHIP

Two computer programmers, Calvin and Dan, have decided to form a company to do free-lance programming and consulting work. They've considered all the factors we've just discussed and have determined that a partnership would be the best form for their new company.

Calvin and Dan want an attorney to help in the formation of their partnership. Even in a simple partnership between friends, there will be problems that an expert can anticipate and help the participants avoid. But Dan figured that he could save himself some attorney's fees by doing some of the work himself and then having the attorney review the papers. What do the prospective partners need to do?

It's really quite easy to form a partnership. First, Calvin and Dan need a partnership agreement. The partnership agreement is a type of contract between the partners that sets out their rights and obligations to each other. The appendix contains the agreement that Dan drafted, after it was reviewed and revised by his attorney. A partnership agreement can be much more detailed than the one in the appendix, but Calvin and Dan's agreement includes the basic provisions found in most agreements. The agreement starts with the name, purpose, and place of business of the partnership. Then the duration is stated; a partnership can last for a specified period of time or until the partners agree to dissolve it. The agreement also indicates how much capital each partner will contribute to the business and how profits and losses are to be shared. Typically, all investments, profits, and losses are shared on an equal basis, although the partners can agree to a different arrangement.

Other provisions in the partnership agreement include details on how the partnership will be managed and records kept and a description of the circumstances under which the partnership will be terminated. The termination paragraph is one of the most important aspects of the partnership agreement. Unlike a corporation, a partnership doesn't have perpetual existence. If a partner retires or dies, the partnership is dissolved. So Dan and Calvin should think about what they want to do if one of them dies or retires. If the remaining partner wants the right to continue the business, the partnership agreement should allow for such continuation. The agreement should permit the remaining partners to buy out the retiring partner's interest or the interest of the heirs of a deceased partner. The agreement should also permit amendments to be made to it, and the partnership to be dissolved, by mutual consent of the partners.

The partnership is created when Dan and Calvin sign their partnership agreement. A partnership can even be formed by an oral agreement. Of course, it's advisable to have a written partnership agreement to avoid later arguments about how to keep the books, split profits, dissolve the business, and so forth. In addition to the agreement, it will be necessary to file a "fictitious business name" statement in the county where the principal place of business is located. It's not likely that Dan and Calvin will do business under their own names. "Dan Dimsdorf and Calvin Small" isn't a very good name for a programming and consulting firm. If they call their company "Caldan Programming" or "High Tech Associates," they'll have to file a fictitious business name statement. There may be other registration, licensing, and tax-reporting requirements, depending on the particular state. Calvin and Dan should check with their attorney to be sure they're complying with all applicable laws.

LIMITED PARTNERSHIP

Dan and Calvin might have formed a limited partnership. Under that arrangement, they would act as the operating general partners, and the limited partners would provide investment funds. Formation of a limited partnership is more complicated than formation of a general partnership. First, a limited partnership agreement must be drafted. The agreement is similar to that for a general partnership, with the addition of provisions for the contribution of capital by the limited partners, the allocation of profits and losses to them, and the transfer of partnership interests. Because of these added complexities, Dan would probably have to leave the drafting of a limited partnership agreement entirely up to his lawyer.

After the limited partnership agreement is prepared, it's necessary in most states to file a certificate of limited partnership. Depending on the amount of capital the limited partnership is trying to raise and the number of limited partners, there may also be reporting requirements under the securities laws. In short, a limited partnership involves a lot of details and requires expert knowledge. You should get your attorney's advice on whether to set up a limited partnership and then let him or her do the work for you.

HOW TO FORM A CORPORATION

Bill was an employee of Businesstech, Inc., a software development company. A year ago Bill left Businesstech and started a company called Companytech. Under the new company Bill developed "Companyplan," a business informa-

tion management program. Bill operated Companytech as an individual proprietor for the first year. He has found a publisher to produce and sell Companyplan, and he now wants to hire a programmer to help him develop other
software. Bill's accountant advises him to incorporate his business.

Bill could hire an attorney to incorporate Companytech. As with any type
of business, it's best to have the benefit of expert advice at the formation stage.
But it's possible to do your own incorporation, and Bill decides to try his hand
at it. Bill will have to contact the secretary of state's office in his state for precise
incorporation details, such as the required number of copies of documents and
the amount of filing fees. Here we'll simply discuss the basic points that Bill
needs to consider and the actions he must take to incorporate Companytech.

STATE OF INCORPORATION

It used to be a common practice to incorporate in the state with the lowest fees
and the most liberal laws governing corporations. For many years Delaware
held this honor, and businesses all over the country incorporated there. Most
states have since simplified and improved their incorporation laws and have
also raised the registration fees for out-of-state corporations doing business in
their state. It's now considered best to incorporate in the state where you have
your principal business activities (headquarters, main offices, and so forth). A
small company like Companytech should be incorporated in Bill's home state
(we'll assume Bill lives in California).

AVAILABILITY OF CORPORATE NAME

Bill wants to incorporate under the name Companytech, the one he's been
using as a sole proprietor for a year. In most states he has to clear this company
name through the secretary of state. Bill should write a letter to the California
secretary of state, inquiring whether the name Companytech is available. The
secretary of state will check the records, and if no one else is already using the
name, will issue a letter or certificate of availability. Usually a name will be
reserved for a period of time (often sixty to ninety days) while you prepare the
incorporation papers. If you don't register the incorporation before the period
expires, the name will be available to anyone who wants to use it. In some
states there's a fee for the search of the records and for the reservation of a
corporate name.

Hagelshaw: The Computer User's Legal Guide (Chilton)

194   OTHER LEGAL ISSUES FOR THE COMPUTER USER

NUMBER OF INCORPORATORS

The modern trend is to allow a single person to form a corporation. For example, Bill could incorporate in California by himself. A few states may require two or more persons. In that case, Bill could ask his spouse or a friend to serve as the second incorporator without that person's having any involvement in the actual operation of the company.

ARTICLES OF INCORPORATION

Bill will have to fill out and file articles of incorporation with the secretary of state. This is a relatively simple procedure. Articles of incorporation are almost like a standardized form in most states. The form contains basic information about the corporation, such as name, purpose, number of shares authorized, place of business, and names of directors. The appendix contains the articles of incorporation for Bill's Companytech.

FEES AND TAXES

Bill will have to pay a filing fee when he sends copies of the articles of incorporation to the secretary of state. The filing fee is usually quite modest, but Bill may also have to pay an incorporation or franchise tax. That may cost him a few hundred dollars. These fees and taxes won't stop you from incorporating a business that should be incorporated. But they do make you think twice about incorporating until it's really necessary.

OTHER FILINGS

Bill may also have to file papers with local governmental bodies. In some states you have to file a notice of incorporation or a copy of the articles of incorporation in the county where the principal place of business of the corporation is located. Some cities may have filing requirements, usually for tax purposes, for corporations and other businesses operating within their boundaries.

ORGANIZATIONAL MEETINGS

Companytech becomes a legal corporation upon approval of the articles of incorporation by the secretary of state. However, the corporation can't start operating until certain other actions have been taken. These actions are accomplished at organizational meetings, held either by the incorporators or by the directors listed in the articles of incorporation. Exactly who should attend is determined by the law of each state (in many cases the incorporators and initial directors are the same people). At the organizational meeting or meetings, directors and officers are selected, and bylaws that give the corporation the capacity to transact business are adopted. The meeting can also be used to authorize issuance of stock and to decide other matters, although much of this can be left for later action by the board of directors.

In a small corporation, in which the incorporators, directors, officers, and shareholders are the same few people, the organizational meeting is basically just a formality to approve decisions already made by the principals of the company. Minutes of the organizational meeting and all other meetings should be kept in the corporate records. Legal stationary stores sell incorporation kits that include a minute book, stock certificates and a stock register, a corporate seal, and other items needed to start your corporation.

The corporate bylaws are very important to the corporation, since they provide the rules under which the corporation is governed. In a small company like Bill's Companytech, the bylaws will grant extensive power and discretion to the officers and directors (i.e., Bill) to carry on the business of the company. Larger companies will have more detailed bylaws explaining the powers and duties of the shareholders, directors, and officers. As an example of the documents for a small corporation, the appendix contains both the articles of incorporation and the bylaws for Bill's Companytech.

RAISING MONEY FOR YOUR BUSINESS

Once your company is organized, you may need to raise money to fund expansion of the company and to develop and market products. Most businesses are started with the personal funds of the founders or with loans from family and friends. If outside funding is needed, it normally comes from commercial loans, traditional investment (e.g., selling stock or limited partnership shares, issuing bonds), or venture capital. From a legal perspective, loans to software or computer product or service companies are no different from loans to other types of businesses. The same is true of investments in limited partnership shares and corporate stock, other standard methods of raising capital. But one specific type of stock transfer—venture capital funding—excites a little more interest and requires a little more explanation.

Many new companies, especially in the software development field, try to get a large infusion of funds from venture capitalists. Venture capital firms are willing to take the risk of investing in a new company for the promise of a great return on their investment should the company prosper. Before approaching a venture capitalist, you have to put together a good business plan and prepare for a major presentation. This requires professional assistance from a law firm or company that specializes in the acquisition of venture capital funding. For now we'll just mention the factors that go into the funding decision, so that you can consider whether raising venture capital is an option worth pursuing.

Venture capitalists are especially interested in software developers. The characteristics that venture capital firms are looking for in a prospective company include experienced and energetic founders, a well-defined product development strategy, and software that's designed for important new applications or is significantly different from current products. The investors also want to be sure that they're funding the actual development of software, not just the creation of a new company. It's sometimes more attractive to them to invest in a going concern than to fund an entirely new company, since having an established management and facilities means fewer expenses in getting a new project under way.

In return for their investment, the venture capital firms get a significant portion of the company's stock. For example, a new company might start with 10 million shares of stock. The venture capitalists might get 3 million shares at a dollar a share, with another 2 million shares going to the founders and future employees. The remaining 5 million shares are reserved for additional investment of private capital through later public offerings of stock. It's the successful public offering of stock, at a price much higher than that paid by the initial investors, that greatly enhances the value of everyone's shares. By "going public" with a company, the venture capitalists (and the founders) expect to make their fortune. Although only a small percentage of new computer-related ventures lead to great wealth, it's the promise of success that keeps all of us interested.

=================================

Postscript: Hiring a Lawyer

WHEN TO USE A LAWYER

This book is called a "legal guide," and it's just that: a guide to the law as it relates to computer users. It's meant to provide you with basic information about legal issues of interest to you, but it isn't meant to replace your lawyer. Remember: Books are good for *information*, but not always for *action*. There are self-help legal books on subjects such as getting a divorce and forming a corporation; such books will be written on computer law subjects as well. These books are fine, as long as you're willing to take the risk of making a mistake. A lawyer, with his or her knowledge of and experience with the law, is less likely to make mistakes. When the lawyer does, you may be able to hold him or her responsible for any financial losses. So it makes sense to consult an attorney whenever you have a legal problem involving an amount of money that's significant to you.

TYPES OF LAWYERS

Some lawyers are still generalists, but the trend is toward specialization. Most lawyers are familiar with warranties and contract law, so problems involving the purchase of computer hardware and software can be taken to almost any competent attorney. Other problems require more specialized knowledge. This is especially true of tax, as well as copyright and trademark problems. You can find lawyers who specialize in these areas in most larger cities.

More and more lawyers are beginning to call themselves "computer lawyers." Be careful of this designation; it could mean almost anything. There's no licensing or testing requirement for most legal specializations. Any lawyer can claim to be a specialist in "computer law." The lawyer might actually be new to the field, so ask if he or she has handled cases or drafted documents similar to the ones you need. Of course, in some situations you'll be willing to hire someone new to the field (if you believe that he or she can figure out what to do), since this person probably will charge lower fees than a more experienced lawyer. But you should ask even experienced attorneys for their background. A computer lawyer who has worked for twenty years for a company in hardware procurement won't necessarily know how to represent you in dealings with a software publisher.

HOW TO CHOOSE A LAWYER

When you find one or more lawyers with the right experience for your task, you need to consider other factors before deciding whom to work with. The most reliable indicators of a good lawyer are your own satisfaction from a previous dealing and the recommendations of friends, family, and business acquaintances. If you're dealing with someone new, you might try the lawyer out during one or two minor consultations. If you're satisfied at that point, then let him or her take on your major task or problem. Avoid lawyers who seem too eager to sue and litigate disputes in court. That approach can create more problems than it solves. Pick someone you like and trust. That can be even more important than professional qualifications. You can always teach a friendly lawyer what he or she needs to know about your affairs. But a lawyer who is stuffy or too busy to spend much time with you can be impossible to work with.

LEGAL FEES

Lawyers charge at an hourly rate for the time they spend on your affairs. The rate varies depending on many factors. It's usually higher in large cities than in smaller cities, and specialization and experience result in higher rates. If you want to sue someone for damages, the lawyer might be willing to take the case on a "contingent fee" basis. Under this arrangement, you won't pay anything unless money is recovered from the defendant. Contingent fees usually range from one-third to one-half of the judgment.

Don't be afraid to ask your lawyer about rates before he or she starts working. If you don't ask, you may be shocked when you receive the final bill. Lawyers will always tell you what their hourly rate is, but they usually won't commit themselves to a total cost until the work is finished. Except in the preparation of certain standard documents, it's difficult to predict how much time will be required to complete a project (lawyers are like programmers in this respect).

You can save your lawyer some time, and thereby save yourself some money, by preparing well for any consultations. If you have time, read up on the legal issues involved in your matter so you'll have answers ready for some of the lawyer's questions. Organize your papers, so that the lawyer doesn't have to spend time sorting them out. Sometimes it's a good idea to send a letter, in advance of the consultation, outlining your problems or needs. That allows the lawyer to organize the work in advance and shortens the time of the meeting.

ALTERNATIVES TO LAWYERS

Lawyers don't have a monopoly on solving legal problems. Problems with defective computers or software can also be taken to various governmental and private consumer organizations. For example, the Lemon Byte Society, P.O. Box 558250, Miami, FL 33155, will do battle on behalf of unhappy members against unsympathetic manufacturers and sellers of computer products. And if you think you're being defrauded, you can contact the state attorney general or local prosecutor. Letters or phone calls from those offices can produce quick results for you.

Of course, before you pay for an attorney's involvement in a legal dispute, you should try to work out a solution yourself. Sometimes there's no substitute for just staying calm and talking things over.

PART FIVE
Appendix

================================

LIMITED WARRANTY

MANUFACTURER warrants this product against defects in material and workmanship for a period of NINETY (90) DAYS from the date of original retail purchase. This warranty applies only to products made by or for Manufacturer, which can be identified by Manufacturer's trademark or trade name affixed to them. Manufacturer does not otherwise warrant any products not made by Manufacturer.

For Manufacturer's products other than software, Manufacturer will repair (or at its option replace) this product during the warranty period at no charge to you, provided it is returned to an authorized service center within the country of original retail purchase.

For software accompanying Manufacturer's products, (1) Manufacturer will replace media at no charge if you discover physical defects in it and return it during the warranty period, and (2) Manufacturer will replace media and documentation for system software (general operating-system software including drivers, utilities and emulators, and programming languages with associated utilities and operating-system programs) at no charge to you if Manufacturer releases a corrective update to such system software during the warranty period and you return the original media and documentation within SIX (6) MONTHS of the date of original retail purchase.

In order to obtain warranty service, return the product to an authorized service center in the country of original retail purchase, transportation charges prepaid (you can obtain the name and address of an authorized service center from your local authorized Manufacturer's Dealer or from Manufacturer directly at the address printed on this certificate). Attach to the product your name, address, telephone number, a description of the problem, and a bill of sale bearing the appropriate Manufacturer's serial number as proof of date of original retail purchase.

This warranty does not apply if the product has been damaged by accident, abuse, misuse, or misapplication or has been modified without the written permission of Manufacturer; or if any Manufacturer's serial number has been removed or defaced.

MANUFACTURER IS NOT RESPONSIBLE FOR INCIDENTAL OR CONSEQUEN-TIAL DAMAGES RESULTING FROM THE BREACH OF ANY EXPRESS OR IMPLIED WARRANTY, INCLUDING ANY COSTS OF RECOVERING, REPROGRAMMING, OR REPRODUCING ANY PROGRAMS OR DATA STORED IN OR USED WITH MANUFAC-TURER'S PRODUCTS; DAMAGE TO PROPERTY; AND, TO THE EXTENT PERMITTED BY LAW, DAMAGES FOR PERSONAL INJURY. THIS WARRANTY IS IN LIEU OF ALL OTHER WARRANTIES. ANY IMPLIED WARRANTIES, INCLUDING IMPLIED WARRAN-TIES OF MERCHANTABILITY AND FITNESS FOR A PARTICULAR PURPOSE, ARE LIMITED IN DURATION TO NINETY (90) DAYS FROM THE DATE OF ORIGINAL RE-TAIL PURCHASE OF THIS PRODUCT.

Some states do not allow the exclusion or limitation of incidental or consequential damages, or limitation on how long an implied warranty lasts, so the above limitations or exclusions may not apply to you.

This warranty shall not be applicable to the extent that any provision of this warranty is prohibited by any federal, state, or municipal law that cannot be preempted. This warranty gives you specific legal rights, and you may also have other rights that vary from state to state.

RENTAL AGREEMENT—COMPUTER RENTAL, INC.

BILLING INFORMATION

Lessee name:	Ben Smith, Smith Enterprises
Address:	100 Main Street, Waygo, Texas
Telephone:	(512) 777-7123

EQUIPMENT LOCATION

Address:	100 Main Street, Waygo, Texas
Contact person:	Ben Smith (512) 777-7123

EQUIPMENT INFORMATION

First item: 1 Pumpkin Computer, Serial # P-569386
Purchase price: $7,500
Monthly rental: $800

Second item: 1 Realfast Printer, Serial # R-701839AX
Purchase price: $1,800
Monthly rental: $250

MONTHLY PAYMENT INFORMATION

Rent	$1,050
Insurance waiver fee:	45
Total monthly rent:	$1,095
(Date due: 15th of each month)	
Delivery/installation:	$ 200
Security deposit:	$1,095
Total due at delivery	$2,390

TERM OF RENTAL

Month-to-month, beginning August 15, 1985 (*delivery date*)
Minimum rental period: One month

ACCEPTANCE

This rental agreement is subject to the terms stated below. Lessee hereby acknowledges that he has read this agreement, is aware of all of the terms contained in the agreement, and accepts the above-described Equipment subject to those terms.

Lessee: _____

Ben Smith
President, Smith Enterprises

Date: August 10, 1985

Lessor: _____

President
Computer Rental, Inc.

(*continues*)

CONDITIONS OF AGREEMENT

1. *Rental Agreement:* Computer Rental, Inc. (*Lessor*), hereby rents to Lessee the items of personal property described above, for use in lessee's business. The initial term of this agreement will begin on the date of actual delivery, even if such date is different from the delivery date stated in this agreement, and will end on the date the Equipment is returned to Lessor or on the date of termination of this agreement as determined under paragraph 6 below. Unless otherwise noted, the minimum rental period is one (1) month. Title to the described Equipment will remain with Lessor throughout the term of this agreement. THIS IS A RENTAL OF PERSONAL PROPERTY AND NOT A CONDITIONAL SALES CONTRACT, SECURITY AGREEMENT, OR OTHER INSTRUMENT.

2. *Rent:* Lessee will pay Lessor as rent for the described Equipment the total monthly rent set forth above, on the monthly rental due date, for at least the number of months indicated, and thereafter until this agreement is terminated. If Lessee fails to make a monthly payment on time, or within five (5) days thereafter, Lessor may (but shall not be obligated to) treat such failure as a default by Lessee and may immmediately take possession of the Equipment without notice to Lessee. If Lessor fails to receive any monthly payment within ten (10) days from the due date, Lessee shall pay to Lessor a late payment charge equal to five percent (5%) of the monthly rent. This sum will become immediately payable together with the delinquent rent, plus interest on any unpaid rental charges at the rate of eighteen percent (18%) annual interest.

3. *Location and Use:* Unless otherwise noted in this agreement, the Equipment shall be used at the specific location set forth above, and no part of said Equipment shall be removed from such location except by Lessor, or with Lessor's express permission. If Lessee wishes the Equipment moved to another location, Lessee will give Lessor seven (7) days' written notice, and Lessor will move the Equipment (at Lessee's expense) or allow Lessee to move the Equipment, at Lessor's sole discretion. A charge of $100 will be assessed for any violation of this section. If Lessor permits the Equipment to be used at any location other than the original Equipment Location, Equipment must be returned to the original location, at Lessee's expense, for purposes of repair, maintenance, or pickup by Lessor.

4. *Lessee's Responsibility:* Lessee will keep the equipment in good and clean condition, use it only for the purposes for which it is intended, treat it with due care, and not misuse, damage, or destroy any of the Equipment or permit another to do so. Lessee will not alter, paint, improve, modify, or decorate any of the equipment and will not modify or deface any of the markings identifying the Equipment as property of Lessor. Lessee bears all risks of damage, loss, theft, or other destruction of the Equipment, for any reason whatsoever, including damage resulting from improper use of the equipment. Lessee acknowledges and warrants that all operators of the Equipment are trained in its use. By executing this agreement, Lessee is acknowledging that the Equipment is received in good condition. Upon termination of this agreement, the Equipment will be returned to Lessor in good condition, excepting only ordinary wear and tear. Lessee will pay Lessor the cost of restoring any damaged Equipment to good condition. If damaged Equipment cannot be repaired, Lessee will pay Lessor the Purchase Price of the Equipment. Lessee shall pay additional rent, at the then-current rate, until all repairs have been completed. Lessor shall have the right to enter Lessee's premises at reasonable times to inspect the Equipment. If

Hagelshaw: The Computer User's Legal Guide (Chilton)

inspection reveals that the Equipment is damaged or improperly maintained, Lessor may (1) service or repair the Equipment, charging the costs to Lessee, or (2) terminate this agreement and take immediate possession of the Equipment, with Lessee remaining liable for rental payments until the Equipment is repaired (repair costs to be charged to Lessee).

5. *Insurance:* (A) At its own expense, Lessee shall insure the Equipment for the term of this agreement against any loss or damage to the Equipment, in an amount not less than the total Purchase Price of the Equipment specified above. Lessee shall maintain public liability insurance in an amount satisfactory to Lessor. Lessee shall deliver evidence of such insurance coverage upon Lessor's request.

(B) *Insurance Waiver:* Lessee may elect, with Lessor's consent, to purchase an insurance waiver by so advising Lessor and by paying the Insurance Waiver Fee with each monthly payment. If Lessee agrees to pay such fee, Lessee need not provide insurance for the Equipment. The insurance waiver fee shall not cover damage or destruction caused by the Lessee or resulting from the intentional acts or failures to act on the part of lessee, or incidental damage caused by Lessee.

6. *Termination:* (A) Lessee may terminate any rental after the original term by giving Lessor two (2) days advance notice of such termination, by paying all amounts due to Lessor, and by returning the Equipment to Lessor. Equipment may be returned to Lessor's offices, or Lessee may request that Lessor pick up the Equipment from Lessee's Equipment Location, for a pickup charge of $100.

(B) If Lessee fails to perform any obligation contained in this agreement, Lessor may, at its option, terminate this agreement and immediately take possession of the Equipment without notice. Lessor may also terminate the agreement and take possession of the Equipment if during the term of the agreement bankruptcy or insolvency proceedings are commenced by or against Lessee, or if a receiver is appointed for the business of Lessee, or if Lessee discontinues business at his current location. In addition to the rights afforded under this agreement, Lessor may exercise any right or remedy available in the law in the event of a default by Lessee. Upon any termination, Lessee shall deliver the Equipment to Lessor, or permit Lessor to enter Lessee's premises to take possession of the Equipment. Lessee expressly releases any claim for trespass or damages caused by reason of entry and removal of the Equipment. Notwithstanding termination of this agreement, Lessee shall remain liable to Lessor for

1) All past due amounts owing Lessor;
2) The current total monthly payment, less an adjustment for any unexpired portion of the month;
3) Payment of the purchase price for any missing Equipment, and payment for repairs to damaged Equipment; and
4) All other applicable charges and penalties, including late payment charges and pickup charges.

7. *Early Cancellation Fee:* If the rental period is other than a month-to-month rental, Lessee may terminate the agreement prior to the stated date of termination upon written notice to Lessor. In such an event, Lessee shall pay Lessor the total rental fees that would have been charged had the rental been on a month-to-month

basis, less credit for payments already made, plus a cancellation fee of 20 percent (20%) of the total recalculated rental fee.

8. *Renewal:* For any original rental term other than month-to-month, this agreement will be automatically renewed, after the expiration of the original term, for successive month-to-month terms.

9. *Security Deposit:* Lessee agrees to pay Lessor the amount set forth above as a security deposit. Such deposit is to ensure Lessee's performance hereunder and is not rent. Lessee agrees that Lessor will not pay interest on such deposit. Lessor may offset against the deposit any amounts due from Lessee at the termination of this agreement (or any other time). Lessor will refund any remaining deposit (after such offset) within fifteen (15) days of the latter of (a) the termination of this agreement, or (b) the resolution of any dispute between Lessee and Lessor arising from this agreement.

10. *No Warranties:* Lessee acknowledges that Lessor is not the manufacturer of the Equipment nor the agent of such manufacturer, and that LESSOR MAKES NO WARRANTY REGARDING THE EQUIPMENT, EXPRESS OR IMPLIED, INCLUDING ANY WARRANTY OR MERCHANTABILITY OR FITNESS FOR ANY PARTICULAR PURPOSE. IN NO EVENT WILL LESSOR BE LIABLE FOR ANY DAMAGES, INCLUDING LOST PROFITS OR OTHER INCIDENTAL OR CONSEQUENTIAL DAMAGES ARISING OUT OF THE USE OR INABILITY TO USE THE EQUIPMENT. Lessor's obligations to Lessee are limited to

a) The delivery of Equipment that is selected by Lessee; and
b) The repair or replacement of Equipment that is defective when delivered to Lessee or that becomes defective while subject to this agreement, provided such defect is not caused by Lessee or by Lessee's negligence.

Notice of any defect must be given to Lessor within five (5) days of its discovery by Lessee.

11. *Waiver and Indemnification:* Lessee hereby releases and waives all claims against Lessor for damages to persons or property in any way relating to the equipment or its use and agrees to indemnify and hold Lessor harmless from all claims, liabilities, costs, or expenses resulting from the use of the equipment or from any breakdown of the Equipment or other failures. It is also understood that there shall be no abatement of rent during any period of breakdown or nonuse of the Equipment, unless Lessor is unable to repair or replace defective Equipment (as defined in paragraph 10 above) within three (3) days of receipt of notice of such defect from Lessee. If defective Equipment is not repaired or replaced by Lessor within three days of the notice, Lessee's only recourse against Lessor is abatement of rent for the period after the notice of defect is given until the Equipment is actually repaired or replaced. Lessee expressly waives any other claims against Lessor for Lessor's inability or unwillingness to replace or repair defective equipment.

12. *Assignment:* Lessee will not assign this agreement or any rights hereunder to another, sublease or loan any of the Equipment, pledge or grant a security interest in any of the Equipment, or otherwise permit the Equipment to come into the possession or control of any third person. Lessee shall not permit or cause any of the Equipment to become affixed to the premises in such a way as to become a fixture. This agreement may be assigned by Lessor.

13. *Credit Approval:* Lessor shall not be obligated to deliver the Equipment unless and until Lessee's credit is approved by Lessor, in Lessor's sole discretion.

14. *Force Majeure:* Lessee's obligations under this agreement are absolute and shall not be affected by any circumstances or events beyond Lessee's control, of whatever nature.

15. *Lessee Representations:* Lessee represents and warrants that it has the power to enter into this agreement, and that this agreement is a valid, binding, and enforceable obligation of the Lessee. Lessee warrants that all information furnished by Lessee now or hereafter is and will be true and correct as of the date submitted to lessee.

16. *Notices:* All billings, payments, and written notices from either party to the other shall be given at the above addresses, or at such other addresses as may be designated in writing by either party to the other, and shall be deemed to have been received upon delivery to the party to whom they are directed.

17. *Miscellaneous Provisions:* This agreement is the entire agreement between the parties concerning the rental of the Equipment. No changes may be made to this agreement except by a written instrument signed by Lessee and Lessor. This agreement will be binding upon and is for the benefit of the parties and their heirs, executors, administrators, legal representatives, and successors (and assigns of the Lessor only). Lessee hereby waives any and all existing and future setoffs and counterclaims against the rental charges and payments due under this agreement.

LEASE AGREEMENT—COMPUTERLEASE, INC.

This is a lease agreement between Jones Associates *(Lessee)* and ComputerLease, Inc. *(Lessor),* for the following described equipment, which shall be delivered to Lessee by Lessor within three (3) days of the date of this agreement:

1 Delta 3010 Business Computer (Serial # 96012)

1 Beta 609 Disk Drive (Serial # D-982644)

1 Alpha Printer (Serial # 98367-YT)

Location of Equipment: Jones Associates
6988 Second Street
Willowby, Mass

PERIOD OF LEASE AND RENTAL PAYMENTS

This lease is for a period of sixty (60) months, beginning on the date of this agreement. The total value of the Equipment is $17,250. The monthly lease payment is $412, due on the 1st day of each month for a duration of the lease period. A lease advance payment of $1,486 is due upon signing of this agreement (this amount includes $412 for the first month's lease payment, $824 as a security deposit, and $250 as a delivery and installation charge).

TERMS AND CONDITIONS OF LEASE

1. *Lease:* Lessee hereby leases from Lessor the Equipment described above. Lessee accepts such Equipment subject to the terms and conditions of this agreement.

2. *Warranties:* Lessor hereby assigns to Lessee, for and during the term of the lease, all manufacturers' warranties and guarantees, and Lessor authorizes Lessee to obtain the customary services furnished in connection with such warranties and guarantees, at Lessee's expense. LESSOR MAKES NO REPRESENTATION OR WARRANTY AND ASSUMES NO OBLIGATION WITH RESPECT TO THE MERCHANTABLE CONDITION, QUALITY, OR FITNESS OF THE EQUIPMENT, OR THE ENFORCEABILITY OF THE MANUFACTURER'S WARRANTIES AND GUARANTEES. NO DEFECT OR UNFITNESS OF THE EQUIPMENT SHALL RELIEVE LESSEE OF THE OBLIGATION TO MAKE LEASE PAYMENTS OR PERFORM ANY OTHER OBLIGATION UNDER THIS LEASE.

3. *Lease Payments:* Lessee agrees to make total lease payments of *$24,720* at the monthly rate and over the period specified above. The first month's payment, the security deposit, and installation charges are due upon the signing of this agreement. Subsequent payments are due monthly, in advance, commencing on the 1st day of the calendar month after the month in which this agreement is signed.

4. *Location:* The Equipment shall be delivered and thereafter kept at the Location specified above and shall not be removed therefrom without Lessor's prior written consent.

5. *Accepted Condition/Notice of Defects:* Unless Lessee gives Lessor written notice of each defect in the Equipment within five (5) business days after receipt

Hagelshaw: The Computer User's Legal Guide (Chilton)

thereof, it shall be conclusively presumed that the item was delivered in good repair and that Lessee accepts it as an item of Equipment described in this lease. If Lessee rejects the Equipment within the five (5) business day period, this lease shall immediately become void, and Lessor shall return all monies paid, with the exception of the installation charge.

6. *Use:* Lessee shall use the Equipment in a careful manner and shall comply with all laws relating to its possession, use, or maintenance.

7. *Labels:* If Lessor provides Lessee with labels stating that the Equipment is owned by Lessor, Lessee shall affix and keep the labels in a prominent place on each item of Equipment.

8. *Alterations:* Lessee shall not make any alterations or improvements to the Equipment without Lessor's prior written consent. All alterations and improvements made to the Equipment shall belong to the Lessor.

9. *Surrender:* Upon expiration or termination of this lease, Lessee, at its expense, shall return the Equipment to Lessor in good condition, ordinary wear and tear excepted. If Lessee fails to surrender the Equipment within ten (10) days after expiration or termination of this lease, Lessor may demand from Lessee the fair market value of the Equipment. If Lessee fails to pay the fair market value of the Equipment within ten (10) days of demand, Lessee shall be responsible for paying the costs of recovering the Equipment, including reasonable attorney's fees.

10. *Loss and Damage:* Lessee shall bear the entire risk of loss or damage to the equipment from any cause whatsoever, and no such loss or damage shall relieve Lessee of the requirement to make lease payments or meet other obligations under this lease. In the event of damage to any item of Equipment, Lessee shall immediately place the same in good repair. If Lessee fails to do so, Lessor may effect repairs and demand reimbursement from Lessee. If Lessor determines that any item of Equipment is lost, stolen, destroyed, or damaged beyond repair, Lessee (at the option of Lessor) shall

a) Replace the same with like equipment in good repair; or
b) Pay Lessor all amounts then owed under this lease, together with the unpaid balance of the total remaining lease payments specified in this lease, and ten percent (10%) of the value of said Equipment.

11. *Insurance:* Lessee shall, during the term of this lease, purchase and maintain insurance covering all leased Equipment against all ordinary perils in an amount at least equal to the actual cost of replacing the Equipment. The proceeds under said insurance shall be payable to Lessor. If Lessee fails to provide proof of said insurance upon request by Lessor, Lessor shall have the right to obtain such insurance. In such an event, Lessee shall repay to Lessor the cost of the insurance with the next lease payment.

12. *Liens and Taxes:* Lessee shall keep the Equipment free and clear of all levies, liens, and encumbrances. Lessee shall pay all charges and taxes that are now or hereafter may be imposed upon the ownership, leasing, renting, purchase, possession, or use of the Equipment, excluding taxes on or measured by Lessor's income. If Lessee fails to pay any such taxes, Lessor may pay them instead, and Lessee shall then reimburse Lessor on demand.

13. *Liability:* Lessor shall not be liable for any loss, property damage, personal

injury, or expense, including legal expense, incurred by any person, regardless of how caused, arising out of the use or possession of the Equipment by Lessee. LESSOR SHALL NOT BE LIABLE FOR LOSS OF PROFITS OR OTHER BUSINESS LOSSES, OR ANY OTHER CONSEQUENTIAL OR INCIDENTAL DAMAGES CAUSED, DIRECTLY OR INDIRECTLY, BY THE INADEQUACY OF ANY ITEM OF LEASED EQUIPMENT FOR ANY PURPOSE OR USE OR BY ANY DEFICIENCY OR DEFECT THEREIN.

14. *Indemnity:* Lessee shall indemnify Lessor against, and hold Lessor harmless from, all claims, actions, proceedings, expenses, damages, or liabilities, including attorney's fees, arising in connection with the selection, delivery, use, or possession of the Equipment.

15. *Assignment:* Lessee shall not assign or transfer any right, obligation, or security interest in this lease, or sublet or permit the use of the Equipment by anyone other than Lessee or its employees, without the prior written consent of Lessor. Lessor may assign this lease or any part of it. This lease is binding upon the heirs, executors, administrators, and successors of the parties hereto.

16. *Late Charges and Interest:* Should Lessee fail to pay any part of the lease payments or any other sum required to be paid to Lessor within ten (10) days of the due date, Lessee shall pay a late charge of $50 for each month for which the payment is delinquent, plus interest on the delinquent payment from the due date at the rate of eighteen percent (18%).

17. *Default:* If Lessee fails to make lease payments or perform any other obligation under this lease within five (5) days after Lessor shall have demanded performance thereof, or if Lessee abandons the equipment or enters bankruptcy, insolvency, or receivership proceedings, or makes an assignment for benefit of creditors, or makes false statements to Lessor in connection with this lease, or allows or suffers an attachment or levy against any of its property, Lessor shall have the right to exercise any one or more of the following remedies without notice to Lessee:

a) *Acceleration:* Lessor may demand the immediate payment of the total lease payments due through the end of the lease period, less credit for amounts already paid. Lessee must pay all costs and attorney's fees associated with the collection of said lease payments. If Lessee makes all such accelerated payments, Lessee may keep possession of the Equipment for the balance of the lease period, subject to the terms and conditions of this agreement.

b) *Repossession:* Lessor may take possession of the Equipment (or any part of it), without notice, wherever it is located, and without incurring liability to Lessee for any damage related to such taking of possession. In the event of repossession Lessor may store the equipment at Lessee's expense for the balance of the lease period, or re-lease or sell the Equipment at such terms as it may decide. Any attempt to re-lease or sell the Equipment shall not be deemed a waiver of Lessor's right to exercise the Acceleration or any other remedy. In the event that Lessor re-leases or sells the Equipment, Lessee shall pay any difference between the total lease payments due through the end of the lease period and the amounts recovered through re-lease or sale, plus reasonable costs associated with the re-lease or sale. In the event of Repossession, Lessor may declare all Lessee's rights under this lease terminated.

c) *Continuation:* Lessor may elect to continue under this lease agreement, with Lessee obligated to bring up to date and continue all lease payments. If Lessor elects to sue to recover past due lease payments, Lessee shall be obligated to pay all legal costs, including reasonable attorney's fees.

d) *Other Remedies:* Lessor may pursue any and all other remedies allowed by law.

18. *Notices:* Any written notice or demand under this agreement may be given by mailing it to the party at its address stated above, or at such other address as may be provided in writing. The notice or demand shall be effective when deposited in the mail properly addressed and with postage prepaid.

19. *Ownership:* The equipment is, and at all times shall remain, the personal property of Lessor. Lessee shall have no right, title, or interest therein except as expressly set forth in this lease. Lessee warrants that Lessee is not leasing the Equipment for personal, family, or household purposes.

20. *Security Deposit:* In all situations, the security deposit paid by Lessee may be used by Lessor to cover delinquent lease payments or any other obligation under this agreement. The use of the security deposit by Lessor in this manner shall not constitute a waiver of any rights belonging to Lessor under this agreement. The security deposit, if any amount remains after setoffs, shall be returned to Lessee, without the payment of any interest, within fifteen (15) days of the expiration or termination of this lease, or the resolution of all disputes between the parties, whichever shall come last.

21. *Entire Agreement:* This instrument, together with any written addendums or amendments signed by both parties, is the entire agreement between Lessee and Lessor. It shall not be amended except by a written instrument signed by both parties.

For Lessee: _____ Date: _____
Sally Jones
President, Jones Associates

For Lessor: _____ Date: _____
President
ComputerLease, Inc.

SOFTWARE LICENSE AGREEMENT (MASS MARKET)

The Enclosed Software is licensed to users for their use only on the terms set forth below. Please fill out the registration form at the bottom of this agreement and return it to Publisher. You will then be entitled to use the software and receive the benefits of the Limited Warranty described below.

   1. *License:* Publisher hereby agrees to grant to you, upon your return of a completed registration form to Publisher, a nonexclusive license to use the enclosed Software, subject to the terms and restrictions set forth in this License Agreement.

   2. *Copyright:* The enclosed Software, including its documentation, is copyrighted by Publisher. You may not copy or otherwise reproduce the Software or any part of it except as expressly permitted in this license agreement. If a backup copy of the Software is not supplied by Publisher, you may make backup copies as required for your own use, provided that you reproduce all copyright notices and other proprietary legends on all such copies.

   3. *Restrictions on Use and Transfer:* The original and any backup copies of the Software are to be used only in connection with a single computer. You may not distribute copies of the Software to others. You may transfer this license together with the original and all backup copies of the Software, provided that you give Publisher written notice, and the transferee completes and returns to Publisher a customer registration form and agrees to be bound by the terms of this license.

   4. *Limited Warranty on Media:* Publisher warrants the disks on which the Software is recorded to be free from defects in materials and faulty workmanship under normal use, for a period of ninety (90) days after the date of original purchase. If during this ninety-day period, a defect in the disk should occur, the disk may be returned to Publisher, and Publisher will replace the disk without charge, provided that you have completed and returned to Publisher the enclosed registration form. Your sole remedy in the event of a defect in a disk is replacement of the disk as provided above.

   5. *LIMITATIONS ON WARRANTY AND LIABILITY:* EXCEPT AS EXPRESSLY PROVIDED ABOVE FOR MEDIA, PUBLISHER AND ITS SUPPLIERS AND DEALERS MAKE NO WARRANTIES, EITHER EXPRESS OR IMPLIED, WITH RESPECT TO THE SOFTWARE, ITS MERCHANTABILITY, OR ITS FITNESS FOR A PARTICULAR PURPOSE. THE SOFTWARE IS LICENSED SOLELY ON AN "AS IS" BASIS. THE ENTIRE RISK AS TO ITS QUALITY AND PERFORMANCE IS WITH YOU. SHOULD THE SOFTWARE PROVE DEFECTIVE, YOU ASSUME THE ENTIRE COST OF NECESSARY SERVICING, REPAIR, OR CORRECTION, AND ANY INCIDENTAL OR CONSEQUENTIAL DAMAGES. IN NO EVENT WILL PUBLISHER OR ITS SUPPLIERS OR DEALERS BE LIABLE FOR DIRECT, INDIRECT, INCIDENTAL, OR CONSEQUENTIAL DAMAGES RESULTING FROM ANY DEFECT IN THE SOFTWARE, EVEN IF THEY HAVE BEEN ADVISED OF THE POSSIBILITY OF SUCH DAMAGE. Some states do not allow the exclusion or limitation of implied warranties or liability for incidental or consequential damages, so the above limitations may not apply to you.

(continues)

Hagelshaw: The Computer User's Legal Guide (Chilton)

APPENDIX

REGISTRATION FORM (RETURN TO PUBLISHER)

I have read and understand the above Software License Agreement, and agree to abide by its terms.

Signature: _____ Date: _____

Name (print): _____

Street/#: _____

City/St/Zip: _____

Type of software: _____

Software license number: _____

Date of purchase: _____

READ BEFORE OPENING

SHRINK-WRAP SOFTWARE
LICENSE AGREEMENT

IMPORTANT: THE ENCLOSED PROGRAM IS LICENSED BY PUBLISHER TO CUSTOMERS FOR THEIR USE ONLY ON THE TERMS SET FORTH BELOW. OPENING THIS PACKAGE INDICATES YOUR ACCEPTANCE OF THESE TERMS.

1. *License:* Publisher hereby agrees to grant you a nonexclusive license to use the enclosed Program, subject to the terms and restrictions set forth in this License Agreement.

2. *Copyright:* The Program and its Documentation are copyrighted. You may not copy or otherwise reproduce any part of the Program or its Documentation, except that you may load the Program into a computer as an essential step in executing the Program on the computer.

3. *Backup Policy:* Publisher will provide you with a backup copy of the Program upon receipt of your completed Registration Card.

4. *Restrictions on Use and Transfer:* The original and any backup copies of the Program and its Documentation are to be used only in connection with a single computer. You may physically transfer the Program from one computer to another, provided that the program is used in connection with only one computer at a time. You may not transfer the program electronically from one computer to another over a network. You may not distribute copies of the Program or Documentation to others. You may transfer this license together with the original and all backup copies of the Program and its Documentation, provided that the transferee completes and returns to Publisher a Registration Card and agrees to be bound by the terms of this License Agreement. Neither the Program nor its Documentation may be modified or translated without written permission from Publisher. YOU MAY NOT USE, COPY, MODIFY, OR TRANSFER THE PROGRAM, OR ANY COPY, MODIFICATION, OR MERGED PORTION, IN WHOLE OR IN PART, EXCEPT AS EXPRESSLY PROVIDED FOR IN THIS LICENSE.

5. *NO WARRANTY OF PERFORMANCE:* PUBLISHER DOES NOT AND CANNOT WARRANT THE PERFORMANCE OR RESULTS THAT MAY BE OBTAINED BY USING THE PROGRAM. ACCORDINGLY, THE PROGRAM AND ITS DOCUMENTATION ARE LICENSED "AS IS," WITHOUT WARRANTY AS TO THEIR PERFORMANCE, MERCHANTABILITY, OR FITNESS FOR ANY PARTICULAR PURPOSE. THE ENTIRE RISK AS TO RESULTS AND PERFORMANCE OF THE PROGRAM IS ASSUMED BY YOU. SHOULD THE PROGRAM PROVE DEFECTIVE, YOU ASSUME THE ENTIRE COST OF ALL NECESSARY SERVICING, REPAIR, OR CORRECTION.

6. *Limited Warranty for Disks:* To the original licensee only, Publisher warrants the magnetic disk on which the program is recorded to be free from defects in materials and faulty workmanship under normal use and service for a period of ninety (90) days from the date the Program is delivered. If during this ninety-day period, a defect in the disk should occur, the disk may be returned to Publisher, and Publisher will replace the disk without charge to you, provided that you have previously returned the enclosed Registration Card. Your sole and exclusive remedy in the event of

Hagelshaw: The Computer User's Legal Guide (Chilton)

a defect is replacement of the disk as provided above. ANY IMPLIED WARRANTIES OF MERCHANTABILITY AND FITNESS FOR A PARTICULAR PURPOSE ARE LIMITED IN DURATION TO A PERIOD OF NINETY (90) DAYS FROM THE DATE OF DELIVERY. If the failure of a disk has resulted from accident, abuse, or misapplication of the disk, then Publisher shall have no responsibility to replace the disk under the terms of this limited warranty. This limited warranty gives you specific legal rights, and you may also have other rights that vary from state to state.

7. *LIMITATION OF LIABILITY:* NEITHER PUBLISHER NOR ANYONE ELSE WHO HAS BEEN INVOLVED IN THE CREATION, PRODUCTION, OR DELIVERY OF THIS PROGRAM SHALL BE LIABLE FOR ANY DIRECT, INCIDENTAL, OR CONSEQUENTIAL DAMAGES, SUCH AS, BUT NOT LIMITED TO, LOSS OF ANTICIPATED PROFITS OR BENEFITS, RESULTING FROM THE USE OF THE PROGRAM OR ARISING OUT OF ANY BREACH OF ANY WARRANTY. SOME STATES DO NOT ALLOW THE EXCLUSION OR LIMITATION OF DIRECT INCIDENTAL OR CONSEQUENTIAL DAMAGES, SO THE ABOVE LIMITATION MAY NOT APPLY TO YOU.

8. *Term:* The license is effective until terminated. You may terminate it at any time by destroying the Program and Documentation together with all copies, modifications, and merged portions in any form. It will also terminate if you fail to comply with any term or condition of this License Agreement. You agree upon such termination to destroy the Program and Documentation together with all copies, modifications, and merged portions in any form.

9. YOUR USE OF THIS PROGRAM OR SIGNATURE ON THE ENCLOSED REGISTRATION CARD ACKNOWLEDGES THAT YOU HAVE READ THE CUSTOMER LICENSE AGREEMENT AND AGREE TO ITS TERMS. YOU FURTHER AGREE THAT THE LICENSE AGREEMENT IS THE COMPLETE AND EXCLUSIVE STATEMENT OF THE AGREEMENT BETWEEN US, AND SUPERSEDES ANY PROPOSAL OR PRIOR AGREEMENT, ORAL OR WRITTEN, AND ANY OTHER COMMUNICATIONS BETWEEN US RELATING TO THE SUBJECT MATTER OF THIS AGREEMENT.

SOFTWARE DEVELOPMENT CONTRACT

This is a contract between Yellowstone Expert Programmers, Inc. *(Programmers)* and Fred's Wholesalers, Inc. *(Company),* for development of software and related services, as specified below.

1. *Duties:* Programmers shall create a computer program, and related documentation and services, in accordance with Schedule A, which is attached to this contract and incorporated herein.

2. *Payments:* Company shall pay Programmers the sum of $20,000 for their services under this contract.

Programmers shall keep a detailed time record of the professional time spent working toward completion of this contract. Should Programmers expend more than 400 hours on the project, the Company shall make additional payments at the rate of $50 per hour for each hour of work beyond the initial 400 hours, up to a maximum of $5,000 in additional payments (for a total maximum payment under this contract of $25,000).

Payments shall be made as follows:

$5,000 upon signing of this contract

$5,000 when the items specified in paragraph 1 of Schedule A are delivered to Company

$10,000 and all additional payments, if any, when Company accepts the software in accordance with this contract

3. *Acceptance Testing/Formal Acceptance:* Company shall have a period of sixty (60) days following delivery of the source code and all materials specified in Schedule A to test the software at Company's business location. Programmers shall provide reasonable support to Company employees during the test period.

No later than the end of the sixty-day period, Company shall notify Programmers whether or not they have accepted the software. The software shall be deemed to be accepted by Company if no notice is received by Programmers prior to the end of the sixty-day period. If Company elects not to accept the software, it shall notify Programmers of that fact in writing, and Programmers shall return, within ten (10) days, all but the initial $5,000 payment. If the software is rejected, Programmers may keep the initial $5,000 payment as their sole compensation under this contract.

Company shall exercise good faith in its decision to accept or reject the software. The sole permissible grounds for nonacceptance of the software are failure to comply with the specifications set forth in Schedule A.

4. *Proprietary Rights:* In consideration for the payments described in paragraph 2 of this contract, Programmers hereby assign all rights in the software to Company. Programmers understand that the software is a "work made for hire," and is and shall be the exclusive property of the Company. Any and all modifications or improvements made to the software by any person are likewise the exclusive property of the Company. Company shall have the sole right to copyright the software and any changes thereto. Programmers understand that they have no right to sell or license the software, or any of its modifications or improvements, to any third party.

5. *Trade Secrets:* All information relating to the software, this contract, and Company's business operations are trade secrets of the Company. Programmers shall

Hagelshaw: The Computer User's Legal Guide (Chilton)

keep all such trade secrets confidential and shall sign any nondisclosure agreements requested by the Company. Programmers shall also comply with all of Company's security rules while on the Company's premises and shall take all reasonable security precautions in the handling of materials related to the development of the software.

6. *Warranty of Original Development/Indemnity:* Programmers warrant that the software developed pursuant to this contract is the original work of Programmers and that such work does not infringe in any way on the proprietary or contractual rights of any third party. In the event that any third party shall bring legal action against Company for alleged infringement of copyright or other rights, Programmers shall indemnify Company for any expenses incurred, including attorney's fees, court or arbitration costs, and any court judgments, arbitrator's awards, or reasonable settlements paid in any legal action.

7. *Remedies:* Prior to acceptance of the software under paragraph 3 of this contract, either party shall have the right to terminate the contract in the event of a breach of one of its provisions by the other party. If the contract is so terminated, neither party shall have any rights under the contract. Company shall be entitled to a return of all payments made under the contract, and Programmers shall own exclusive rights in the software. Neither party shall have any other rights or remedies in the evnt of a breach prior to acceptance.

If the contract is breached by either party subsequent to acceptance of the software by Company, the breaching party shall be allowed a period of ten (10) days within which to correct any deficiencies in his performance. If the breach is not rectified within the ten-day period, the nonbreaching party shall be entitled to pursue any and all remedies allowed by law for breach of contract.

8. *Arbitration:* All disputes relating to the performance or interpretation of this contract, if they cannot be resolved by the parties themselves, shall be resolved through binding arbitration. Either party may request an arbitration, which shall be conducted in accordance with the rules of the American Arbitration Association. Arbitration shall be the exclusive forum for any disputes arising out of this contract, and neither party shall have the right to file a lawsuit in a court of law.

9. *Miscellaneous Provisions:* Programmers are considered independent contractors, and not employees of the Company. Programmers shall not subcontract any work under this contract without the written consent of the Company.

Programmers shall pay all sales and other taxes incurred in connection with the work performed under this contract.

Any and all amendments to this contract must be made in writing, signed by both parties.

Date: _____

For Company: _____
Fred Farmer
President
Fred's Wholesaler's, Inc.

For Programmers: _____
Stan Stansky
Yellowstone Expert
   Programmers, Inc.

(continues)

Hagelshaw: The Computer User's Legal Guide (Chilton)

SCHEDULE A

1. Programmers are to provide the following items no later than (*the completion date*):

Two copies of machine-readable object code in magnetic disk form, and one copy of source code in printed form, and documentation, for the computer program described in paragraph 2 below. The program shall be written to run on a Pumpkin 1000 Computer.

2. Programmers are to design and produce a computer program that performs the following functions for Company:

  a) Accepts entry of customer orders, producing printed request forms for action by shippping department;
  b) Accepts entry of shipment information, making automatic changes in inventory records and producing supplier reorder forms;
  c) Produces weekly reports of customer orders and shipments by customer name and type of product, and monthly summaries showing volume of product type ordered and shipped, and total dollar value of orders and shipments.

3. Programmers shall provide training services to Company's staff during the acceptance testing period specified in paragraph 3 of the contract. The training shall be sufficient to enable Company's employees to learn all aspects of the software.

4. Programmers shall correct all defects and otherwise maintain the software for a period of one (1) year after its acceptance by Company. Programmers shall make all corrections to the software within ten (10) days after being notified of the problem. After the one-year maintenance period expires, Company shall be responsible for all further maintenance of the software.

Hagelshaw: The Computer User's Legal Guide (Chilton)

SOFTWARE MARKETING AGREEMENT

This agreement to publish and market software is entered into this date by Ellen Wilson (*Developer*) and SoftPublishing, Inc. (*Publisher*). The computer program that is the subject of this agreement is known as "Comput-A-Point" (*Program*).

1. *Delivery:* Developer shall furnish to Publisher, no later than (delivery date), a copy of the Program in machine-readable object form, and one copy of the Program documentation. These items shall be the same as those provided to Publisher pursuant to the parties' Software Evaluation Agreement signed (date), together with the improvements and modifications suggested by Publisher in its letter to Developer of (date).

2. *Acceptance/Royalty Advance:* Following delivery by Developer of the items specified in paragraph 1, Publisher shall have sixty (60) days to test the Program. No later than the end of the sixty-day test period, Publisher shall determine whether or not it accepts the Program. Publisher shall exercise good faith in its determination as to acceptance. If the Program is not acceptable to publisher, Publisher shall notify Developer of this fact, in writing, prior to the expiration of the sixty-day test period. If no notification is received by Developer within the sixty-day period, the Program shall be deemed accepted by Publisher. The notice shall contain an explanation of the deficiencies in the Program and the actions needed to correct those deficiencies. After receiving notice of nonacceptance, Developer shall have thirty (30) days within which to correct the deficiencies. If the corrections are not made within the thirty-day period, Publisher may terminate this agreement.

Upon acceptance of the Program in accordance with this paragraph, Publisher shall pay to Developer an advance of $3,000 on the royalties specified in paragraph 7 of this agreement. Developer shall be entitled to keep such advance even if insufficient copies of the Program are sold to earn $3,000 in royalties.

3. *Marketing Commitments:* Acceptance of the Program by Publisher is not a guarantee by Publisher that the Program will be published and sold, although Publisher shall exercise its best efforts to publish and sell the Program. Publisher agrees not to sell any software designed primarily to record and monitor the personal appointments of the user, within one (1) year of the date of this agreement.

4. *Training and Maintenance:* For the first year following the commencement of this agreement, Developer shall provide ten (10) days of her services to train Publisher's staff in the operation of the program, at times requested by Publisher, upon two (2) weeks' notice to Developer. If additional training is required, Publisher shall pay Developer for such training services at the rate of $50 per hour.

Should any program errors appear in the program during the first year after the commencement of this agreement, Developer shall correct such errors within fifteen (15) days after receiving notice (oral or written) from publisher. If the errors cannot be corrected within fifteen days, Developer shall work a minimum of four (4) hours per day on the Program each working day until the errors are corrected. The Publisher has full responsibility for maintaining the Program beyond one (1) year after the commencement of this agreement.

5. *Source Code Escrow:* On the one-year anniversary of the signing of this agreement, Publisher and Developer shall sign a source-code escrow agreement, and De-

veloper shall deposit into the escrow a printed copy of the source code for the Program, such that Publisher is able to maintain the Program thereafter.

6. *License:* Developer hereby grants to Publisher an exclusive license, for a period of eight (8) years from the date of this agreement, to publish and market the Program through any distribution channel within the United States only. Publisher may publish and sell the Program only for use on any Pumpkin computer, as well as on the Watermelon 500 computer. Publisher shall not sublicense the Program without the prior, written consent of the Developer. Developer shall not grant a competing license to any third party during the term of this license and shall notify Publisher of any noncompeting licenses for the Program within ten (10) days after they are granted.

7. *Royalties:* Publisher shall pay to Developer a royalty of 17.5 percent (17.5%) of the net sales price (the total price received by publisher, less shipping charges and allowance for copies returned) received by Publisher for the first 5,000 copies of the Program. Developer shall be paid a royalty of 20 percent (20%) of the net sales price for all additional copies sold. No reduction shall be made for the portion of the net sales price of the software package that represents the user's manual, although such manual shall be developed by and belong exclusively to the Publisher. No royalties shall be paid on dealer demonstration copies or other free copies distributed at the discretion of the Publisher.

Royalty payments shall be made to Developer within thirty (30) days after the end of each calandar quarter, for the copies of the Program sold during such calendar quarter.

8. *Proprietary Rights/Copyright:* Developer shall continue to hold all rights in the Program for the duration of this agreement, modified only by the license granted to Publisher in paragraph 6. The user's manual shall be developed by and be the exclusive property of the Publisher. Publisher is entitled to act as the agent of Developer for purposes of registering a copyright in the Program. The copyright shall be registered under the name of the Developer. All copies of the Program that are sold shall contain an appropriate copyright notice. Developer shall take all reasonable actions to protect its copyright in the Program, and hereby permits Publisher to protect against copyright infringement at Developer's expense.

9. *Warranties/Indemnification:* Developer warrants that the Program is a work of her original development, and that no third party holds any proprietary or contractual rights in the Program. Developer further warrants that she has the legal right to grant the license specified in paragraph 6 of this agreement. Developer further warrants that the Program has not been previously published in such a way as to destroy its eligibility for copyright protection, and that there are no lawsuits pending concerning the Program.

In the event that legal action of any sort is taken against Publisher in relation to proprietary rights in the program or any license to publish and sell the Program, Developer shall indemnify Publisher against all expenses incurred in such legal actions, including attorney's fees, costs, judgments and awards, and reasonable settlement payments. In the event that any legal action is taken against Developer by any user of the Program, or by a customer or client of any user, for losses suffered because of purchase or use of the Program, Publisher shall similarly indemnify Developer against all expenses and losses incurred by Developer.

10. *Termination:* Developer shall have the right to terminate the agreement, upon thirty (30) days' written notice, in the event that Publisher fails to make the Program available for sale during any sixty (60)-day period following the first sale of the program or in the event that no program is sold within six (6) months of the date of this agreement. Publisher may terminate the agreement at its will upon thirty (30) days' written notice to Developer. In addition, either party may terminate this agreement, at his option and upon thirty (30) days' written notice, in the event of a material breach by the other party. Prior to the expiration of the thirty-day notice period, the breaching party shall have the right to rectify his breach, in which case the agreement will continue as if there had never been a breach.

Upon termination of the agreement, the publisher's license shall become void, all copies of the Program code and documentation shall be returned to Developer, all royalties owing shall be paid to Developer, and all unsold copies of software packages containing the Program shall be destroyed by Publisher.

11. *Arbitration:* All disputes involving this agreement that cannot be resolved by the parties shall be submitted to binding arbitration. The arbitration shall be conducted under the then-existing rules of the American Arbitration Association. Neither party shall have the right to file a lawsuit in a court of law to resolve any question concerning this agreement.

12. *Miscellaneous:* Neither party shall assign any right or obligation under this agreement without the prior, written consent of the other party.

This agreement is the entire agreement between the parties, is binding upon the legal successors and assigns of the parties, and may be amended only by a written instrument signed by both parties.

Dated: _____

Developer: Publisher:

_____   _____

Ellen Wilson   President
                                                       SoftPublishing, Inc.

SOFTWARE LICENSE AGREEMENT (CUSTOMIZED)

This Software License Agreement is entered into *(date)* between Pleasantville Unified School District *(District)* and Calvin Small *(Developer)* for the license to District of use of Developer's school attendance software *(Software)*.

    1. *License:* (A) In consideration for the payment of $300, Developer hereby grants a nonexclusive license to District to use the Software for a period of sixty (60) days. During this sixty-day period, District will use and test the Software and determine whether it wishes to return the software to Developer. If the Software is returned to Developer prior to the expiration of the sixty-day period, this agreement shall immediately terminate. If the software is not returned by the end of the sixty-day period, it will be assumed that District is continuing to hold and use the Software under the license specified in paragraph 1 (B) of this agreement. District may notify Developer at any time during the test period that it intends to use the software under the license specified in paragraph 1 (B).

    (B) District is hereby granted a nonexclusive license to use the Software for an indefinite period of time, such license being contingent on payment to Developer of a monthly license fee of $200, due, in advance, on the *1st* day of each month. This license begins on *July 1, 1985* and shall continue from month to month for as long as District shall pay the monthly license fee and comply with the other provisions of this license. This license is not assignable without the prior, written consent of Developer.

    (C) Within three (3) days of the signing of this agreement, Developer shall deliver to District one set of magnetic disks containing the machine-readable object code, and two copies of the user's manual for the Software. At no time is District entitled to receive a copy of the source code.

    2. *Place of Use:* The Software shall be used only at the District's adminsitrative offices located at (address), unless prior, written consent is given by Developer to use the Software elsewhere.

    3. *Training:* Developer shall provide training in the use of the software to District's employees, in the form of a twenty (20)-hour course of instruction, at an additional payment of $300 per employee.

    4. *Maintenance:* Developer shall maintain the Software during the entire term of this agreement. District's only remedy for Developer's failure to maintain the software is termination of the agreement as provided in paragraph 9.

    5. *Modifications and Improvements:* District may modify or improve the Software at any time. Such modifications and improvements are the property of the Developer and must be surrendered to Developer in the event this agreement is terminated. Should Developer make any modifications or improvements to the Software, an updated disk or disks containing such changes will be provided to District, free of charge, if they are provided to any user of the Software.

    6. *Proprietary Rights/Copyright:* It is understood by District that the Software, including the computer program and the user's manuals, and any modifications or improvements made to the Software by the District or the Developer, is the exclusive, copyrighted property of the Developer. District shall not sell or relicense the software or any part of it to any third party, or publish the software or any part of it in such a way as to affect the Developer's copyrights. District may not make any copies of the

12. Amendments: This agreement may be amended at any time by a written instrument signed by both partners.

_____   _____
Calvin Small   Dan Dimsdorf

ARTICLES OF INCORPORATION

The undersigned, acting as incorporators of a corporation under the laws of the State of _____ , adopt the following articles of incorporation:

1. The name of the corporation is Companytech, Inc.
2. The principal place of business of the corporation shall be (address).
3. The corporation shall have perpetual duration.
4. The purpose for which the corporation is formed is the development of computer software, and all other purposes allowed by law.
5. The corporation shall have authority to issue one hundred thousand (100,000) shares of common stock. No other class of stock is authorized.
6. The number of directors constituting the initial board of directors is two (2), and the names and addresses of the persons who are to serve as directors until the first annual meeting of shareholders are

Bill Johnson (*address*)
Mary Johnson (*address*)

7. The name and address of each incorporator is

Bill Johnson (*address*)
Mary Johnson (*address*)

Date: _____ Incorporators: _____
                                          _____

Hagelshaw: The Computer User's Legal Guide (Chilton)

CORPORATION BYLAWS (OUTLINE)

ARTICLE I. Location of principal office and branch offices

ARTICLE II. Stockholders
    Section 1. Date, time, and location of annual meetings
    Section 2. Conditions under which special meetings of stockholders will be held
    Section 3. How and when notice of stockholders' meetings will be given
    Section 4. Quorum requirements for stockholders' meetings
    Section 5. How shares are to be voted; proxies

ARTICLE III. Board of directors
    Section 1. Powers and duties
    Section 2. Number of directors; how elected
    Section 3. Date, time, place, and frequency of regular meetings
    Section 4. Special meetings
    Section 5. Notice of meetings
    Section 6. Quorum requirements for directors' meetings
    Section 7. Decisions of board; voting rules
    Section 8. Compensation of directors

ARTICLE IV. Officers
    Section 1. Number and type of officers
    Section 2. Selection, term of office, removal, method of filling vacancies
    Section 3. Powers and duties of officers
    Section 4. Compensation of officers

ARTICLE V. Conduct of business
    Section 1. Entering into contracts
    Section 2. Real estate transactions
    Section 3. Incurring indebtedness
    Section 4. Bank accounts

ARTICLE VI. Corporate stock
    Section 1. Issuing of certificates for shares of stock
    Section 2. Transfer of shares of stock

ARTICLE VII. Dividends

ARTICLE VIII. Miscellaneous provisions
    Section 1. Corporate seal
    Section 2. Fiscal year
    Section 3. Amendments to bylaws

Index

Internal Revenue Service (IRS), 86, 165, 167–69, 189–90
Inventory control system, 84
Investment capital, raising of, 187–90, 196–97
Investment management, 169–70
Investment tax credits, 42–43, 47, 167
  for hardware, 164
  for software, 166
  tangible personal property and, 164, 166
Itel Corp., 33

Japan, IBM secrets taken to, 112

K. C. Munchkin, 101

Languages, computer, 87, 125
Lawyers, 47, 198–200
  alternatives to, 200
  choosing of, 199
  cost of, 25–26, 199–200
  incorporation and, 188
  prejudice against, 1
  software development and, 72, 73
  types of, 198–99
  when to use, 198
Lease agreements, 44–47, 208–11
  assigned to third party, 46
  location of use in, 45
  negotiating the terms of, 46–47
  period of, 44–45
  provisions of, 44–46
  renewal clause in, 46
  repairs and maintenance in, 45, 47
Leasing companies, financial difficulties of, 33
Leasing computers, 33–34, 41–47. See also Lease agreements
  advantages of, 41–44
  buying compared with, 33–34, 43–44
  tax benefits of, 42–44
Licenses. See also Software license agreements
  exclusive vs. nonexclusive, 149
  software, 76–77, 148–49, 152
Limited liability, 186, 187, 189
Limited partnerships, 186–87
  corporations compared with, 189
  formation of, 193
  tax advantages of, 187
  termination of, 190
  transfer of ownership in, 191
Liquidated damages, 183

Macintosh computer, 34, 128
Magnetic tapes, 87, 114, 115
Mail-order companies
  computers from, 32
  selling software through, 136
  software from, 50, 61–62, 66
Mainframe computers, 15, 33
Maintenance
  contracts, 31–32, 42, 64
  of leased computers, 42, 45

of rented computers, 36, 39
of software, 64, 77–78, 145, 155
Malpractice (negligent misrepresentation), 27, 28–29, 178–79, 181
Management and Computer Services, Inc. (MACS), 128
Manuals, 57, 87, 100, 103, 143
  copyrighting, 113, 115, 116
  writers of, 94, 143
Marketing of software. See Software marketing; Software marketing agreements
MicroPro International Corp., 67
Minnesota, software disputes in, 84
Misrepresentation, 8–9, 27–29, 130
  intentional (fraud), 8, 21, 27–28, 58, 59, 181
  negligent (malpractice), 27–29, 178–79, 181
Mitsubishi Electric Corp., 112

Negligence
  contributory, 179
  ordinary, 177–78
  professional, 27, 28–29, 178–79, 181
Net sales revenue, 150
Networks, computer, 50–51
Nondisclosure agreements, 106–8, 125, 126, 141–42
Notice, copyright, 116–17, 120, 156

Object code, 114, 115, 119, 145
  defined, 87
  registration of, 120–21, 125–26
Offer and acceptance, 8
Offices, home, tax deduction for, 171
Office Supply Co. v. Basic/Four Corp., 25
Operator's manuals. See Manuals
Original works, meaning of, 115
Ownership. See Proprietary (ownership) rights

Pac-Man video game, 101
Partnerships. See General partnerships; Limited partnerships
Passwords, 104–5
Patent and Trademark Office, U.S., 86, 128–31
Patent law, 113, 130–31
Pensions, 190
Performance warranties, 78
Personal computers (PCs), 15
  defects in, 21–26
  IBM, 14, 25, 34, 35
  recalls of, 25
  repairs of, 26, 31–32
  software packages with, 50
  typical purchase of, 16–17
Piracy, 56, 67–68, 86, 154
  copyright infringement and, 122–23
  economic protection against, 133
  legal protection against, 100–31
  technological protection against, 132
Printouts, 87, 103, 145

Profit-sharing plans, 190
Programmers. See also Software development; Software development contracts
  bankruptcy or dissolution of business of, 83
  cost of, 69, 75
  independent, 92–95
  liability of, 73, 74, 80, 173–84
  notes of, 87, 103
  proprietary rights of, 76, 89–95, 96
  self-employed, 96
  spare-time, 96
  staff, 89–92
Programs, 88
  backup copies of, 52, 55–56, 63, 68
  "breaking the lock" on, 68
  copyrighting of, 113–17, 119
  defined, 87
  locked, 67–68
  "made for hire," 76
  original, 115
  patented, 131
  profitability of, 85
  source code of. (See Source code)
  technological protection of, 132
  trade secret protection of, 102–3
Property, real vs. tangible personal, 164
Proprietary (ownership) rights. See also Copyright; Patent law; Software development; Software development contracts; Trademarks; Trade secrets
  assignment of, 97, 98
  in corporations, 190, 191
  customized software and, 75–76
  of independent programmers, 92–95
  for leased computers, 45
  meaning of, 96–97
  in operator's manual, 94
  protection of, 98–133
  of self-employed and spare-time programmers, 96
  in software, 75–76, 85–133, 143, 144, 148, 152, 154, 156
  of staff programmers, 89–92
  transfer of, 89, 97, 98, 190, 191
  "Published," meaning of, 116
Publishers of software
  choosing, 138–39
  dealing with, 137–39
  evaluation of software by, 139–43
  marketing agreements with. (See Software marketing agreements)
  protection of, 141–42
  selling through, 135

Quality control, 180

Racketeer Influenced and Corrupt Organizations Act (RICO), 111–12
Registration
  of computers, 17–18
  of copyright, 118–26, 151–52
  of trademarks, 128–29

Hagelshaw: The Computer User's Legal Guide (Chilton)

Hagelshaw: The Computer User's Legal Guide (Chilton)